HEDDA AND LOUELLA

"A sparkling book on the big studio era . . . narrated in popular style and definitely a part of American film history."

—*San Francisco Chronicle*

A DUAL BIOGRAPHY

"Behind-the-scenes delving into their private lives, marriages, secret loves, and how each [got] the scoops on which her power depended."

—*Publishers Weekly*

OF HOLLYWOOD'S JOURNALISTIC SUPERSTARS

"Thoroughly engrossing, meticulously researched, and extremely well written."   —Rex Reed

"Rich in anecdote."   —*Philadelphia Inquirer*

BY GEORGE EELLS

Born in Winslow, Illinois (population 399), GEORGE EELLS became fascinated with show business at an early age. Filled with the memories of the circuses, carnivals, and repertoire companies that passed through his hometown, he attended Northwestern before coming to New York. After being entertainment editor for *Parade* and *Look,* he was editor of *Signature.* He now lives in Manhattan but spends a good deal of time in Los Angeles.

HEDDA
AND
LOUELLA

by George Eells

**WARNER
PAPERBACK
LIBRARY**

A Warner Communications Company

WARNER PAPERBACK LIBRARY EDITION
First Printing: June, 1973

Library of Congress Catalog Card Number: 70-174638

This Warner Paperback Library Edition is published by arrangement with G. P. Putnam's Sons, Inc.

Warner Paperback Library is a division of Warner Books, Inc., 315 Park Avenue South, New York, N.Y. 10010.

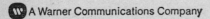 A Warner Communications Company

For my mother, my sister and Aurand

HEDDA
AND
LOUELLA

Acknowledgments

In addition to those quoted in the text grateful acknowledgment for assistance is made to my editor, Harvey Ginsberg; Mrs. Herbert Humphrey; Mrs. William Simon; Mr. and Mrs. George Schmidt; Miss Stella Eells; Mrs. Irene Burns; Mrs. Marjorie Brose; Mrs. Edward Ganshirt; Warren Weaver; Tom Clapp; George Leigh; Jack Langdon; Leonore Silvian; Dick Segel; Jack Hamilton; Howard Hughes; Bob Thomas; Hy Gardner; Sylvia Rabin; Mrs. Lucy F. Smith; Conrad Smith; Henry G. Dodds, Samuel Taub, Jack Aaron of the New York *Morning Telegraph;* press agent Nat Dorfman; Mayor A. B. Silbertson, Redfield, South Dakota; Mary Jane Higby's *Tune in Tomorrow;* Father Joseph C. Harrison, Trinity Episcopal Church, Tallulah, Louisiana; Carolyn Younger, *Madison Journal* of Tallulah, Louisiana; Deputy Clerk Dorothy Layman, Stephenson County, Illinois; The Dixon, Illinois, Free Public Library; Dixon, Illinois, Public High School; Attorney Robert L. Warner, Dixon, Illinois; Laura E. Rogers, Mount Morris, Illinois; Mrs. C. B. Fowler, Mount Morris, Illinois; Edwin L. Glessner, Dixon, Illinois; Stanley Gordon, Los Angeles, California; County Clerk George Knott, Des Moines County, Burlington, Iowa; reporter

Lloyd Maffitt, Burlington, Iowa; Maurice Rich Fischer, Chicago, Illinois, Press Club; Clerk of the Court Winifred I. Diehl, Thompson Falls, Montana; County Clerk James McGurrin, New York County, New York; numerous Cook County, Illinois, clerks; Deputy Clerk Louise S. Brownlee, Missoula, Montana; The Blair County Historical Society of Pennsylvania; Altoona, Pennsylvania, Public Library; and the Lincoln Center Theatre Collection Staff of New York, New York. Special thanks to Mildred Simpson, Lilliam Schwartz and the entire staff of the Library of the Academy of Motion Picture Arts and Sciences and to the staff and family of Hedda Hopper—especially Patsy Gaile and Honor Traynor. In addition, my gratitude to Harriet Parsons and Dorothy Manners, whose decision to withhold cooperation made me dig that much harder. I would like to extend my special thanks to Samuel Stark for compiling the index.

GEORGE EELLS

June 6, 1971

Prologue

HOLLYWOOD'S life-style has always been rich, exciting and absurd.

In what other place, in what other time could a woman who decorated her white baby grand with an enormous blue bow gain a reputation for chic? Yet Lilyan Tashman *was* chic.

Reality and illusion have always been inextricable.

Rudolph Valentino's leading lady Nita Naldi might snort at his reputation as a great lover as she held up a pinkie to twit the measure of the man. But for millions of women, Valentino represented the ideal.

There is no denying that Hollywood's fabled tycoons began as furriers, pitchmen, junk dealers and ne'er-do-wells, but in the end they proved themselves showmen. They understood how to put together a series of moving pictures that extracted nickels and dimes from the pockets of unsophisticated audiences. Eventually some of them consolidated those nickels and dimes into big business— major studios. And from these studios came masses of kitsch, quantities of light entertainment and at least a few genuine works of cinematic art.

To the general public, movies meant stars. Even when

Florence Lawrence's identity was unknown, fans worshiped her as "The Biograph Girl." They made Mary Pickford "America's Sweetheart," Clara Bow and Colleen Moore symbols of flaming youth, and Pola Negri, Mae West, Rita Hayworth, Ava Gardner and Marilyn Monroe love goddesses—of one kind or another.

Stars shared, in varying degrees, exciting personalities, photogenic features, an aura of excitement, a certain amount of talent and (to use a favorite adjective of yesteryear) colossal amounts of publicity. At one time in excess of 400 accredited newspaper and fan magazine correspondents (more than were assigned to any other U.S. city except Washington, D.C.) covered Hollywood hijinks. Enough printer's ink to pollute the Atlantic and the Pacific poured from the presses, bringing the "scoops" of such columnists as Sidney Skolsky, Sheilah Graham, Army Archerd, Mike Connolly, Jimmy Fidler, Jimmy Starr, Radie Harris and Edith Gwynn. But the two who still stand out in bold relief, who managed to become "stars" in their own right are Louella Parsons and Hedda Hopper.

In their heyday Hedda and Louella claimed a combined readership totaling 75,000,000.* Intellectuals might —and did—question what readers in Bangkok made of the squib that Marion Davies was enjoying a new typewriter or that "Daroes (a well-known astrologer) says Cobina Wright Jr. will have a happy future if left to her own devices." Still there is no gainsaying that more than 600 newspapers printed Louella's columns, which were avidly followed in cities ranging from Los Angeles to Peking, from New York to Beirut, or that at the beginning of World War II, when paper shortages forced the Honolulu *Advertiser* to reduce its content by one-third, the editor wrote Hedda to assure her that her column was indispensable.

In a society where everyone was either on the way up

* Like most figures connected with the film industry, this may have been exaggerated. Amusingly, both downgraded publicity. Hedda flatly stated publicity never made a star. Louella once credited it with 20 percent responsibility, later reduced the figure to 15 percent.

or on the way down, Louella and Hedda shared a determination not to lose footing. It earned them a few devoted friends, many collaborators and a host of enemies.

Who were these women, these phenomena?

To find out, one must first know that there were two Hollywoods. The first was lit by arc lights and inhabited by stars. The second generated the power to produce the illumination. It was the Hollywood of the moguls. In their day, Hollywood moguls functioned as despots. They ruled by will, made policy by whim and hired out of pique.

When agent Charles Feldman became a rival for the affections of the glamorous Jean Howard, Louis B. Mayer simply barred him from the lot. That was Metro-Goldwyn-Mayer, the Rolls-Royce of the studios.

Mogul Herbert J. Yates habitually thought up and assigned "box-office" titles. One grim morning he handed writer Gertrude Walker a piece of paper upon which she found "Sing, Dance, Plenty Hot." She protested that was a review, not a title. Yates gave her a choice of writing the script or checking off the lot. That was Republic, the jeep of the studios.

Whether a tycoon headed MGM, Republic or some other studio, he ruled. Should an employee seriously offend a tycoon, he might be unofficially blacklisted throughout the industry. Only a star of enormous box-office appeal could sometimes give the back of his hand to a tycoon.*

To keep these benevolent dictatorships functioning, it took an army of directors, writers, designers, publicity agents, specialists, "gofors," † adventurers and adventuresses whose duty it was to see that the stars twinkled.

Louella and Hedda linked these two worlds. Just as

---

* A highly popular screen juvenile was once reportedly called into Mayer's office and informed that so much gossip was circulating about him and his male companion of several years' standing that the juvenile must get rid of his friend. The juvenile refused. Mayer insisted. The juvenile regarded the studio head coldly, then asked: "Mr. Mayer, what would you do if I told you to get rid of Mrs. Mayer?" Then he walked out. There were no repercussions.

† Flunkies: "Howie, go for Miss Grable's cigarettes. Oh, and while you're at it, go for my. . . ."

they became "star" columnists, so were they "star" adventuresses. Hollywood abounded with adventuresses on many levels and of many types. These were vivid, unconventional women, who thrived amid power, glamor and wealth. Their pasts were often veiled in mystery. Even close friends could only guess their ages, what their origins had been or how they had become connected with the industry. In the telling, their lives were reshaped to conform with what *ought* to have been.

In the case of some, details seem too improbable for fiction. Take Anita Loos. Did her career as a short-story writer, novelist, playwright and scenarist begin at thirteen when she dashed off a story which she sent to D. W. Griffith, who used it as the basis for Mary Pickford's *The New York Hat*? Or bold, beautiful, imaginative Frances Marion—what a fictional heroine! She arrived from San Francisco in her teens, painted theatrical posters for Morosco. Eventually, she wrote scenarios for such stars as Mary Pickford and Marie Dressler, married Army chaplain Fred Thompson and converted him into a popular screen cowboy. "I wrote over 300 stories that were filmed," she said. "Some of the best ones were terrible when they reached the screen and some of the worst went through the mixmaster and turned out to be very good." She also won two Oscars; the last she saw of them her grandchildren were using them to crack nuts.

There were June Mathis and Natacha Rambova. Miss Mathis masterminded Rudolph Valentino's career until Miss Rambova, née Winifred Hudnut, married him. Not content to create sets and costumes, Miss Rambova also tried her hand at scriptwriting and producing and advising her husband. Before they were divorced, she had almost ruined his career. When he died prematurely, his "fiancée" Pola Negri swooned, but June Mathis magnanimously provided a resting place for his body. Louella had plenty to say about that—as did Hedda.*

There was also Elsa Maxwell. One year, she was em-

---

* Hedda later claimed that when newsreelmen missed Miss Negri's grief-stricken histrionics, the actress obligingly reenacted the scene for them.

ployed as a "writer," another as an "actress," and on still another as a "technical adviser." The truth was, according to friends, the moguls hired her to spice up the social scene. Since Louella loved Elsa, Hedda naturally grew to despise her.

Both Hedda and Louella accorded Countess di Frasso, née Dorothy Taylor, lots of space. A worldly society woman, the countess settled in Hollywood for a time and found in bucolic, young Gary Cooper just the instrument to banish boredom. When she lost him to a younger woman, the countess titillated film society by taking up with Benjamin "Bugsy" Siegel, who was warmly accepted despite his gangland connections.

Adventuresses then were both respectable and raffish. They might be scenarists, story constructionists, playgirls or reporters. It was Hedda's and Louella's personal styles that put them in such company. Otherwise, they might have remained hard-working, respected professionals comparable to Grace Kingsley, Florabel Muir, Agnes Underwood, Ruth Waterbury, Katherine Albert and Jane Ardmore—to name a few.

It was not to be. They were phenomena, the likes of which we are not likely to see again. Both columnists were relentless in demonstrating their influence. During her life-time, Hedda used to point dramatically at her home on Tropical Drive in Beverly Hills and chortle: "That's the house that fear built."

Hedda wasn't kidding. Although her ashes are interred at Rose Hill cemetery in Altoona, Pennsylvania, and Lou-ella (as of 1971) rocks aimlessly back and forth in a Santa Monica rest home, their names still evoke real, if irrational, uneasiness among some Hollywood veterans.

Judging from the responses I received when I began researching this book, I might have been preparing an exposé on the CIA or a Mafia chieftain.

For instance, while I was a guest at the Del Mar home of Navy Commander and Mrs. William Robinson, Audrey Robinson suggested that I call actor Victor Mature, who had told them some humorous and hair-raising anecdotes about the two columnists. I phoned him and stated my business. Mature at once said that he was just leaving for Palm Springs and anyway Audrey must have him confused with someone else. Audrey took over the telephone. After a somewhat prolonged exchange, she hung up. "Vic wasn't happy about what I'd told you," she explained with evident disbelief. "He said that as far as he was concerned, he was finished in Hollywood, but if you do anything to those two old broads, that town'll mess you up good."

"Talk to Jules Dassin," a magazine editor advised me. "When Hedda was on her pinko purge, she never let up. Also, he's very astute about Louella. It's his theory that the tragedy of Hollywood is that for over a quarter of a century the filmmakers were harried by these two illiterate, vindictive women."

I sent a letter to Mr. Dassin, requesting an interview. Shortly after, I received a reply which represents the ulti- mate in polite understatement: "In all candor," it goes in part, "I had so little sympathy for Miss Parsons and Miss Hopper that I don't think I could make any contribution— even if I had the time to do so."

I also wrote to Dore Schary, former head of Metro- Goldwyn-Mayer. It was during his tenure that Hedda re- ferred to it as "Metro-Goldwyn-Moscow." Mr. Schary never bothered to respond to the letter or to a subsequent attempt to contact him.

Letters seemed ineffective. I called writer Leonard Spi- gelgass, who was direct and charming. "I was not a friend of Miss Hopper's," he said. "I must tell you that. And I can only tell you that if Miss Hopper was at a party, I left. I just never wanted that confrontation. Because a woman who has the Los Angeles *Times* and all those other outlets—how do you fight her? What she used to do was to run an item saying that the Hollywood Ten and other Communists have been given film assignments. Paragraph. Leonard Spigelgass has been assigned to write *Gypsy*. There was never anything I could put my finger on. She could say it was just a news item that followed the other by chance. But the column had that kind of continuity. Then in Chicago at a luncheon attended by Adlai Steven- son's sister, Miss Hopper said that Dore Schary, Humphrey

Bogart, Lauren Bacall,* and I were the four most dangerous men in America."

I had hardly finished speaking to Spigelgass when Patsy Gaile, one of Hedda's devoted staff, rang me. She explained that she had read *The Life That Late He Led,* my biography of Cole Porter, and she wanted to be helpful. "I want you to hear how Hedda's staff felt toward her," she said. "I want to tell you some of the things we knew about her. I know you'll get plenty of the other."

In an optimistic mood, I placed a call to Dorothy Manners, Louella's former assistant who had taken over the column upon Louella's retirement in 1966. Miss Manners said that she would prefer not to cooperate. She explained that she had been approached by several magazines to do pieces but had turned them down. She felt it wasn't fair to be "in someone's confidence for over thirty years and then talk about it."

I assured her I was no hatchet man.

"Probably not," she conceded. "But I know what publishers want to print, and I just don't want to get into that."

My exchange with Lola, the funniest of the once-popular Lane sisters, proved eerie. Lola and her sister Rosemary had starred in *Hollywood Hotel,* a Warner Brothers' film inspired by Louella's popular weekly radio program. In the film, Louella had portrayed herself. I had heard numerous stories about her demands, gaffes and tantrums.

When I explained to Miss Lane what I wanted, she begged off on the grounds that she felt it would be professionally unwise for her to discuss Louella. Lola Lane's last film appearance was in 1946.

Three big-league press agents were also reluctant to talk. One didn't want to risk having his remarks about Louella misinterpreted by Dorothy Manners. The second had "just stepped out" the first time I called. A week later he was "on vacation." Finally, he had "retired." The third said that two or three other writers had approached him on the subject and he couldn't play favorites. "Anyway, I loved

---

* Lauren Bacall's reaction: "I think it's time for Hedda to shut up."

Louella and Hedda," he said. "I don't think it would be fair to talk about them."

Meanwhile, I met Louella's daughter, Harriet, or Parsons Jr., as she was billed in the Hearst press, and Hedda's son, William.

Bill Hopper, who played Paul Drake on the Perry Mason television series, made every effort to be helpful. His relationship with his mother had always been capricious. In speaking of her (he always called her Hedda), Bill was candid and objective and was sorry that he could be of little help in regard to her family, since he had hardly met them.

During the interview, I told him that I had once gone to a nightclub with a party including his mother at a time when she and Louella were ostensibly friendly. The occasion had been the appearance of opera star Helen Traubel at the old Moulin Rouge at Sunset Boulevard and Argyle Street in Hollywood. At the climax of the show, the director had devised a visual treat which consisted of setting loose a covey of pastel-dyed doves which were to fly to the stage and position themselves strategically upon the bodies of the seminude showgirls. For some reason (perhaps the lights, the music, the crowd or a combination of the three) the birds became frightened and began to circle about in confusion. When Hedda saw a pastel feather drifting through the colored lights toward one of the tables, she leaped up, hissing, "Let's get out of here! Those birds are going to shit! And if they do, I hope they hit Louella's bald spot!"

Bill roared. "You've got to use that," he said. "It's so Hedda."

Louella!
Hedda!
They are legendary. They are neither the angels that friends paint nor the two viragos depicted by their enemies. But who were these sometimes terrifying, sometimes misguided, often pathetic women?

What lies beneath the rumors, innuendos and distortions that surround them? And what of the suppressed facts? Where do posturing and self-dramatization end? What of their cruelties? Their frustrations? Their longings? What of their much vaunted power? Who was susceptible to it, and who was not? And what of the society that created them and made them both rich and celebrated?

On the surface, they could not have been more dissimilar. One was a slightly dowdy brunette; the other, a stylish blonde. One accented her kindliness; the other, her bitchiness. One was the daughter of a successful merchant; the other, of an irresponsible butcher.

Fittingly, the daughter of the clothier was inclined to cover up for the industry, to hide its naked underbelly from the world, while the butcher's daughter slashed away at it, spilling Hollywood's guts with seemingly careless abandon.

Yet whatever the dissimilarities, both were driving women born into a world not yet ready to accept the feminist point of view. Both were repressed by the conventional mores of small-town Midwestern America in the early 1900's. There is a hint of Sinclair Lewis' *Main Street* heroine, Carol Kennicott, in each of them. They longed for the glitter of the great world where they would no longer have to struggle against what Lewis once called "the village virus." They rebelled against what they considered the smugness and provincialism of those who scoffed at their artistic ambitions.

One was to invent a new kind of business—the gossip column—and for decades to practice it with bedazzling material success. For forty years, fear of her disfavor was to haunt stars and press agents. The other, Hedda "The Hat" Hopper, was even more ambitious, but she was always regarded as second-rate—in acting, in the game of loving and living, in whatever she undertook. Finally, however, she harnessed her frustrations into a drive for power that succeeded in establishing her as a superpersonality or, as one crude film star whom she had worked over in print put it, "a super cunt." Almost at retirement age, Hedda began writing a gossip column that she rode successfully until sudden death provided her with an exit far more stylish and dramatic than any she had ever made on stage or screen.

Louella was a plump, clear-skinned young woman, with

liquid brown eyes, even white teeth and an all-consuming curiosity. She took to newspaper work at a time when women reporters—Nellie Bly notwithstanding—were rare. Concentrating at first on the arts and social events, she eventually made forays into the sob sister field which led to her first association with the first mechanized art, motion pictures. This, in turn, led back to newspaper work, first in Chicago, then in New York, before a major illness and publisher William Randolph Hearst sent her to the California desert to recuperate.

Concurrently, Louella had lived through an unhappy marriage, mothered a daughter, secretly divorced her philandering husband, made a second unhappy marriage, which until now has been concealed in stories about her, secured a second secret divorce and carried on a deeply felt but humiliating love affair with a man who was not free to marry her. All this occurred before she finally arrived in Hollywood, where her unique qualities and connections enthroned her as the undisputed, if uncrowned, queen for twenty years and made her, with the advent of Hedda, the embattled ruler of a large part of the movie colony for still another twenty.

Small-town Pennsylvania was no more compatible to Elda Furry, the woman who was eventually to be known to the world as Hedda Hopper, than Illinois was to Louella. The Quaker butcher's daughter soon grew restive selling meat over the counter of her father's shop and hounding customers to settle their unpaid bills. Even while she wore a bloody apron, Elda must have dreamed of owning Worth gowns.

At twenty-two (not as the seventeen-year-old runaway she later pretended to have been), she went to New York, where step by step she progressed from the chorus to leading roles in musical comedy—despite a severely limited vocal range. Along the way Elda became the fifth wife of DeWolf Hopper, a Broadway musical star, who was four or five years older than her father. Eventually, she changed her name to Hedda and presented Hopper with a son.

Eventually, too, Hedda's fresh, doelike beauty photographed better than her aging husband's bags, pouches and blue-tinted skin. Her nonexistent acting technique also proved more compatible to the camera than his exaggerated theatrical gestures. These unpalatable facts were rammed down his throat when Hedda's salary inched up and finally matched what DeWolf Hopper was earning after forty-three years on the legitimate stage. It was an intolerable situation. They divorced.

From that point on, Hedda hopscotched between success and failure—with periods of affluence matched by periods of poverty. The pattern was broken only after she finally began to sell what she had previously given away—gossip.

Yet in the beginning her efforts were so negligible that her friend Louella noted that Hedda was writing a weekly fashion column for Cissy Patterson's Washington *Herald*. But as the column's popularity grew, the friendliness disappeared. And when "Hedda Hopper's Hollywood" began appearing in the prestigious Los Angeles *Times*, the New York *Daily News* and the Chicago *Tribune*, Louella and Hedda inevitably came into conflict with each other, and the rivalry soon became fierce.

Louella had the power of the Hearst press behind her, and many maintained that she was still queen. But there was a choice. Even Hedda wittily acknowledged Louella's superiority as a newspaperwoman. "Louella Parsons," she said, "is a newspaperwoman trying to be a ham. I'm a ham trying to be a columnist."

Louella's complaint was: "She's trying to do in two years what took me thirty and I resent some of the things she says about me."

Both were often startlingly vindictive with major stars. The truly first-rate seemed to infuriate them. Charlie Chaplin, Orson Welles, Greta Garbo, Katharine Hepburn, Laurence Olivier and Vivien Leigh all received harsh treatment. Lesser players, possibly because they represented less news potential, were treated better, especially by Louella.

A minor incident involving actress Joan Evans clarifies the contrasting attitudes of the two. When Joan was about to announce her approaching maternity, she confided in her mother, Katherine Albert Eunson, that since Hearst columnist Harrison Carroll had always been kind to her, she had decided to give the story to him.

Katherine Eunson, erstwhile fan magazine writer, a script-writer and a longtime Hollywood campaigner, suggested that after calling Carroll, Joan also telephone Louella and Hedda, pretending to be unaware of such realities as deadlines and such unethical acts as triple planting. "Pretend," she said, "you have no mother to guide you."

Joan followed the advice, spoke to Hedda and left a number for Louella, who happened to be absent from home. The next day Carroll used the item as the lead in his column.*

That afternoon Louella called Katherine Eunson apologetically. "Oh, Katherine," she cried. "Poor little Joanie! She called to give me the news, and I didn't get back to her. I know how excited she must have been. Just bursting to tell someone. So she called Harrison. Now she probably thinks I'm mad. But I'm not. I know she wanted me to have it, and you thank her for thinking of me first!"

Later Hedda, who had conveyed the impression to Joan that the world was not waiting breathlessly to receive news of the approaching event, also called Katherine. "That daughter of yours!" she spluttered. "That sneaky little bitch! I'm onto her. She gave the story to Harrison, and then she tried to foist it on me too! Now she's hiding. Well, she doesn't fool me for one minute! She's a bitch! And I'll never use her name again!"

Even in the "new Hollywood" mention of Hedda and Louella seldom fails to stir up old rumors and elicit an enormous number of conflicting points of view that run something like this:

WHAT THEY SAY ABOUT HEDDA:
*That she didn't recognize a news story when she saw one
*That she used her column to make the film industry suffer for failing to make her a star

---

* Carroll was noted for his fondness of illness, accident and disaster stories. Upon seeing the prominent position the columnist had given the pregnancy, Dale Eunson, Joan's father, quipped, "He must have thought it was an accident."

*That she was a social climber and a snob
*That she was politically to the right of the John Birch Society and/or that she was an old-fashioned American who had attacked Communism when it was unfashionable to do so
*That she was a sentimentalist who hid her good deeds and/or that she was a sadistic bitch
*That she was stingy
*That she was anti-Semitic and antiblack
*That she hated men and/or that she gave a journalistic boost to young actors who "gave her a poke" now and then

WHAT THEY SAY ABOUT LOUELLA:
*That she held her job because William Randolph Hearst knew she knew where the body was buried
*That she held her job because she had introduced Hearst to Marion Davies
*That she was Hearst's hatchet woman
*That she was the best newspaperwoman in Los Angeles and/or that she was "consistently the least accurate reporter who ever lived to draw $600 a week"
*That she was scatterbrained and vague and/or she only pretended vagueness to cause people to lower their guard
*That she was a freeloader and/or that she was wildly generous
*That her copy was marked MG—"Must Go as Is"
*That she began the day with a tumblerful of whiskey
*That she suffered from a tragic kidney malfunction and that one sat where she sat at his own risk

WHAT THEY SAY ABOUT HEDDA *AND* LOUELLA:
*That they cold-bloodedly destroyed anyone who crossed them
*That they used their journalistic power to promote their families
*That they sold major studios unusable material for huge sums
*That they paid off stars for appearing on their radio and television programs through publicity breaks
*That they encouraged filmmakers to regard their endeavors as commodities rather than art

*That they only pretended to feud to draw attention to themselves

This mixture of fantasy and fact which refuses to be put to rest testifies not only to the controversy which the two columnists engendered but also to their success in establishing themselves as figures who made as well as reported news.

Louella, despite her favored position as a showy performer in Hearst's troupe of journalistic novelty acts, always managed to create the impression that she was somebody's maiden aunt from a small Midwestern town who had dropped in for a visit and stayed on. Someone once asked, "Isn't it possible she is a nice lady who happens to be involved in a dirty business?"

"Yes," was the rejoinder. "Except that she happened to invent the business."

No one would have made such a mistake in assessing Hedda. Even when she was clinging desperately to the fringes of show business, eking out a living selling real estate, dabbling in cosmetics, briefly representing other actors, running for political office or trying to write a play, she acted as though she had been born to the purple. Her appearance was such that in only a few films (once, incredibly, as Mona Lisa) was she ever cast as anything except a brittle, worldly woman.

After one was dead and the other retired, a mutual acquaintance said, "I think Hedda was harder to forgive in the things she did because you felt she knew better. Louella was unworldly in terms of the position she held and never seemed to progress much from the struggling young newspaperwoman. Except that she was determined to have the news first, she always seemed to be muddling through."*

What would Louella and Hedda have had to say about this?

In her biography, *The Gay Illiterate,* Louella wrote: "I have been sniped at by experts. And why not? Almost anyone who has ever attained any kind of public stature

* In a letter from Alex Tiers, a friend of both.

in his or her profession can expect sometimes to see a reflection in a cracked mirror. It would be strange indeed if Louella Parsons were to be the exception."

Not long before she died, Hedda granted an interview to London columnist Donald Zec. In discussing herself, she turned the tables and demanded that Zec give his candid impressions of her. "I don't mind your being unkind. Sometimes the truth is very brutal. . . .

"I want an answer to my former question: what makes me tick? I'd really like to know. There are times when I hate myself."

This, then, is the story of Hollywood and its people, and of two women that the film community either tolerated or created. It is also the story of what happens when two basically simple people are feared, catered to and given enormous power.

I

The first person I ever cared deeply and
sincerely about was—myself.
                          —LOUELLA PARSONS
                          in *The Gay Illiterate*

HAD Louella Parsons been an actress, no talent agent
would ever have considered suggesting her for the role of
a world-famous newspaperwoman. Yet the Parsons by-line
sold millions of papers, and publisher William Randolph
Hearst said that although she might not be his best writer,
she was his best reporter.

If Louella was relentless in exposing other people's
secrets, she was equally deft in concealing her own. Assessing all the incidents that she had so successfully hidden,
you have to admire her for her bravado. It takes real
chutzpah for anyone with a hidden past to respond as she
did in a January, 1942, column. She announced that after
reading a new book on Hollywood, she was weary of seeing the "same old wheezes" about herself. She said that if
only the writers had called her, she would have given them
new material.

There was an abundant amount to give. For Louella's
early life has always remained largely obscured by her
own fantasies. For example, when Cleveland Amory included a short sketch about Louella in his *Celebrity
Register,* she was quoted as saying: "I happen to know
on very good authority that I was born Louella Oettinger

26

in Freeport, Ill. 6 August 1893, and that I have been widowed twice—John Parsons, one daughter Harriet, and Dr. Harry (Docky) Martin. . . ."

To begin at the beginning, Louella Rose Oettinger was not born in 1893. In fact, she barely made the early 1880's. Stephenson County Courthouse records show her birthdate as August 6, 1881.

Freeport was then a pleasant county seat town of 15,000 citizens, located on the banks of the Pecatonica River, in rich northern Illinois corn country.

That Louella intended to give the impression that the Oettingers were individualistic can be gathered by the tale in her autobiography on how she came to be named. As she told it, her dainty, blue-eyed mother, Helen, and her usually mild-mannered father, Joshua, got into a disagreement whether the new baby should be called Jeanette after Helen's mother or Sarah Louise after Joshua's. Finally, Helen announced the infant would be named for neither, but for the first person who entered their door. By chance it was Louella Bixler, saving the child from such possibilities as Clorinda Jane and Lena.*

Mrs. Bixler, who lived at 225 West Clark Street in the house adjoining the one occupied by the Oettingers, had another version. She claimed that when Helen Oettinger went into labor, no doctor was available, so she delivered the baby. In gratitude, Helen named the baby Louella.

Louella's father, Joshua, had come to Freeport from Danville, Pennsylvania. Although Louella became a deeply devout Catholic convert, the Oettingers were originally Jewish. Strangely enough, in an industry dominated by Jews, Louella never publicly acknowledged this.

Possibly she never considered herself Jewish. There was no synagogue in Freeport. Like many other Midwestern Jewish families, the Oettingers began to attend another place of worship. In their case, it was the Zion Episcopal

---

* Louella, the first of five children, was four years older than her brother Edwin. Three other children died in infancy: Florence, born April 4, 1883, died August 3, 1883; Freddie, born May 20, 1887, died July 7, 1888; Rae, born August 26, 1889, died December 1, 1889.

Church, and in later years Louella identified herself as a former Episcopalian.

Joshua, upon arrival in Freeport in 1879, clerked briefly for a clothier before he and his brother Eli took over a portion of the room occupied by Chamberlin Hats and opened a small store of their own. It prospered, and the Oettinger brothers, by marrying the Stine sisters, Helen and Hattie,* absorbed the Stine Clothing Store located in the Tarbox Block. This was another step upward. For a short period, Joshua and Helen, Eli and Hattie, and two other Oettinger brothers, Gus and Louis, all were involved in the management of what they now called the Star Clothing House.

Then, in 1888, despite poor health, Joshua moved his wife and children to Sterling, Illinois, where he opened a branch store—advertised as the largest clothing house in that county. Buoyed up by the excitement of the ambitious undertaking, Joshua's health seemed to improve.

Nevertheless, Helen Oettinger worried. There were still chest pains, abscesses and night sweats that her husband had to endure. Without alarming him, Helen tried to assume as many of his duties as possible.

It was a futile effort on her part. The harder she worked, the more Joshua drove himself. And in the latter part of 1889 his health began a precipitous decline. By February, 1890, it was apparent that he was suffering from a terminal case of tuberculosis.

Even so, Joshua refused to recognize the seriousness of his condition and doggedly continued going to business each day. This must have made a deep impression on eight-year-old Louella, because years later she too bravely attempted a business-as-usual policy whenever she suffered from one of her several serious illnesses.

On the morning of May 25, 1890, Joshua arose after spending a restless night. His ashen face so frightened Helen that she begged him to remain at home in bed. He refused. It was Saturday, and as owner and manager of the

---

* Their father, Isaac Stine, emigrated from Württemberg, Germany, arriving in the United States in 1847 and in Stephenson County, Illinois, in 1852.

store he felt that it was his duty to be on hand to greet his farm customers on their weekly trip to the county seat.

During the day, he was wracked by chills and fever but refused to go home. Then, in the early evening, he collapsed. He was taken home in a semiconscious state, suffering, the newspaper said, from "brain congestion" and died the following morning at the age of thirty-one.*

With the help of her brothers-in-law, Helen quickly disposed of the Sterling business and moved her bewildered children back to Freeport. Following Joshua's death, Louella, who had always been somewhat self-possessed and withdrawn, became openly hostile toward her paternal grandfather, who drank excessively, and was sullen toward her uncles and aunts. She had ambivalent feelings about her mother.

Of her relatives, there were but two for whom she felt deep affection: her maternal grandmother, Jeanette Stine, and her brother, Eddie. In later years, there was also her cousin Margaret "Maggie" Ettinger,† the Hollywood publicist, who was fifteen years her junior. Ed Ettinger used to say with a twinkle: "Oh, yes, I used to be Louella's little brother, but I'm much older than she is now."

Eighteen months after her father's death, Louella was faced with another major adjustment. On December 16, 1891, Helen Oettinger married John H. Edwards, one of the best-known and best-liked traveling salesmen in northern Illinois. Everyone was happy about this except Louella, but even she enjoyed the wedding ceremony. In fact, it is easy to detect where she developed some of her ideas of glamor by reading the account of the event in the Freeport *Daily Journal*:

THE CLIMAX OF LOVE

A Charming Home Wedding Celebrated This P.M.

Nuptials of Mr. John H. Edwards of Chicago and Mrs.

---

* One obituary notice gives his age as thirty-three.
† Maggie and Ed simplified the spelling upon entering the business world.

Helen Oettinger of this city were celebrated at the home of the bride on North Van Buren Street at 5 o'clock this afternoon. While the wedding was attended by only the relatives and a few intimate friends of the bride and groom, it was a very elaborate and elegant affair in its every detail. The parlors were prettily adorned with smilax roses, pinks and other flowers and the effect was very beautiful as well as artistic. The curtains had been drawn and the parlors were brilliantly illuminated with artificial lights which added to the scene.

At precisely 5 o'clock Mrs. G. M. Sheetz touched the piano keys and the strains of the Lohengrin Wedding March rang out in joyful notes. This was the signal for the appearance of the bridal party in the parlor where the wedding ceremony was performed by Rev. Marcus Lane, Rector of the Zion Episcopal Church.

The fair bride was attired in a traveling suit of rich imported broadcloth of the Russian red shade cut princess style with jet trimming. She wore a bonnet and gloves and diamond ornaments.

The groom was faultlessly attired in conventional black and looked supremely happy as the words were spoken which made him the husband and life protector of the lady at his side.

The newly made bride and groom accepted most gracefully the congratulations of the guests after which friends were invited to the tastefully decorated dining room where they were served with a most palatable array of dainties in which were found such viands as only a skilled caterer knows how to prepare.

The bride was most handsomely remembered by her friends as she received an elegant assortment of wedding gifts consisting of many pieces of solid silverware, rare pictures, decorated china and bric a brac. Her home is always furnished in an elegant style and it will puzzle the bride to find places for the many gifts she received from her admiring friends.

She is a lady who possesses both grace and beauty and her friends are legion. The bride is the daughter of the late Isaac Stine, who during his lifetime was known as one of Freeport's most respected merchants. . . .

Mrs. Edwards' bridal trousseau is one of the most elegant

of any bride who has ever been married in this city. Besides the traveling suit described above, she has a wave bengaline heavy-corded silk with gold and black jet trimmings, an evening dress of black and yellow silk with yellow ostrich trim, a pearl grey street suit, black silk dress with black ostrich trimming, a Nile green and white china silk house-dress trimmed with chiffon, a brown broadcloth suit, besides several elaborate tea gowns. . . .

Other of Louella's ideas of glamor may have come from her mother's secret love of the theater. With her small daughter in tow, Helen Edwards would travel by train to Chicago, register at a Loop hotel and enjoy the latest offerings. Upon her return home, Louella would present her own version of the play in the carriage house behind the Edwards' residence.

Louella always saw herself as a literary peacock caged among crows, even claiming that she was a published author at ten years of age.* As she told it, she had written a mournful tale entitled "The Flower Girl of New York." Since the Oettingers lived near Dwight Breed, editor of the Freeport *Journal,* she submitted her story to him, and he gravely told her that it would be published someday— perhaps when she was dead. Shortly afterward she fell through a hay hole with "a pair of scissors in each hand," breaking a tooth, fracturing an elbow and cutting a gash in her chin. Certain that she was dying, Louella insisted that her mother summon editor Breed, who informed her that in case she didn't survive, she could rest assured that her story would be printed. Breaking your neck for a story, Louella concluded, is newspaper legend, but something she almost achieved.

According to her, three other stories appeared in the rival *Daily Democrat,* and she also wrote several prize-winning essays. All this furthered her ambition to be rec-ognized as, if not the best, the youngest author in the country.

* "It's possible," said a Los Angeles newspaperman who handled her column for a time. "She always wrote good, solid fourth-grade prose."

What a fitting beginning for a little girl who was to grow up to be the world's most famous motion-picture gossip columnist. It is unusual. It is colorful. It is inaccurate. "I noticed that she said her first published story appeared in the Freeport paper," said Donald Breed, who succeeded his father as editor of the Freeport *Journal-Standard*. "I am afraid that her memory was erratic. She may have submitted a story to the *Journal,* but her nice complimentary remarks about my father and the help he gave her do not convince me. I have always thought it was something that she wished had happened."

Since so many of her Freeport contemporaries are either dead or unreachable, most of her statements about her childhood are unverifiable. Karl Kae Knecht, two years her junior, who was to become editorial cartoonist for the Evansville (Indiana) *Courier* and whose father was in business with the Oettingers, said, "She was a grade or two above or below mine. But I don't remember there was any reason to remember her."

Louella attended River School and later Freeport High School, but the records do not survive. Among the second-hand tales, however, there is a literary skein.

A Hollywood co-worker recalls that Louella said that her mother introduced her to sentimental novels and detective stories when she was very young and that *Little Women* and *Little Men* and all the Sherlock Holmes adventures enthralled her. In her column, she claimed to have read *"The Murders in the Rue Morgue"* after retiring and to have been almost too frightened to put out the light.

Old settlers in Freeport report that she did win a prize for a seventh-grade composition. They recall this not so much for her literary accomplishment as for the fact that she was so thrilled she wet her pants. The contention that she had an insatiable curiosity about her neighbor's business also prevails, but it seems likely that this rumor developed after she made gossip her business.

Yet it is undeniable that in some obscure way, she began at an early age to regard writing as the magic carpet which would whisk her away from humdrum small-town life into the great world of adventure. So it was that when John Edwards decided to leave Freeport, Louella welcomed the move. After marrying, Edwards had quit his job as a traveling salesman and opened a grocery at 121 Stephenson Street which soon ran into financial difficulties. Real estate and tax records show that in 1897, he transferred stock, fixtures, horses and a wagon to his wife's name. Shortly thereafter the Edwardses left Freeport and took up residence in Dixon, Illinois. A salesman who sometimes roomed with Edwards later said, "His greatest achievement was marrying a widow with money."

The interval that Louella passed in Dixon represented a problem to her. If, as she claimed, she had been born in 1893, not only would she have been graduated from high school at eight, but she would have married at twelve. Louella solved the problem by ignoring it. She portrayed herself as a minor Midwestern tornado who swept through Dixon streets snatching news from every crack and cranny and dropping it into the printing presses, carrying a reporter's notebook in one hand and schoolbooks in the other.

In the magazine story on Louella, Howard Dietz once observed that "doubtless she learned her own futuristic grammar (at Dixon High School) . . . . Louella can spell anything right but words, although she gets names wrong occasionally. . . ."

Nevertheless, while attending high school, Louella did review musicals, traveling repertory companies and social events. And her essay, *When Is Revolution Justified?*, won first prize—busts of Washington, Lincoln and Daniel Webster—in the local chapter of the DAR's contest. Louella donated the prizes to South Central School.

She was one of twelve members of the thirty-seventh class to graduate from Dixon High. She claimed that she had been valedictorian, but no mention of this was made in newspaper accounts. In the class day exercise (in which all members either spoke or sang), Louella delivered the prophecy, and at commencement, held at the Dixon Opera House (admission 15 cents) on June 3, 1901, Louella gave "Great News," an oration on distinguished men who had come from Illinois.

At graduation then, Louella was unusually ambitious and energetic, but otherwise unexceptional. She was neither brilliant nor stupid, neither remarkably pretty nor painfully plain. She was simply an incurably romantic girl who never hesitated to touch up reality when it failed to meet expectations. Those who had known her during her Dixon days later described her over and over as "silly," "a big sentimentalist" and "always had a gooey personality."

Take, for instance, teacher W. G. Turnbull. None of Louella's contemporaries recalled him as particularly handsome. But in 1944, when Louella published *The Gay Illiterate,* Turnbull, then superintendent of the Philadelphia General Hospital, wrote her a jovial letter: "I take the title of your book as a personal insult. Why do you think I spent those years in Dixon teaching you Latin, algebra or anything else?" In response, Louella rhapsodized over the young teacher, so good-looking that even to be seen walking with him was "heaven." Recalling this, ninety-year-old Sadie Mack laughed and said, "Oh, Louella always was kind of silly."

The only practical attitude to take toward Louella is that she was an enthusiastic role player and that nothing happened the way she claimed. She always said that at seventeen she became the child bride of a middle-aged roué.

The fact is that two months and three days after graduation, Louella celebrated her twentieth birthday, and it was not until four years later that she married. Meantime, she had attended Dixon College and Normal School, spent a year teaching a country school * and worked as a reporter.

It may have been through her newspaper work that her romance with John Parsons began. Parsons is generally described as a real estate man, but apparently he also worked as a reporter. The *Dixon City Directory of 1900* lists him as a reporter on the *Evening Telegraph.* At that time Louella was a part-time employee of the *Star.*

In any case, the two met, fell in love and applied for a marriage license on October 31, 1905. Louella gave her

---

* Gwendolyn Bardell, another teacher, recalled in 1941 that their monthly salaries "probably wouldn't pay for a new fall hat for Louella now."

age as twenty-four and John Dement Parsons, her "middle-
aged" husband-to-be, was thirty-two. For some inexplicable reason, the wedding was held in the home of the
groom's, not the bride's, parents in North Dixon. Only
relatives were present in the parlor that had been banked
with autumn leaves, chrysanthemums and bittersweet. At
8 P.M. the pianist struck up Mendelssohn's "Wedding
March," and Louella, wearing a white china silk gown,
slowly descended the stair on the arm of her stepfather.
She and John Parsons were wed by the Reverend John
Ericsson of St. Luke's Episcopal Church.

Soon after, the newlyweds moved to Burlington, Iowa,
where John Parsons installed his bride, who was innocent
of domestic skills, in "a genteel boardinghouse." Louella
admitted she was not happy there, but the reasons for her
discontent had little to do with those she gave.

She claimed that as a child bride she embarrassed her
middle-aged husband by prattling girlishly, skipping happily about and innocently suggesting word games or follow-
the-leader when Parsons entertained business associates.
Behavior of that sort would have earned Louella a reputation for extreme eccentricity, if not downright insanity.
Yet in describing her, most Burlington contemporaries
remembered her as mousy, sentimental, soft-hearted and
maladjusted.

Burlington, one veteran resident explained, had been
settled by Easterners and had aristocratic pretensions un-
common in the typical easygoing Midwestern community.
According to this observer, Louella had no patience with
their life-style. They honored precedent; Louella considered it something to be broken. They judged a woman
by the tidiness of her house; Louella, if she thought about
the subject at all, regarded housework as something to be
ignored.

She had few women friends, and she found conversation
about business a bore—unless it promised to bring
enormous returns to John and indirectly to her. There
was no possibility of this. As manager of the Parsons
Block, a real estate development built by his grandfather,
John Parsons was not in a position to share directly in

any profits—no matter how big. So it was that Louella found herself trapped in an unsatisfactory environment.

Sensing his ambitious wife's dissatisfaction, John Parsons moved her out of the boardinghouse. In the ensuing months, they occupied a succession of houses, but Louella remained despondent.

"Louella was awfully unhappy," said Margaret Clark, whose family lived directly across from a house the Parson rented on North Third Street. "I didn't know her awfully well." She paused. "I wasn't allowed to associate with her. It was whispered they served drinks. We were very *pious* in those days," Miss Clark said, with a self-mocking laugh. "Once though I sneaked over to a party, and all they were serving was beer. I was bored to death."

A closer friend of Louella's was Miss Clark's mother. "I suppose Mother realized Louella was lonely," Margaret Clark said. "You see, John Parsons' grandfather and father had a lot of money. John and Louella should have fitted in. But John wasn't the most stable man in the world, and Louella made a lot of boners socially.

"She used to come over and read poetry she'd written. Mother thought it was perfectly terrible, but she was awfully polite about it. I know when Louella succeeded later, everyone was very much surprised. Of course, they admired her intestinal fortitude, but they were very much surprised."

One Burlingtonian who was not surprised was Martin Bruhl, a local pianist who was later to appear with the New York Philharmonic. Since Bruhl's musical aspirations also made him something of an outsider, he was sympathetic to Louella.*

Bruhl's advanced deafness made direct conversation with him difficult, but through his wife he recalled that Louella had often cried on his shoulder. She had been pregnant at the time and neglected. "She hated the idea of getting pregnant so soon," Mrs. Bruhl quoted her husband

* "It's easy to see why they became friends." Margaret Clark laughed. "The crazy poetess and the crazy musician. That's catty. But kind of fun. And true!"

as saying. "And John Parsons was boosting around with his secretary, so Louella didn't know where to turn."

When Bruhl left town to pursue his musical career, he rented his home in the North Hill section to Louella. But her indifference to such mundane matters as keeping the lawn trimmed and looking after the disposal of garbage triggered a controversy with her neighbors. "They tried to evict her," Mrs. Bruhl said. "But Martin always thought it was because she didn't accept small-town living." In later years, Louella explained to him in a letter that she seldom mentioned Burlington because those years represented the unhappiest period of her life.*

Certainly the brightest event of that period occurred when Harriet Oettinger Parsons was born on August 23, 1906.† Louella, deeply feminine and weepily sentimental, gloried in motherhood. "It's been said before, but it's true —it was as if she had invented it," a Burlingtonian said. "Of course, the divorce was tragic from her point of view."

Once again fact and fantasy collide. Louella chose to ignore the divorce in later years, attributing her problems with John Parsons to her immaturity. What happened to him cannot be clarified at this point in time. Presumably he enlisted in the Army during World War I. Louella claimed he died aboard a transport ship. Another person said he died of influenza at an Army camp in St. Louis, while a third party maintains he committed suicide. Had he survived World War I, Louella thought they might have worked out their problems.

"Worked out their problems!" exclaimed a source who asked not to be identified. "How, might I ask? She must have taken that idea from some old movie. They couldn't. Not in a million years. By the time the little girl was born he and Louella were practically finished. He had another interest. I knew him—more by reputation than anything

* In 1939 when the *Saturday Evening Post* published Tom Wood's frank appraisal "The First Lady of Hollywood," the Burlington Chamber of Commerce threatened to ban the magazine.

† Inexplicably, the filing date was delayed until January 15, 1907.

else. But he was spoiled rotten. His family was well-to-do, but he just dissipated the money. Anyway, Louella and he were divorced. I knew the girl he married. His secretary, I believe. She was a nice little thing. The person you should talk to is Adeline Churchill."

It turned out that Adeline Moir Churchill, several years younger than Louella, had played a brief but significant role in Louella's life. Her feelings about her friend of long ago were obviously complicated. "I knew Louella, Louella's mother, her brother—all of them," she said, as if establishing her credentials. "And I knew John. John was very likable and very intelligent, but he was not one to make Louella happy, I'm sure.

"Louella herself was certainly a queer mixture. It puzzled me. She appeared so, well . . . naïve isn't quite the word. Nor stupid, because she had a brain, but she didn't always show it. I knew her here in Burlington and when she worked at Essanay in Chicago. I visited her, and she visited back. Frankly, when I went out to Hollywood, I didn't attempt to see her, because I thought she wanted to forget Burlington and all her unhappy associations."

Mention of the mysterious divorce brought immediate confirmation. Mrs. Churchill was certain there had been one and was under the impression Louella had obtained it while visiting a relative in Missoula, Montana. In Missoula, Deputy Louise Brownlee checked civil and judgment documents between 1906 and 1917, without positive results. Nor did the records of Ravalli, Mineral or Lake counties produce anything. The Bureau of Vital Statistics in Helena carries no Central Registration prior to 1943, and no record of the court action could be found in either Des Moines County, Iowa, or Cook County, Illinois.

Nevertheless, Mrs. Churchill remained firm and in so doing referred to a husband whom Louella had previously never acknowledged publicly. Louella, on a visit from Chicago, had met him at the Moir residence. "What has always irritated me a little was that she seemed unwilling to mention her second husband, Jack McCaffrey," Mrs. Churchill said. "Jack was a fine man. He loved Louella, and he adored Harriet."

She described Captain McCaffrey as a handsome, intelligent riverboat captain—"very much a gentleman." He had worked for her father on a small steamboat used for towing a houseboat on which her father went up and down the river buying shells for several button factories in which he was interested. She thought that Captain Jack and Louella were probably married in Chicago sometime in 1915. A search of Cook County records between 1912 and 1916 proved futile.

How Louella managed to conceal the existence of so colorful an Irishman as Captain Jack is almost inexplicable. Powerful connections might have expunged records of divorces and marriages, but a living, breathing human being is something else. Nevertheless, conceal him she did.

Captain Jack, who was born in Le Claire, Iowa, on March 21, 1873, was, by all accounts, extremely attractive. In recalling him, even those who met him when he was well past the prime of life described him as handsome, courtly, charming, gentle and beguiling. Yet he was thought to be a confirmed bachelor.

To Louella, a woman who always needed to be in love, he must have represented a splendid replacement for her errant ex-husband. Like John Parsons, Captain Jack was a few years older than she was, and he was infinitely better-looking than the husband who had rebuffed her in favor of his secretary. Luckily, too, the McCaffrey family was rich.

As the neglected wife, Louella had been miserable enough to flee Burlington. Older residents recall that when she returned to visit, she flowered under Captain Jack's compliments. He praised her complexion, her expressive brown eyes and her pretty smile. He commented on her intelligence and vivacity. All her life when in the company of casual acquaintances, Louella might seem withdrawn, even somewhat stupid, but when she was intrigued by anyone, especially a man, she sparkled. And toward any romantic attachment, she managed to project a helpless charm combined with an unbounded admiration that made a man know he was a man.

At the time that Louella and Captain Jack met, he was experiencing financial difficulties and may possibly have been regretting the opportunities he had jauntily cast aside in his youth. For his parents had made an effort to provide him with advantages. They sent him to Northwestern University, but he was young and high-spirited and found academic pursuits tedious. Life on the Mississippi promised escape, and he signed to work on a boat. Thereafter he followed the river, operating almost every type of vessel found on the Mississippi, including such steamers as the *Natchez, Cairo* and *Memphis*.

When Captain Jack decided to give up bachelorhood, it came as a surprise to his acquaintances, but he happily accepted Harriet, as well as Louella, taking both to the South immediately after the marriage.

"I imagine Captain Jack and Miss Louella got married in that little town up there, Le Claire, Iowa. Or they might have got married in Chicago," Mrs. William P. Sevier, Jr., the former Martha Boney, said. "I know when they went on their honeymoon to Biloxi, they left Harriet with my family. I think Harriet was about eleven and I was about ten. Harriet was crazy about Captain Jack. She wanted to change her name to McCaffrey."

Some residents of Tallulah, Louisiana, where the Mc-Caffreys had a plantation, were under the impression that Captain Jack had brought his new family there to live. "I'm quite sure he came here with the idea of staying on," said Miss Katharine Ward. "But Louella wasn't having any of it. My uncle Andrew Sevier used to tell of Captain Jack bringing her into the office to introduce her. Uncle Andrew was very much taken with her. He liked her. He liked her very much. In fact, everyone who met her liked her. At the time she was on the plump side, but pretty. But she just couldn't tolerate the country. She was a big-city girl, and she just couldn't put up with this small-town stuff."

No amount of digging unearthed either marriage or divorce records in Tallulah, Chicago or New York. Was it possible they had never been legally married? The answer turned up in an undated letter on her International News Service stationery to Captain Jack at the Federal Barge Line offices in New Orleans. She was asking "a big favor." She had been happily married for thirteen years now,* she told Captain Jack, and had attended a Catholic church regularly. What she needed was an affidavit from him "to prove you were never a member of the Church."

Obviously, Captain Jack had been her legal husband in the eyes of the state, if not in the eyes of the church.

If the Burlington years provided some painful episodes for Louella, they also exposed her to the great passion of her life: motion pictures.

While living in Burlington, she saw her first "flicker." She claimed that it was *The Great Train Robbery,* but taking into consideration her tendency to associate herself with important people and momentous events, it may have been something else entirely. No matter. Whatever the film was, exposure to it was to alter her perception and her existence permanently.

Her first thought was that she wanted to be a part of "this new Art form." It was flourishing in Chicago, so when her marriage to John Parsons and her visit to Montana were over, what could be more natural than that she should settle in that city? Especially, since her favorite cousin, Maggie, was living there?

The picture that Louella paints of her Chicago years is once again difficult to reconcile with verifiable facts. Louella's versions: She was a poor war widow, alone in the world, often hocking the diamonds that she inherited from her mother to support her beloved daughter.

It is easy enough to point out that pawning the diamonds supposedly inherited from her mother was an especially neat trick since her mother lived on until 1922, at which time Louella had finished her Chicago sojourn and was well established in New York.

However, Louella may have struggled before—and even after—marrying Captain Jack. As Katharine Ward pointed out: "Perhaps he was temporarily financially embarrassed, although in later years he was quite prosperous. And I do know that even after the divorce, he sent Harriet a check every month for many years."

* To Dr. Harry Martin. This would presumably have made the date 1942.

Beverly Bayne, who with Francis X. Bushman formed the screen's first popular romantic team, confirmed that Louella probably had financial problems. "I know at Essanay she doubled as part-time secretary for Bushman," Miss Bayne said. Did she recall Captain Jack? "Oh, my, yes. He and Louella often came to play cards with my mother and stepfather," the silent star recalled.

Certainly Louella was a role player: first a Betty Bronson type sprite; then during the Parsons marriage a Mae Marsh innocent suddenly brought to maturity by harsh realities; now in Chicago a combination of Belle Bennett-Lillian Gish, a woman whose sole interest lay in protecting and providing shoes for baby. Later in life, she found it convenient to appear fluttery, feminine and slightly addle-pated. Let the world laugh. While others laughed, this shrewd, pragmatic young woman plodded on, never questioning that she was destined for greater things. Probably late in 1910, Louella began her career in Chicago at $10 a week working for a stereopticon company, but she shrewdly accepted a job at $1 a week less in the syndication department of the Chicago *Tribune*. At night she wrote scenarios.

Louella claimed she got her job at a film studio by allowing her cousin Maggie to read a screen story based on a sensational case she had covered as a newspaper reporter in Dixon. Maggie was impressed enough to give it to her college roommate, Ruth Helms, who gave it to her mother, who gave it to a member of her card club. This woman, Mrs. George Spoor, gave it to her husband. Spoor, who was the "ess" of Essanay (formed with "Bronco Billy" Anderson), bought the scenario and hired Louella as a combination story editor and writer.

Actually, Maggie Ettinger had heard Essanay was looking for a story editor and persuaded Ruth Helms to help Louella get the job through Mrs. Helms' connection with Mrs. Spoor. Louella proved herself able enough to be included among the established screenwriters discussed by Roy McCardell in an August 16, 1915, *Saturday Evening Post* Article.

She always claimed that her first scenario was *Chains,*

starring Francis X. Bushman.* As synopsized in the November 2, 1912, issue of the *Moving Picture World,* the movie asked this question: What happens to an innocent girl who foolishly marries a condemned murderer before he is sent off to serve a twenty-six-year prison sentence and then requests that out of the goodness of his heart he free her so she can wed his lawyer?

Louella once estimated that she read 20,000 submissions and wrote 125 one- and two-reel scenarios a year while at Essanay. Exaggeration or not, she impressed Spoor enough so that he raised her salary from $18 to $20, then $30 and finally to $45 a week before an efficiency man, Homer Boushey, persuaded Spoor the studio couldn't afford her.

It came as a blow to Louella. For Essanay provided an unpredictable, stimulating environment. The studio lacked all the stultifying small-town conventions that had kept her unhappy. She gloried in her contacts with the stars and future stars. In later years, she never tired of telling how she bawled out "scrawny, young Gloria Swanson" and Agnes Ayres when the two $3.25-a-day extra girls distracted her by giggling outside her window. She recalled the career crisis of Francis X. Bushman when his fans discovered he was married and the father of five little Bushmans. Both Louella and Charlie Chaplin remembered his refusal to accept the shooting script she provided, but since his first picture at Essanay was made in 1915, Louella must have left in that year, not in 1914 as she claimed.

Apparently Louella had had some premonition that her days with the company were numbered, because she spent her evenings working on a book, *How to Write for the*

---

* Whether written before or after *Chains, Margaret's Awakening* for which Louella supplied the scenario, was advertised in the May 25, 1912, issue of *Moving Picture World*. The studio described it as a "bright, brisk, animated and thoroughly satisfying comedy-drama, featuring a romping little tot, who is gloriously refreshing in her childish enthusiasm and pantomimic perfection. . . ." That tot was Baby Parsons, as the six-year-old Harriet was billed. Harriet also appeared in other Essanay films of Louella's authorship, including *The Magic Wand*.

Movies, and she had almost completed it when she was fired. She placed the book with the Chicago-based A. C. McClurg publishers and it appeared in 1915, selling for $1 a copy. Advertised as "the most helpful book for amateur photoplay writers ever written . . . invaluable to beginners and those who aren't acquainted with the rules of the game . . ." it was such a success that it was revised and reissued in 1917 at $1.25.

She was also able to sell it for serialization to former associates on the *Tribune* who were now editing the *Herald,* and at one time it was used as a textbook in a college course on scenario writing.

In all probability, the first person to write critiques of "shadow plays" was Frank E. Woods, whose criticism began appearing in the New York *Dramatic Mirror* in June, 1908.

In Chicago, by 1914 the *Tribune* had assigned Jack Lawson as its critic. Shortly after taking over the job, he was killed accidentally and succeeded by Audrie Alspaugh, who took the alliterative and easily remembered "Kitty Kelly" as a pseudonym. She in turn was succeeded by Frances Smith, whose by-line was the visual pun Mae Tinee.*

Louella conceded that she had not been the first critic to write about films in Chicago, although interviewers sometimes made the claim for her. But she did insist that after leaving Essanay, she had originated the motion-picture gossip column for the Chicago *Record-Herald*.

In later years, she said that she suggested "behind the scenes" coverage to William Handy, publisher of the *Herald,* and convinced him that it would be a boon to the paper's circulation. The result was a column "Seen on the Screen" and an "Answers to Questions" feature. Exactly when these features started is difficult to ascertain since only scattered issues of the paper are on file in the Chicago Public Library and Louella cunningly clipped off all dates in her earliest scrapbooks.

While Louella may have intuitively understood the

---

* Mae Tinee before switching to films wrote interviews with visiting stage stars for the *Tribune.*

public's curiosity about the personal lives of screen actors, a perusal of her early columns reveals a focus on production news plus occasional interviews with screenplayers who were working in or passing through Chicago.

On occasion she undertook to cover general news stories, such as the Eastland boating disaster. Here she was far from successful. Her emotional copy was at best supplementary material which added human interest to factual accounts of the tragedy. Most of her energy was expended on films, however, and gradually gossip began to dominate her work.

Surprisingly, in the earliest columns there is a considerable amount of skepticism. Speaking of the screen's first vamp Theda Bara (Bara was "Arab" spelled backward; Theda, an anagram of "death"), she reported that it was being whispered that Miss Bara believed herself to be the reincarnation of Lucrezia Borgia and other feminine fiends and that the star always delved deeply into the occult when acting. Louella wryly commented that this seemed an excellent angle to complement Miss Bara's "dark, weird beauty," but she left no doubt that she was not taken in by such press agent folderol. This skepticism soon disappeared on the apparent—and accurate—assumption that fans preferred to have her tell it as it wasn't.

Soon after she began writing the column, those mannerisms that made her so easy to parody began to develop. By the late 1920's she was developing them consciously on the theory that a phrase or adjective applied to an entertainer often enough made him identifiable. Thus, one inevitably found "madcap Mabel Normand," "fascinating Marie Dressler," "the irresistible Charlie Chaplin," and "fickle-hearted Mary Garden." Lillian Gish was "the lily-like Lillian," Mary Pickford "the golden child," Jetta Goudal "that temperamental cocktail" and the early Garbo "the Scandinavian vamp."

The image-making terms created an unintentionally humorous effect. Nevertheless, Chicago contemporaries, including Gene Fowler, Ashton Stevens, Charles MacArthur and Carl Sandburg, admired her tenacity in bulldogging a story, even though they did not always admire her style.

Jack Lait, later a Hearst editor, was with the *Record-*

Herald in 1915. At the time, Chicagoans were vitally interested in the plans of Mary Garden, who had been closely associated with the development of opera in Chicago. Lait attempted to run down the story but failed. Later that day Louella turned in her Sunday copy. In the eighth paragraph, he found: "The latest recruit for film is Miss Mary Garden, formerly a singer, who will act in two photoplays directed by Tom Ince, the well-known, popular and wonderful director . . . ," a reflection on both her reportorial abilities and her news sense.

With or without adjectives, Louella's forte was never understatement. Her boundless enthusiasm permeated her column. Even mild criticism of the medium angered her. In 1915 she attacked the legitimate theater, claiming that the "quick action of shadow scenes" makes stagecraft seem sluggish. Films offered a "latitude" not present on the stage and provided "exhilaration" absent from live performances.

When Richard Henry Little, the *Herald's* star drama critic, rebutted that movies were only a passing fad, adding, "They have certain elements that make them popular for the moment, but Art alone endures, and there is no more Art in the movies than there is in a bronze guinea pig," Louella was outraged, not at his pomposity but that he dared criticize films. Although their offices were on the same floor, she ignored the six-foot-four critic for a week. When he finally spoke, she hissed, "Assassin!" and swept by.

Later "Art" did not particularly concern Louella, but in the early days she took producers to task for lack of aspiration. The Morosco Company's *Peer Gynt* (1915) offered "silent proof that nothing is impossible in 'movies' today . . . Poetical fancy has been thought to be lost in the movies, but *Peer Gynt* has proved that all pictures are not composed of the commoner sort of material. If we only might have some Grieg music, the *Peer Gynt Suite,* we might have felt that movies had accomplished their mission," she added.

She also rallied to D. W. Griffith's side when controversy arose over *The Birth of a Nation.* Louella idolized the director and sometimes attached more than one of the common adulatory catchphrases to his name—"The Master," "The Edison of the Cinema," "The Marconi of the Screen" or "The Shakespeare of the Movies."

When the *Record-Herald* joined the attack on *The Birth of a Nation* as inflammatory and racist, Louella was outraged. Since James Keeley, owner of the paper, was one of the chief attackers in Chicago, Louella faced a dilemma. But she summoned up her courage to beg him to see the film. He saw it and was won over.

Soon Louella's column was filled with laments that this work of art should be viewed on racial grounds. Why, Griffith asked, if the villain was white, couldn't there be a black rogue? But as he talked on, his Southern background exposed his prejudice. "The most active workers against this film have been people who believe in intermarriage of the races. The Negro should be as much opposed to this as the white man. . . . The intermarriage of any two races has never been attended with good results," he said.

Griffith's social views were actually of little interest to Louella. Overwhelmed by the film's cinematic qualities, she threw herself into the fight against the forces of censorship which were attempting to ban the picture. "I felt a thrill of happiness to know that I'd lived to see a day when such marvelous photography, such acting and such marvelous productions should come under the head of a motion picture. Only we who have started at the beginning and have grown with the pictures can understand what this development of the newest Art means—a screen epic as someone aptly called it. . . . I went away feeling that I had seen the most stupendous achievement of this age, and if I may be pardoned for saying so, a photoplay whose wonder in the years to come will stand with Homer's *Iliad* and Wagner's operas and Milton's *Paradise Lost*."

Louella afterward proudly pointed to her stand against censorship. Yet her attitude was ambivalent. For example, when the Pennsylvania Board of Censors allowed the seal of approval to Elinor Glyn's *Three Weeks,* only to be reversed by the National Censor Board, Louella hoped that the film would be consigned to "a nice dark shelf in the closet. Sin is sin whether committed by a peasant or a king, and no amount of decoration can ever make *Three Weeks* anything but an immoral tale."

By 1916 Louella was considered enough of an authority on "shadow plays" to be booked as a lecturer on them after giving assurance that her talks would be educational and contain nothing offensive to Chautauqua audiences. Through writing and lecturing her reputation grew. In late 1917 she was sent to New York to cover a motion-picture ball and to report on the studios located there and across the Hudson River in New Jersey.

While Louella's career boomed, the *Record-Herald's* circulation sagged. At last in May, 1918, the inevitable could be staved off no longer. The *Herald* was absorbed by William Randolph Hearst's *American.*

Despite the success she had achieved, Louella was apprehensive about her chances of finding a new job. When she mentioned her fears to "assassin" Richard Henry Little, they were walking along the street. Did he think there would be a place for her with Mr. Hearst?

Hearst!

Little dramatically pointed to a delivery truck. "See that milkman?" he asked. "Well, go take *his* job—do any damned thing, but don't ever work for Hearst."

Nevertheless, Louella tried to place her column in the new publication, pointing out that in addition to her work for the daily paper, her Sunday page was syndicated in eighteen other cities. Louella's first version was that Hearstling Arthur Brisbane turned her down flat. Later she changed it to his saying that there was $25 but not $45 a week's interest in films—an estimate she refused to accept.

One way or another, Louella left Chicago for New York with, according to her, only $200 in cash. It must have been somewhat more complicated, for Captain Jack was still in the background. In New York, Louella, armed with letters of introduction, set out to find a job. She toyed with the idea of joining Pathé's publicity department but decided against it. Her attitude is expressed in an item she was to run in her column a few months later about Janet Flanner, whose letters from Paris in the *New Yorker* magazine under the pseudonym Genêt, were to make her celebrated. "Janet Flanner, another perfectly good news-paper person, has gone and sold her birthright for a fat salary. . . . She is leaving for a seven week trip into the West where she will exploit the advantages of *Hearts of Humanity.*"

Louella held out for a newspaper job. Her opportunity came when Richard Watts, the motion-picture editor of the *Morning Telegraph,* was called into the service during World War I. On June 9, 1918, Louella was appointed to take his place. Editor and publisher W. E. Lewis hired her at $75 a week, and the announcement he issued makes it clear that before Louella ever met, let alone worked for, Hearst, she was considered a prominent reporter of motion-picture news. The release emphasized that she would continue her "chatty, intimate interviews. . . . She will tell what is happening each day in moving picture circles. Not stereotyped paragraphs of events, but live current gossip, such as everyone from property boy to film president likes to read. The entire industry will be her field and everyone with a motion picture secret to tell can send or give it to Miss Parsons for the *Morning Telegraph.*"

At once what writer Ruth Waterbury called Louella's wonderful "political instinct in the widest sense" went to work. She began cultivating valuable contacts. "I don't believe she consciously worked it out. It was absolutely instinctive," Miss Waterbury observed. "For instance, she dined with someone tonight because she was thinking way ahead. She was aiming at something way over there. And all this worked. If she happened to be going to New York or London, she got to know people who had contacts—and now suddenly her hotel is set up and introductions are made. She got what she wanted and she paid off in what her contacts wanted—which was to see their names mentioned in her column. I think it is so interesting to see this instinctive reaction at work."

It was in exactly this same manner that Louella assembled her first staff, which she called "my garden of cats." Among them was Helen Pollock, daughter of playwright Channing Pollock (whose most enduring achievement may have been to inspire Dorothy Parker to say one of his works "*The House Beautiful* is the play lousy.");

Aileen St. John Brenon, niece of a successful film director; Dorothy Day, ex-Belasco actress; Gertrude Chase, fiancée of a famous artist; and Frances Agnew and Agnes Smith, whom Louella considered the best writers working for her.

These were young women with valuable connections, and Louella intended to make maximum use of them. She visualized her column format as being similar to "Happenings of Local Interest" in Freeport, Dixon, Burlington and other small-town newspapers. Condensed and punched up, it was also used by Walter Winchell in what was eventually to become the most influential gossip column ever published.

Unlike Winchell's, Louella's early approach was for the most part benign. She wished Marian (*sic*) Davies a happy California vacation. Louis Mayer was planning to spend five days in New York, two in Boston, now that he was becoming a film producer. She chronicled the metamorphosis of Samuel Goldfish into Samuel Goldwyn. And when the Goldwyn Studios moved to California, Louella wistfully hoped "the warm weather next spring will bring them back to New York to make pictures." Because now that Louella was in New York it seemed the center of the universe to her, just as Chicago once had and as Hollywood eventually would.

In New York, she relentlessly cultivated people who could further her career. When she did a story on Mrs. Heywood Broun, Louella and Broun became friends. Theodora Bean taught her to make up a newspaper page. When O. O. McIntyre was still a press agent for the Majestic Hotel, Louella predicted he would become a great success and encouraged him to drop into the old car barn which the *Morning Telegraph* occupied. She made it a point to see novelist Fannie Hurst often. In fact, she lunched with Miss Hurst and Lillian Lafferty, better known as Beatrice Fairfax, at the English Tearoom, a gathering place for literary and theatrical people, the day the Armistice was signed, November 11, 1918.

By her own admission, Louella had a tendency to feel herself the center of things. She spent a great deal of time at 14 Fifth Avenue, the home of the Smith family, whose daughters included Agnes and Sally Smith Benson. On the day General Pershing returned from World War I, Louella was leaning out the Smiths' window, waving, when suddenly she cried, "Look! He's waving at me!"

"Nonsense," said Mrs. Smith. "He's waving at everyone." But Louella was unconvinced.

Louella made every effort to ingratiate herself with people who could help her in publishing. Captain Jack might not feel totally at home in the new surroundings, but if not, he would have to change. Given her new salary and her new social and professional contacts, Louella, with the most amiable intentions, began to rile him with what he considered incessant criticisms, for Louella was determined that "the little girl who lives at my house," as she customarily referred to Harriet, was to have the advantage of the best schools, clothes and friends. Because of his fondness for his stepdaughter, Captain Jack went along with Louella's ambitions, but her openhandedness often irritated him. When she began buying him expensive wearing apparel and other gifts, he rebelled. "Next," Captain Jack told his cousin Mrs. A. R. Baillie, "she'll be wanting me to stay home and wear an apron, while she goes out to make the living."

Although Louella was an intensely feminine woman, she never let personal problems interfere with her career. She was tireless in stalking a story, gathering tidbits about the stars and fighting to get those highly prized "scoops." Sometimes increasing activity in California posed problems. More and more often, she was forced to quote from the Los Angeles *Times*' Grace Kingsley. Still, frequent visits to New York by actors kept her fans in touch.

Among mentions of rising favorites, there was one item about a young woman, who in Louella's wildest dreams could not have loomed as a possible rival. On May 4, 1919, this paragraph appeared: "When one has youth and good looks, one doesn't mind telling a story on one's self. So Hedda Hopper, now cast as the mother in Norma Talmadge's *By Right of Conquest*, tells this one on herself. 'I asked Mr. Hopper [Mr. Hopper being DeWolf] if he thought it would be all right for me to play a mother in Miss Talmadge's picture. You see, I do not grey my hair or really look very much older. He said, "My dear, if you are as rotten as you were in the last picture I saw you in, I don't think it will make any difference," ' which husbandly frankness was quite undeserved, we who have seen and liked Hedda Hopper in pictures will say."

II

Elda Furry has always sounded like a small blonde animal with soft skin that people like to stroke. Being stroked makes my hair rise on my head.

—HEDDA HOPPER

A FAN magazine writer once observed that Hedda Hopper looks "as the Queen of the Nile should have looked—and very likely didn't. She has a sort of serpentine grace which would fit very well with the Palmolive complexion ad's conception of Cleopatra."

There is no blinking the fact that Hedda lived by her wits—and her wit. While Hedda had no more intention of telling her real age than Louella did, she tried to conceal it even more completely. She wasn't content merely to change the year from 1885 to 1890. She also switched her birthday from May 2 to June 2—thereby altering her astrological sign from Taurus, the Bull, to Gemini, the Twins.

Like Louella, Hedda was not one to adhere scrupulously to facts. In addition to her real name, Elda Furry, she sometimes called herself Elda Curry, Ella Furry and Elda Millar. In an August, 1909, interview with a New York *Telegraph* reporter as *Elda Curry, she had been born in Boston, educated there and then had attended Miss Carter's Seminary for Young Ladies in Pittsburgh.* By December, 1909, she informed an interviewer that *she had been born in Nebraska, but at the age of eight, she and her sister had been taken to England.* In 1919, she told Delight Evans of *Photoplay* magazine that *she had been born in Pittsburgh* and as a child in England she had sung for the American ambassador to London, a Mr. Bayard. Ambassador Bayard had asked whether she wanted to be a great singer. When she replied that she did, he requested a lump of sugar for his tea. Some day, he promised, he would tell the world that the famous prima donna Elda Curry had sweetened his tea.*

Fairly early on, Hedda stopped claiming Boston, Nebraska and Pittsburgh as birthplaces, admitting that she had been born in Hollidaysburg, Pennsylvania.

David Furry had been born in New Enterprise, Pennsylvania, one of twelve children. David's father, who had managed to accumulate several large farms, practiced a peculiar form of paternal favoritism. Six of the twelve children were chosen to have college educations at the expense of the other six.

Unluckily for David, he fell into the "have-nots." The expectation was that he would help work the farms, but David had other ideas. He ran away from home three times before he finally stayed away. Then he married Margaret Miller, opened a meat market and fathered nine children, seven of whom survived.

Elda, who was named for a character in a novel her mother was reading at the time, was the middle child. Elda resented that. From the first, as someone once observed, she considered her place stage front and center. But with all her sibling rivals, this was not easy to achieve.

In 1888, when Elda was three years old, the family moved to 2901 Maple Avenue in what is known as the Millville section of Altoona, and Elda found further cause for resentment. Her mother now undertook to help out in the butcher shop. Even though she was only three, Elda expressed her displeasure. At first she sulked, and when no one noticed, she yelled. From the beginning, according to her family, Elda felt more intensely than the other Furrys.

She *worshiped* her mother, a woman so diffident that all

---

* At least it was the right state.

her life she allowed everyone to call her Maggie, never revealing until she was an old, old woman that she detested the name.

Elda *loathed* her older sister, Dora, who consistently borrowed Elda's belongings, including her new clothes, until the younger girl flew at her and scratched her face so severely that Dora couldn't leave the house for two weeks. Even then she had to explain to friends that "a cat" had clawed her. "She was right. I had," Hedda wrote years later. "Yes, it broke the habit."

Elda *adored* her baby sister, Margaret, to whom she played substitute mother when big Margaret was ill after giving birth to this, her ninth child.

Elda *despised* her paternal grandfather, who rewarded her with a single silver dollar after her devoted nursing had saved his eyesight.

Elda *idolized* her Uncle John, her mother's twin, whose easygoing sense of humor was an effective antidote to her father's authoritarianism.

Elda *hated* her father. It was, in her opinion, his selfishness that had caused her saintly mother to be burdened with the irritating Dora, as well as her brothers Sherman, Cammon, Frank and Edgar—whose offense in Elda's eyes was their maleness. Because of them, her mother was too exhausted to give her the attention she craved, and because of her father's self-indulgence, assembly-line techniques had to be applied to the family when illness struck. When one of the little Furrys came down with measles or mumps, the rest of the flock were cooped up with the patient so that the illness would spread rapidly and subside more quickly. She blamed her father too for having made it necessary for her to clean, cook, wash dishes (she hated dishwashing for the rest of her life) and assist in the butcher shop. She received no wages but helped herself from the till—and saved the money.

The result of all this was a childhood in which there was almost no coddling and few good-night kisses. Thus, it was not by chance that Elda grew into a woman who found it difficult, if not impossible, to express any kind of tenderness, who viewed expressions of emotions as signs of weakness and who gloried in a reputation for bitchiness.

"Elda, as I recall, never had any dolls or other girl playthings," said her brother Edgar, seventy years later. "She enjoyed boys' games and sports more."

Elda saw it another way. She observed that boys got all the breaks; girls, nothing. Her grandfather exploited her grandmother. Her father misused her mother. And her brothers enjoyed life while she and her sisters, even the greedy Dora, were expected to stand back.

Incredible as it may seem to those who knew her either as a child or later, Elda regarded herself as shy, timid and frightened.* In her isolation she learned to place little value on what she felt or said, assuming no one paid any attention unless she became obstreperous. She might tremble within when she behaved outrageously, but she was determined to draw attention to herself.

A photo which was taken when she was eight years old illustrates this. In it, a triumphant Elda exhibits her scandalous bangs. She had suggested her hairstyle be changed, but her mother was too distracted by more pressing concerns to respond. So Elda took the scissors to her locks. Naturally she botched the job, and the Furrys had to hire a barber to repair the damage. The result: bangs. Her mother, amused, had had the determined mite's portrait taken—thus unconsciously rewarding her for her willfulness.

Appropriately enough, Elda's favorite holiday was Independence Day. "Orators weren't ashamed to stand up and say what America meant to them and as kids we were pretty proud," she was to say later. But as Elda stood there on Altoona's main street in the hot July sun, she always envied the beauty who played the Goddess of Independence. When she grew up, she was determined that she would grace that float. She never made it, but perhaps that is one of the reasons she eventually became an international personality.

Perhaps not, too. From the time her youngest brother, Edgar,* can remember, Elda was a leader. "When she

---

* "Timid? As timid as a buzzsaw," said ex-newspaperman and press agent Casey Shawhan.

* Elda helped finance his college education but, typically enough

started something, every person followed through and went ahead with it," he said.

Elda's education was terminated at the eighth grade. Her mother was ill after Baby Margaret's birth in 1898, and shortly thereafter David Furry closed the butcher shop and started overland for the Klondike, leaving the family with handfuls of accounts-payable bills to subsist on.

With the children's father absent and their mother ill, thirteen-year-old Elda offered to work in the silk mill, an idea that horrified her mother, who maintained that Sherman's salary and the money that he and Cammon would collect from former customers would tide them over.

Mrs. Furry was wrong. The boys tried and failed. Elda's smoldering resentment against the ineptitude of men flamed. She was certain she could do better. She was, step by step, becoming a take-over woman. She begged her mother to let her try her hand with their recalcitrant customers. Her mother finally, if reluctantly, agreed.

So it was that Elda became the "fightingest fourteen-year-old bill collecter ever seen in Altoona." At first, she tried sweet-talking the customers, following her mother's admonition that you catch more flies with honey than vinegar. When that tactic failed, the inequity of the Furrys' position overwhelmed her. She yelled, threatened, bullied —and eventually collected.

There was no time for attending school, but Elda wasn't disturbed. "She was always a good student of human nature," Edgar said, "but disliked the monotony of school."

The adult Hedda put it more succinctly: "The only [school] prize I ever received was a dunce's cap."

"School wasn't important to Elda," Margaret Furry Mitchell, her sister, said. "From the time she was very young, she was determined to escape from the big family. To leave Altoona. To find a place in the world she knew in her imagination."

---

where her kindlier actions were concerned, she was adamant that he tell no one.

"She built dreams and made them come true," was Edgar's analysis.

The relationship between David Furry and Elda was troublesome before he left for the Klondike, and it certainly did not improve after his return. "Elda was such an independent person," Mrs. Mitchell recalled. "Always. Our father was rather—well, German. And we thought that when father spoke that was *the* word. All the rest of us jumped, but not Elda. She had a mind of her own."

In her mind, the obsession that women were exploited grew. Her antennae were out for injustices. "I hated men because I thought all of them selfish, grasping, overbearing," she told interviewer Alice Tildesley of the Philadelphia *Public Ledger* in speaking of her girlhood. "They were my natural enemies. I wouldn't speak to boys I met on the street, but just looked right through them as if they didn't exist. High-hatting men was my favorite sport."

They had let her mother, her sister and her down. It was a lesson that she would forget only once in her life.

What of Elda's social life? If one believed Hedda, it had all been work, work, work. No pretty dresses. No parties. Fun? Church on Sunday morning. Entertainment? Reading the scandal and fashion notes in the Sunday paper. Beaux? She claimed one, a local dentist. She implied that romance fled when she glimpsed his bathing-suit-clad body which was "covered with fur" and reminded her of an "emaciated orangutang." But she allowed him to escort her to the Mishler Theater to see *Captain Jinks of the Horse Marines* with Ethel Barrymore. At that moment, she decided to go on the stage—and romance was put out of her life. She had had a vision of what rewards acting could bring.

Actually Elda's social life need not have been any less fulfilling than that of most girls in Altoona. The difference was that she refused to settle for coined metal, preferring to dream of pure gold. While she somewhat jocularly claimed in later life that she developed muscles wrestling sides of beef in her father's shop, photos reveal a tall, slim, young blonde with a patrician nose, a high brow, beautiful eyes and a humorous mouth that lends distinction but denies the highest beauty to a face.

There were only two beaux—the dentist and Ralph Dalton, a youth who often came to the Furrys for musical evenings and was regarded as Elda's special friend. But it was a mutual interest in music, rather than romance, that united them. "Young men didn't court girls who were too independent—they didn't like that," Mrs. Mitchell said.

Although they might not court Elda, everyone in the Millville section of Altoona knew her because she was the only girl in the neighborhood who could ride well. Hedda claimed she learned on Fanny, an "old plug" that threw her off the first time she used a side saddle she'd ordered from Sears, Roebuck. "Nonsense. Fanny was a thorough-bred Kentucky mare that Elda loved and rode many times," Edgar said. "She made her own habit and bought a side saddle from Sears to ride through the Allegheny Mountains surrounding Altoona."

Hedda and Edgar also differed on what happened to the horse. Hedda said that over her protests her father sold Fanny to the glue factory. Edgar recalled that Hedda insisted on sending the mare to their Uncle John's farm to live out her days.

This was Elda's favorite uncle, according to her cousin Kenton R. Miller. "They both had wonderful senses of humor. And when they were together, there was lots of fun and jokin'. I think he had a great influence on her. He was what is called a ridin' preacher in the Brethren sect of the Quaker church. He farmed during the week and on Sunday preached in the little churches in nearby villages.

"Elda was a live wire. She'd try anything. Once she was at our house after we'd threshed. There was a big straw stack beside the barn. We were jumpin' out of the hayloft and slidin' down the stack. The cows were runnin' around to scratch off flies. Well, darned if she didn't jump and slide right on top of a cow. It threw her all over the place. But it didn't bother her none.

"Even then she had this idea of gettin' into show business," Miller continued. "I must have been around four years old. And me, bein' a farm boy, I couldn't understand her. When the upstairs barn floor was empty, Elda'd go up there, take off most of her clothes and start dancin'.

You see, she saw these shows in Altoona and her ambition was to be a show girl. She was practicin'."

Although David Furry was personally fond of the theater and often took his family, he discouraged his daughter's theatrical ambitions. "I wanted to go on the stage, but my father discouraged me," Hedda told Alice Tildesley. " 'What would you do on stage? You haven't any talent. Certainly nobody would pay to see you,' he would say. No doubt this was in accord with his ideas of putting down vanity, keeping his daughter modest and so on. But it only made me more determined to find out if I could do it. . . ."

Increasingly Elda's daydreams centered on the theater. Whatever else she might be doing, she never lost sight of her goal, and the one image that continued to awe her was that of the glamorous Miss Barrymore. So much so that sixty years later she described in detail a costume from the ermine tippet with black tails to the black velvet barrel muff trimmed with ermine tails—but hardly mentioned the star's performance.

The Barrymore glamor and the admiring reaction of at least part of the congregation when Elda appeared in her first "store-bought" Easter hat—bright-green straw with red velvet geraniums—probably made it inevitable that Hedda "The Hat" Hopper would become better known for her clothes than her acting talent. (In her sixties, she said, "If you wear a crazy hat, no one notices the tired old face beneath it.")

The sequence of events between her escape from her parents' domination in 1903 and her arrival in New York in 1908 is hopelessly scrambled because she dropped those five years from her official life and condensed her experiences. The mature Hedda claimed she left Altoona and went to Pittsburgh to enroll at the Carter Conservatory of Music with her father's permission. Another source dimly recalls that at the time of Elda's disappearance, her destination was unknown. Later, this source says, the family heaved a collective sigh of relief when Elda was found playing with a theatrical troupe in Pittsburgh. She may or may not have gone back to Altoona before returning to enroll in the conservatory.

However, Mrs. Mitchell says that Elda did go to the conservatory with the family's blessing. While there, she formed a close friendship with Hattie Carter, whose parents ran the school. While Elda studied piano and voice, the two girls planned theatrical careers.

When she was twenty-two—rather than the seventeen she claimed—she went to New York.

Once again, there are different versions of the story. In one, the two girls went to New York together. In the second, Hattie went ahead and Elda joined her. In the third—and least likely—Elda left for New York with $250 she had lifted from the till in recompense for her labors in the meat market years before and by sheer coincidence ran into Hattie, who was already working in the Aborn Light Opera Company.

The one seemingly constant fact is that she left for New York without her parents' knowledge. They had no idea of her whereabouts until they were contacted by her psalm-singing uncle, Samuel Furry, head of the New York Bible Association, who operated the Sunshine Mission on the Bowery. He informed them Elda was in New York and promised to look after her. Since he had several daughters, some near Elda's age, the Furrys were relieved. They were convinced that Elda would soon become disenchanted with show business.

Almost immediately, however, Hattie Carter arranged an audition with the Aborns. Elda couldn't dance, her voice consisted of a high C and a low C—with nothing in between—but her figure wasn't bad, she had a good complexion, and she was pretty.

Those who knew her then say that she was that exceptional creature, a pretty woman who could pass a mirror and not look into it. Screenwriter Charles Brackett claimed that in his youth, Elda had the most beautiful legs in the New York theater. She might be told she was pretty. She might even claim that she was pretty, but those who knew her well maintain that it was obvious she never *felt* pretty.

With all her inhibitions, Elda tried out for the chorus, proceeding upon her lifelong assumption that "you can't be hanged for trying." She was readily accepted—and later claimed there was a shortage of chorus girls that year. The company opened in Baltimore, and Elda was extremely well satisfied to be working at $15 a week. (After she became famous, she inflated it to $25 a week.) It was an adventure. "Just being behind the footlights was wonderful," Elda told an interviewer as she reminisced about the experience twenty years later.

With a season on the road behind her, Elda Curry (as she now called herself) first appeared in New York on December 3, 1908, in *The Pied Piper,* a musical comedy produced by Sam S. and Lee Shubert at the Majestic Theater for a run of fifty-two performances. What distinguished the occasion for Hedda was that dance director Ned Wayburn singled her out as the awkwardest cow who ever tried kicking chorus. She claimed that she looked up his rival Vincenzo Romeo, who taught her enough basic steps to get by.

This was the production in which Elda met her future husband. Just as there is the actor's actor, the painter's painter and the writer's writer, DeWolf Hopper qualified as the roué's roué. Of him, John Barrymore said, "I hate to admit this, but if that old bastard and I saw a girl at the same time and had the same idea, I learned to sadly bow out. And I'll be damned—so did my father before me."

"The frontiers of old age have been so extended in my lifetime that I never caught up with that receding boundary," Hopper boasted.

Never was there an unlikelier physical candidate for a ladies' man. Hopper was tall. Hedda said he was six feet three inches. Others said six feet four and even six feet eight inches. He had bold features and was without a hair on his body or his head—even eyebrows and eyelashes. Furthermore, his skin had a slightly bluish tint. Hopper believed that if one aspirin was good, three were better. At one period, he and actor-crony Digby Bell lived at the Algonquin. One morning, Bell cried, "Good God, Wolfie! Look at yourself!" Hopper looked in the mirror and discovered his skin had a bluish tint. After undergoing a series of medical tests, he learned that while gargling silver nitrate for a throat condition he had swallowed so much that it had permeated his skin, giving it a bluish cast. Yet he married so often that it was facetiously suggested that he be designated "The Husband of His Country."

In 1908, he was fifty years old. He had been born in New York in the then-fashionable Bowery section to a couple that had been childless for twelve years. His father, John, was a Philadelphian, whose family figured prominently in abolishing slavery, and his mother, Rosalie, was from the socially elite branch of the DeWolf family. He was a pampered baby who became an indulged child after his father's death, which took place when DeWolf was five, and he grew into a spoiled young man who took for granted that the best was not really good enough for him.

As a youth, he was a big fellow, with a haystack of hair, a mellifluous voice and an eye for the ladies. When he was fifteen, a severe case of typhoid fever destroyed the hair on his body but failed to diminish his sex appeal.

School bored him. He used to say he went in one door of Harvard and out the other. What didn't bore him was the stage. After savoring applause at the Lyceum Theater on Fourteenth Street in an amateur performance of *Conscience* in 1878, he spent his time studying leading and juvenile roles in standard plays. Late in that summer, he turned professional in *Our Boys*.

Our Daughters and *One Hundred Wives* swiftly followed. Disturbed by his sexual drive which he feared might disrupt his career by entrapping him in an unsuitable marriage, he solved the problem with originality. His first wife, Ella Gardiner, was his second cousin on his mother's side. She, too, hoped to prevent romance from wrecking her career. Naturally, that marriage was doomed.

Ella gave way to a saucy chorus girl, Ida Mosher, who captured Hopper's heart, when, one day at rehearsal, he asked what the chorus would do if he increased their salaries. "Drop dead," quipped Ida. The two married and produced a son, Jack, before Ida gave way to Edna.

Edna was that alluring singing-comedienne Edna Wallace, who appeared with Hopper in several productions. When they divorced, Edna asked no alimony but she kept his name. As Edna Wallace Hopper, she became the symbol of eternal youth in the 1930's.

Edna gave way to Nella Bergen. Hopper and Nella met in London during the Boer War, and it was to her that he was still married when Elda Curry joined *The Pied Piper* company.

Hopper was a ham and a legend—as well as a star. He had been a member of the Weber and Fields Company and throughout his career, he was acclaimed for his characterizations in Gilbert and Sullivan comic operas. In addition, in 1890, when he spontaneously interpolated a poem about baseball called "Casey at the Bat" into a musical production* attended by New York and Chicago baseball players, he scored such a hit that he and the poem became inextricably linked.

Hopper was a serious professional, who claimed that any comedian who needed to resort to dirty material didn't deserve the name, but he was not above hamming. In *Trial by Jury,* he played the judge. While the scenes went on below his bench, bewigged and bored, he pretended to slap mosquitoes, catch flies and follow the paths of moths.

His wit found expression both on and offstage. During rehearsals when he was with the McCall Opera Company, a puritanical chorine wept at being required to wear tights. Hopper comforted her, "Don't worry, my dear. No one ever looks at legs in opera."

Actor-writer Fitzroy Davis wrote Hedda in the 1950's, quoting a 1913 Burns Mantle review of *The Beggar Student.* "When Viola Gillette, playing a shapely Lieutenant Poppenburg in white tights, dropped her hanky, tenor Arthur Aldrich, a perfect gentleman (and knowing how tight her tights might be), stooped to pick it up. . . . Mr. Hopper remarked quite casually, "She's a boy. Let him pick it up."

His ad-libbing was well known. In 1963, Selian Ufford wrote to Hedda, recalling a Gilbert and Sullivan matinee in Spokane, Washington, sixty years earlier. Hopper played the Lord High Executioner, and when he sang "I've Got

---

* Hedda claimed the name of the show was *Castles in the Air* at the Broadway Theater. Hopper produced it on May 5, 1890. Della Fox was in the cast, which may have given rise to the old joke: "Do you know Della Fox?" "Yes, I saw DeWolf Hopper."

a Little List," he ad-libbed a verse which he directed to the little boy in an aisle seat in the thirteenth row. "I don't think he'd be missed, I'm sure he'd not be missed. . . ." He sang so persuasively that the child bolted into the lobby and had to be brought back by his mother. "I've never been so impressed by an actor before or since, and I jump at the name of Hopper today," Ufford wrote.

Hopper was a spellbinder. That appealed to Elda. "I kept so steadfastly away from men that Mr. Hopper was the first man I had ever really seen," she told a reporter. "I remember my first glimpse of him, a tall, striking-looking man with a marvelous voice. Everyone within earshot was leaning toward him worshipfully. Everyone was paying court to him."

She was in the Hopper company of *A Matinee Idol,* which began its tour late in 1909 and went as far west as Chicago before opening for a run of sixty-eight performances at Daly's Theater in Manhattan on August 28, 1910. Elda claimed that she was in the chorus and her dancing had improved vastly. Joseph Santley, the eighteen-year-old who played the title role, disagreed in 1970. "Elda wasn't in the chorus. She was a show girl, who played a bit in the second act," he said. "That is, she aged some and played Mrs. Somebody. But she wasn't a chorus girl. In those days there were three sets of girls. They had show girls, who wore clothes and stood around. Then you had mediums, who were there for their voices. They could sing. And then you had the ponies. The little ones that danced. In a show of Wolfie's type, there would probably be eight, eight and eight. With eight chorus men. Elda was a show girl."

Santley confirmed Elda's contention that she was somewhat intimidated by Hopper. "She certainly wasn't assertive around Wolfie. No young girl would be. He was too imposing. After the show, we'd go to the Baltimore Daisy Lunches, because he wasn't a big drinking man. He preferred a baked apple to booze. But he would be—he was always—'on' and I don't mean in an offensive way because everyone always wanted him to be on—because of his knowledge and all. And Elda most of all. That was the start of their romance."

"I fell in love with his voice and I believe that is what all women who ever loved him surrendered to—his voice," Elda told Alice Tildesley in 1928. "He could play on it as if it were an organ.* And with it, he worked on women's emotions so that they trembled if he looked at them."

Given Elda's lifelong hunger for affectionate attention from her harried parents—to say nothing of the antagonism that existed between her and her natural father—it is easy to understand that she might mistake the glow she felt in DeWolf Hopper's presence for love. His attentiveness, small compliments and casual flatteries must have satisfied, at least partially, the hunger she had felt all her life.

On Hopper's part, Elda's slightly prudish outlook, her naïveté and her inability to express emotion, combined with her wit, verve and innate sense of style, must have had an aphrodisiacal effect on a jaded voluptuary.

They were the right people brought together at the right time—but for the wrong reasons.

Conversely, Elda's early stage career—apart from the Hopper productions—seems to have been a case of being at the right place at the wrong time or vice versa.

Producer Frank Hennessy opened *The Motor Girl* at the Lyric Theater in New York on June 15, 1909. But Elda Curry didn't join the cast until August 7, 1909. A replacement.

Edgar Selwyn wrote and directed *The Country Boy,* which had its Broadway debut on August 30, 1910. On September 27, 1911, Elda played her first dramatic role—in the touring company of the hit. Years later she fondly reminisced: "In your youth, it's all adventurous and wonderful. There's something quite gay about getting into town at 7 P.M., hopping a ride on a delivery sled, grabbing a sandwich and a cup of coffee—couldn't have done with-

* In 1953, when *From Under My Hat* was published, she amended that to: "Every woman he ever won fell in love with his voice. It was like some great church organ. This giant of a man was all music and traded joyously on his voice. . . ."

out it—and then rushing to the theater to unpack your clothes, press them, crack the ice in your wash basin so you could wash your hands. . . . I'll never forget Minneapolis when it was 42 below on New Year's Eve, someone gave me one of those silly little paper parasols and as a joke I carried it open over my head to the station. . . . Everyone laughed at it and that started the New Year with a spirit of camaraderie that's been too long lacking. Looking backward on those days, it's hard to realize it happened to you."

It was the same story with *The Quaker Girl,* which opened in Manhattan late in 1911. Elda played the second lead on tour in late 1912 and early 1913, following the peerless Ina Claire in the role. Everyone in the company, including Theodosia de Coppet (to become better known as Theda Bara, the silent screen vamp) and Olga Petrova, who looked like Elinor Glyn, realized that Elda had been friendly with DeWolf Hopper while she was with his troupe, but none of them connected him with the weekly letters that always awaited her at every stand.

Nevertheless, the day before *The Quaker Girl* closed in Albany, New York, Elda purchased a wedding ring. The morning after the show's final performance, she arose early, boarded a milk train to avoid the rest of the company and returned to New York. There, the twenty-eight-year-old Elda was met by the fifty-five-year-old Hopper, fresh from his fourth divorce. They were driven to Riverside, New Jersey, where Elda surprised everyone by becoming his fifth bride. Recalling the ring later, she wryly said that it had paid for itself many times over when she used it in motion pictures—as a prop.

On May 8, 1913, after a ninety-second marriage ceremony, the newlyweds returned to the Algonquin Hotel and imparted their secret to Frank Case, the owner, who obligingly installed them in adjoining suites with a connecting door. (That the marriage did not get off to an auspicious start can be guessed by the only advice Hedda gave her son prior to his wedding: "For God's sake, don't take your wife by force like your father did.")

Nineteen days later, the New York *World* was asking:

WHAT'S HER NAME? MISS ELDA FURRY OR MRS. DEWOLF HOPPER? Hopper was still spending a great deal of time at the Lambs Club, the paper said, and was registered alone at the Algonquin. Rumor had it that Miss Furry's real name was Curry and that she came from Indiana. In response to all questions, Hopper replied: "Domestic affairs are private property." It was nobody's business whether or not she was or would be the fifth Mrs. DeWolf Hopper.

Elda could understand her husband's embarrassment, but as a properly brought-up Quaker girl, she felt compelled to wire the news to her parents. Despite a religious abhorrence of divorce, Margaret Furry smilingly accepted her daughter's marriage and kept her own counsel about any reservations she might feel. Not so with David Furry. He raged and ranted, threatened to horsewhip his new son-in-law and finally issued a statement to the Altoona *Gazette*: "The Furrys for generations have revered the sacredness of marriage vows, and the report that my daughter, Elda, has been married to DeWolf Hopper pains me greatly. . . . If Hopper loves my daughter and means well, I will be satisfied, but if he married her like he took up with his other four wives, as he would a plaything, it will be an outrage her old dad will not stand for."

Elda was humiliated. She had eagerly anticipated the neighbors' astonishment that the butcher's daughter had had the great good luck to marry a big Broadway star. But as usual, her father had succeeded in robbing her of her triumph.

Of course, reality failed to live up to her daydreams. Before their marriage, her future husband had promised as a honeymoon a grand tour of the Continent. After the wedding, she had to wait five weeks while he fulfilled a forty-performance contract with *Iolanthe,* and only then did he agree to a short trip to the White Mountains, accompanied by their mutual friend Mrs. Derby Farrington.

It would have been uneventful except that while they were returning to Manhattan, auto trouble developed, and they were forced to lay over in Goshen, New York, where a racing meet was in progress. The trio fell into the social whirl with such gusto that the aging bridegroom developed an uric acid condition. Once the automobile was repaired, the honeymooners dropped Mrs. Farrington off in Manhattan and proceeded to French Lick, Indiana, to take the cure at the famous health spa. Instead of silk sheets and champagne, Elda found herself settling for mud baths and pluto water.

Nevertheless, she *was* Mrs. DeWolf Hopper—and, as she often remarked later, show business is a world of make-believe whose very soul is publicity. Her position provided the opportunity to mingle with rich, powerful personalities who could be of value to her professionally and socially.

She was a sharp observer and saw that those who succeeded in the "Profession" thought about themselves 95 percent of the time—and she was willing to conform. She learned how important it was to put in an appearance at the right parties; to be on a first-name basis with Douglas Fairbanks Sr., Laurette Taylor, John Barrymore, John Drew, Alice Brady, Billie Burke, and Ethel Barrymore; and to be in a position to entertain D. W. Griffith, Arthur Hopkins, John Golden and Cecil B. DeMille.

Her husband introduced her to Lillian Russell, and they became friendly. Elda admired Miss Russell, but cast a cool appraising eye on the star's too ample proportions and resolved never to indulge *her* appetite until she lost her figure. Indeed, she began then a series of exercises which she continued until the end of her life. Looking one's best was an actress' obligation. Elda had come a long way for a girl who only a few years before had been selling hamburger in a small-town Pennsylvania meat market.

Girls, Elda confided to an interviewer, sometimes fall in love with the glamor of a big name and wonder what he can see in them. His friends sometimes reinforce that doubt. For instance, at a reception following the opening of Sir Johnston Forbes-Robertson's 1913 season at the Shubert Theater, the *Dramatic Mirror* reported that Elda's "unusually fetching hat practically stole the show." In fact, during her husband's introduction of St. Johnston, the impish Laurette Taylor, who never deigned to squander her artistic energies on anything so ordinary as her wardrobe, nudged Elda and whispered, "I think Wolfie married that hat, not you."

Elda, whose self-image was not yet strongly developed, must have suffered often. Sometimes her spouse would absentmindedly call her Edna or Nella or Ida. He criticized her ideas. He mocked her Altoona accent. Under his tutelage, she stopped rolling her *r's* and began clipping them so short that she later claimed she sounded "like an inbred British dowager" mated to "a Boston terrier." It was this manner of speaking that earned her a career as an "affected society slitch" after sound films arrived.

Olga Petrova, with whom Elda had toured in *The Quaker Girl,* wrote in her autobiography* that once Elda, "DeWolf Hopper, Dr. Stewart† and I met for luncheon at the Algonquin. My principal recollections of that luncheon are that Mr. Hopper occupied the first part of the session with a monologue in which he related the most intimate sayings and doings of each of his previous wives." Miss Petrova, whose real name was Muriel Harding and whose act encompassed everything from birdcalls to a scene from *The Shulamite,* was clearly not charmed,** and given Elda's staid background, it is doubtful she was either.

Relations can never have been smooth for two such outspoken, witty and frequently embittered people. For instance, when a guest at their home jocularly cautioned Elda that her practice of lighting her husband's pipe might stunt her growth, Hopper howled: "Stunt her growth! I wish something would!" It was a joke, but his predilection for small women was well known.

Nor could it have been any easier for him to accept her

* *Butter with My Bread* (Bobbs-Merrill, 1942).
† Miss Petrova's husband.
** Miss Petrova had a reputation for being temperamental. There is a perhaps apocryphal story about her appearance at a theater in Albany, New York. All week she raised hell about her billing, her dressing room, her lighting—everything. On closing day, when the stage manager came around, she said, "I have been difficult, but you have been sweet. You may kiss my hand." The stage manager shrugged. "Why not?" he asked. "I've kissed your ass all week."

wisecrack that on opening night "Wolfie never turned a hair. How could he? He didn't have any." Nor her telling him, "Nobody could say I married you for your money— you don't have any."

But when Hopper took to the road with his Gilbert and Sullivan company, including Alice Brady and the future opera singer John Charles Thomas, Elda traveled along. Since she was an established actress, she could not demote herself to the chorus, yet neither could she sing well enough to do justice to the songs. For forty weeks, she played married lady, star's wife. It was perhaps the only uninterrupted vacation she ever permitted herself.

When it was time for Hopper to tour again in the fall of 1914, Elda suspected that she was pregnant. She and her doctor estimated the baby would be born on February 17, 1915. Having seen her mother through several pregnancies, the dauntless Elda pledged her husband to secrecy and again accompanied him on tour.

They reached the West Coast and had returned as far as Cleveland before Elda began to find it difficult to conceal her condition. She was in excellent health and good spirits, although she did admit to one nagging worry. Would their son—for she never doubted the baby would be a boy—be born hairless? To conteract the possibility, she spent her free moments staring at bushy-haired individuals with luxuriant eyebrows and long lashes.

In Cleveland, although her camouflage costumes were still effective, her physical stamina began to decline. At a party, she suddenly became ill. It was decided that she would accompany her husband to Toronto, the next engagement, and then return to New York alone to await the baby's birth.

When she put in a solo appearance at the Algonquin, Frank Case jumped to the conclusion that Hopper's latest marriage was over. So did the couple's other acquaintances. To set rumors to rest, Elda arranged an announcement luncheon for twelve of her closest friends on January 26, 1915. While assisting in arranging the table in the Algonquin dining room, she suddenly felt a sharp pain. It was severe enough that she called her doctor. He ordered her to take a cab to Lying-In Hospital at once.

"But I can't," she reported saying, "I'm giving a luncheon and I've ordered orchids."

Orchids or no orchids, a second severe pain convinced her that there had been a miscalculation. At seven that evening, her child was born. As Elda had predicted, it was a boy.

The first thing that she recalled doing when she saw him was to check whether or not he was hairless. Then she named him William DeWolf Hopper, Jr. The event caused a considerable stir. Telegrams to the fifty-seven-year-old father (including John Barrymore's "I didn't know you had it in you") inundated Hopper, who was appearing in Chicago.

Hedda claimed that Hopper rushed home at once, but actually the tour continued well into March. On the fourth of that month, Hopper told a reporter from the Pittsburgh *Leader*: "It's terrible to be the father of a bouncing boy and not be able to spend every minute of your time with him. . . . You know I expected a Greek God, but according to many, many reports I have received, he has all the gods of mythology lashed to the mast. . . . I wanted a daughter and Mrs. Hopper wanted a boy. However, I was not really particular which it was. I am just as well satisfied that it is a boy, although I do not know why in the name of all that is good, they wished that name upon him, poor kid. In letters, telegrams or messages that I have received and that includes several hundred of each, everyone remarks about the uncanny resemblance between the child and myself. Now why DeWolf Jr. elected to look like me I cannot understand. Perhaps his youth has deceived them or perhaps he will see the error of his ways and reform. His mother, who was Elda Furry, a well-known actress, is a wonderfully beautiful woman. If DeWolf Jr. inherits her good looks and my luck, he will be some boy, some boy. Just to show you what a sacrificing father I am going to be, I am going to spend the summer with Mrs. Hopper and DeWolf Jr. at Nantucket, Mass. Perhaps that will mean nothing to you, but when you understand that I am passionately fond of motoring and the officials will not allow a motor within smelling distance of the island, you will get the drift of the argument."

Hopper said that almost every day since the birth of the baby he had received a book-sized letter from his wife describing every yell (Elda thought she detected a perfect New York accent) and a recital of every minor development.

That summer Hopper accompanied his wife, their son and his sister-in-law Margaret to Siasconset, Nantucket Island, where a colony of famous actors summered. But the experiment in domesticity was cut short. Hopper, along with some sixty leading theatrical stars, including Billie Burke, Marie Dressler, Sir Herbert Beerbohm Tree and Texas Guinan, succumbed to the blandishments of Harry Aitken's Triangle Company in California.* Hopper received a year's contract at a reported $1,500 a week and an opportunity to play Don Quixote. There were no plans for Elda to appear professionally since she would have enough to do taking care of their infant son.

As it turned out, Mrs. Hopper had hardly anything to do. Douglas and Beth Fairbanks had located a house complete with a Japanese couple to look after the Hoppers even before they arrived in Hollywood. A nurse, whom Elda dubbed "The Dragon," jealously guarded little De-Wolf.

Fred Allen complained that in Hollywood no matter how hot it gets in the daytime, there is never anything to do at night. Elda's evenings were filled with activity. In 1915 the movie colony was almost self-contained, and its members entertained one another lavishly. But during the day she had nothing to occupy her time.

She seldom visited her husband's sets, choosing instead to attend the filming of prestige pictures. The two sequences that impressed her most were the crucifixion scene in Griffith's *Intolerance,* during which the wire-borne angels became airsick, and the climax of *Joan the Woman* in which opera-star-turned-silent-film-actress Geraldine Farrar was burned at the stake.

Hopper was going through his own crucifixion and ordeal by fire (and by extension Elda suffered too) because

* Directors D. W. Griffith, Thomas H. Ince and Mack Sennett made up the triangle.

the camera seemed intent upon revealing all 114 years of debauchery that Hopper had crowded into 57. In addition, his impeccable stage technique registered and registered on film. The camera became a persecutor in his eyes, and perhaps in an unconscious effort to escape it, he constantly walked out of its range. Chalk lines were drawn to guide him, making him feel as if he had been straitjacketed. He had expected to work with D. W. Griffith, but instead had drawn Edward Dillon as director of both *Don Quixote* and *Sunshine Dad*. In the latter ten-month-old DeWolf Jr. made his acting debut.

Nor were Hopper's other three films—*Mr. Goode, the Samaritan, Stranded* and *Casey at the Bat*—any more gratifying to him. He became both paranoid and childish. "I have to get up early in the morning," he complained. "I never get any applause no matter how well I play a scene. Griffith won't let me recite 'Casey at the Bat' in the picture *Casey at the Bat*." How he expected to recite the poem in a silent film, he didn't bother to explain.*

He was somewhat mollified when he recited the poem over the telephone to the membership attending the International Circulation Managers Association Banquet 3,000 miles away, thereby establishing a 1916 long-distance telephone speaking record, but Elda found life increasingly difficult.

Given her ambitious nature, her claim that at her husband's behest, she turned down a role in a D. W. Griffith picture seems implausible. The fact is that tall women weren't in demand. Mary Pickford, Lillian Gish and Gloria Swanson—all petite—were the fashion. Elda, who admitted to five feet seven and 135 pounds, was like a chrysanthemum among daisies.

Finally, the Hoppers' good friend William Farnum hired Elda to play opposite him in *The Battle of Hearts*. For the female Scandinavian ship's captain, she was just what was required—a big beauty. Fox executives agreed, and so eventually did writer Frances Marion.

Miss Marion, a great beauty, flirted with painting and

---

* In 1921-22, Lee De Forest's Phonofilms produced a talking version of "Casey at the Bat" as part of its filmed vaudeville series.

acting before deciding to write. When one of her stories "Woman Against the Sea" attracted an offer of $5,000 from the Fox Company, Miss Marion excitedly called her friend Marie Dressler to announce that she had hit the jackpot but was confused. Fox had bought this story about a woman for their popular he-man star William Farnum. The movie-wise Miss Dressler advised her to take the money and ask no questions.

Miss Marion agreed, went to Fox Studios to sign the contract and inquired whether they had decided to change the ship's captain from a dominant female into a male role for Farnum. Not at all. Farnum was to play the lusty first mate, who helped the captain control the crew. Miss Marion predicted they would never find an actress for it. "Tall girls didn't appear on the screen then," she recalled. "They slumped to appear shorter. And when I saw Hedda, she seemed enormously tall. She stood up straight, wore heels and big hats that made her seem even taller. She was very beautiful, had this wonderful complexion and great poise and bearing. But she didn't remotely seem rawboned, and I said so."

Elda gave her a scornful look and informed her that she was an actress. What was more, she had been schooled by one of the greatest actors in America, her husband, DeWolf Hopper. She said she felt competent to handle any role and was eventually signed for $100 a week.*

The company set out for Santa Catalina Island. There, awaiting the arrival of an antique three-masted schooner, which was being sailed from San Francisco, director Oscar Apfel filmed a scene in which Elda drove a team of oxen around the beach, gathering firewood. It went well, but it was the only thing that did. The schooner never arrived. It and two seamen aboard were presumed lost during a storm. The fishing-village set was blown down three times,

---

* The movie marked the beginning of a lifelong friendship—if that is the word for the relationship between Hedda and Miss M. In the early 1950's the two of them and David S. "Spec" McClure, who off and on was Hedda's legman, attended a social function. That night as they let Miss Marion out of the car and she made her way up the walk, Hedda shook her head in wonder and said, "My God! What a story I can write about her when she dies."

and finally Apfel decided to switch the location to Santa Cruz, where another sailing vessel had been located.

The company arrived in Santa Cruz to discover there was no harbor. Everyone had to be transported through choppy waters and small boats, and Farnum's craft capsized. The $6,000-a-week star was saved, but much valuable equipment was lost.

Once ashore, the company found they had arrived a day ahead of schedule. No accommodations were available. Elda and Mrs. Apfel shared a tent, sleeping in blankets that dogs and goats had nested in. During the night, ravenous field mice scurried over the two women to get to the bars of soap stashed at the head of their cots.

To complicate the already complicated nature of things, Elda was terrified of water. "I am a brave woman," she once boasted to a fan magazine writer. "I can ride most any kind of horse. I can drive a car anyplace, and any speed. I am not shy of snakes. And if a burglar entered my room and said, 'Hands up!,' I'd laugh at him, but I am as fond of water as some Greenwich Villager. . . . I was never made for a mermaid."

She was petrified when told she was scheduled to plunge from the boat into the sea. Apfel assured her that two deep-sea divers, Black Joe and Squirrel, were on hand to rescue her. While preparing the shot, Apfel accidentally fell into the ocean and came up with a baby octopus on his arm. After calming the hysterical Elda, they faked the scene.

Throughout the picture, the future fashion plate wore either a stocking cap or a southwester, men's pants, Army turtleneck sweaters, cotton dresses and oilskins, prompting the film critic for the Cleveland *Leader* to observe in his May 22, 1916, review, "Miss Furry proves a large-boned young woman, masculine to a certain extent, who looks exceedingly well in trousers and boots. She is clearly intelligent and displays ingratiating charm."

If Elda's career seemed off to a promising start, the same could not be said for her husband's. Like most of the legitimate stars signed by Triangle, he was proving a critical and box-office dud. In September, he set out for New York by automobile. Elda and the baby were to follow by train. Stopping over in Kansas City, Hopper granted an interview in which he claimed that the only excuse for real actors appearing in films was the high salary scale. Personally he had also been grateful for the opportunity to spend a year with his wife and small son.

Whatever else the year in California demonstrated, it showed that, despite his initial cock-of-the-walk strut over fathering a child at fifty-seven, Hopper had little aptitude or interest in parenthood. For her part, Elda focused whatever attention she had left after pursuing her career on Billy, demanding that when they returned to New York, they buy a house in the country for the boy to grow up in. Hopper fully intended to return to the Algonquin—which they did.

Elda's career immediately boomed in New York and New Jersey studios. She made *Seven Keys to Baldpate, Her Excellency, the Governor* and *The Food Gamblers* in 1917. *Seven Keys* starred George M. Cohan and Anna Q. Nilsson. Like DeWolf Hopper, Cohan had trouble adapting to the camera,* but Elda, as Myra Thornhill, was praised. In the other two films, director Allan Dwan had cast Elda in leading roles, and Elda had done well enough so that one of the staff from the *Morning Telegraph* did an interview with her under her new name, Elda Millar.† Before Dwan could star her in further pictures, Triangle sank.

In order to remain in New York, Hopper accepted *The Passing Show of 1917*. It played the Winter Garden, where Al Jolson's broad technique was needed to project to the upper reaches of the second balcony. Hopper's more restrained style, which possibly had been further refined by film acting, seemed pale by comparison. Years later Hedda dismissed the show as a quick flop, but the production achieved a run of 196 performances, which was more than

---

* One reviewer thought Cohan's work in *Keys* an improvement on past performances on the grounds that he acted as much with his face as his hands.

† Elda later claimed Dwan gave her the name, but it is transparently an adaptation of her mother's name Miller.

respectable in those days. When it closed, Hopper toured with the production.

His condescending attitude toward movies still somewhat intimidated his wife. Publicly, she said, "Despite my brief experience, I'm firmly convinced that motion-picture work is the most fascinating form of acting. It develops all one's resources and every day's work means a new adventure." Nonetheless, she now abandoned the name of Elda Millar and billed herself as Mrs. DeWolf Hopper.

Whatever she called herself, she went from one supporting role to another—with Madge Kennedy* in *Nearly Married* and Billie Burke in *Twin Souls,* as well as with such other stars as Mae Marsh, Alice Joyce and William Faversham. Of greatest moment was *Virtuous Wives.*

This was Louis B. Mayer's first foray into production. Having discovered that the beautiful and ambitious Anita Stewart felt unappreciated at Vitagraph, Mayer lured her away by meeting her financial demands and forming a production company in her name. As her first vehicle, he bought *Virtuous Wives,* which had been serialized in *Cosmopolitan* magazine.

Elda had read it and detected in the other-woman role an opportunity to establish herself with the public as a menace. "I like to play bad women, frankly," she said. "Oh, of course, I like to reform at the fatal last moment, because that gets you sympathy, but I like to be wicked throughout the picture. Good women are so deadly dull. . . ."

When Elda heard that George Loane Tucker, whom she had met at the Fort Lee, New Jersey, studios, had been hired to adapt the serial and direct the picture, she donned what she considered her smartest gray chiffon gown and an

---

* Miss Kennedy, appearing in *The Baby Maker* in 1970, said that filmmaking, in her opinion, had come full circle. In 1919 producers relied heavily upon existing locations. As major studios undertook more ambitious productions, elaborate sets, complicated lighting and the addition of sound equipment necessitated the building of huge stages. Then space-age technology made it possible to pack lighting, sound and other equipment into one large van, and natural locations could be used again. "So," she concluded, "we're back where we began."

ostrich feather hat. Sweeping into his office, she announced that she was ideal for the society woman. Tucker agreed but added that Anita Stewart, who had cast approval, might consider her too visually compelling. It was agreed that the next day she should meet Miss Stewart at the Vitagraph Studios in Brooklyn.

That night Elda prepared for the encounter. Being a woman who viewed acting as a contest rather than ensemble work, she discarded the chiffon and feathers for a well-cut, but subdued, dress, a slightly outmoded hat and sensible shoes. Her cunning paid off. Miss Stewart took one look at the plain creature in front of her and apologized that it had been necessary to make the trip. Elda thanked her. It was their last civil exchange for the next quarter of a century.

Elda immediately betook herself to Lucile, Inc., where she spent the entire $5,000 she would earn on gowns designed by Lady Duff-Gordon. Her plan was simple: to play a startlingly callous society woman of such chic she would steal the picture.

In her first scene with Miss Stewart, the star took one look at Elda's floating gray chiffon tea gown, turned to director Tucker and demanded what "she" was wearing.

Elda spoke up, haughtily informing the star that it was a tea gown designed by Lady Duff-Gordon, the kind of thing she often wore when entertaining.

As DeWitt Bodeen pointed out in a career story on Miss Stewart in *Films in Review,* Anita Stewart was within her rights. "The second woman does not outdress the star," Bodeen noted. "Miss Stewart could have held up production and had Lady Duff-Gordon or any other couturier design a special wardrobe for three times the sum the extravagant Hedda had spent." By not doing so, Anita Stewart allowed Elda to score a hit. Elda became identified as "The Worst Cat on the Screen"—a woman who was capable of callously kicking aside her child's toys as she relentlessly pursued another woman's husband.

Now Elda had made her point. It was no longer necessary to trade on her husband's fame. Sometime in 1918 she decided that Mrs. DeWolf Hopper and Elda Millar fitted her no better than Elda Furry or Elda Curry. She decided she needed a new name. In a 1919 interview, she claimed that she hoped to boost her career by a change of cognomen, and a friend had steered her to Mrs. Cochrane, who had successfully renamed illustrator Neysa McMein. Mrs. Cochrane, variously described as an astrologer, a numerologist and a psychoanalyst, using one technique or another, came up, for the modest sum of $10, with HEDDA HOPPER.*

Later Hedda said she was motivated by the fact that to her husband she wasn't a name, but a number. His previous four wives' names had consisted of two syllables, the second ending in *a*.† She tired of being called Edna, Ida, Ella or Nella and got in touch with Mrs. Cochrane. When her husband heard her new name, he said: "Hedda cheese, Hedda lettuce, Hedda—nothing. I don't like it." But he never confused her with the others again.

When his wife's booming film career was mentioned to Hopper in Cleveland where he was appearing in *The Passing Show,* he replied: "Movies. How I hate 'em, hate 'em, hate 'em. Posing for the camera is certainly a weird and wondrous life, but not for me. I've had my share of it, thank you, and never again." He exaggerated his earnings, saying he had earned $100,000 for ten months' work, but that films were a medium for amateurs. Legitimate actors needed a stage, audiences, applause.

While he was still on tour, Hedda was cast as the nurse in the play *Be Calm, Camilla.* This was indeed a compliment to her since the legitimate theater was experiencing a slump and roles were difficult to find even for established players. Better still, this was no shoestring production. The producer was Arthur Hopkins, one of the theater's most distinguished managers and directors, and the author was Clare Kummer, whose *Good Gracious, Annabelle* had run

---

* Whether or not either Mrs. Cochrane or Elda was familiar with Ibsen's neurotic modern woman, Hedda Hopper never made clear. Undoubtedly they were, since *Hedda Gabler* had had several New York stage productions by that time, and in 1918 Nazimova's film version of the play had been made.

† So Hedda is also a two-syllable name ending in *a*? Well, whoever accused the volatile Miss Hopper of being either logical or consistent?

for 111 performances during a world-wide depression in 1916 and had forshadowed the wisecracking comedies so popular in the 1920's and 1930's.

Be Calm, Camilla opened at the Booth Theater on October 31, 1918. The New York *Times* described it as a typical Clare Kummer comedy. "It has the charm of gossamer or a woodland spider web until it shines forth in the morning sunbeam studded with diamonds," the unidentified reviewer wrote. ". . . Hedda Hopper," he noted, "lent a vigorous and sympathetic touch as Camilla's trained nurse."

The general consensus among reviewers was that this play was even better than *Good Gracious, Annabelle*. Among the cast were Lola Fisher (the original Annabelle), Carlotta Monterey (a stylish actress who eventually married Eugene O'Neill) and Walter Hampden (who was taking a rest from the classics). There was also an actor named Arthur Shaw, talented but unstable. Soon after the opening, he disappeared. When he reappeared five performances later, he was forgiven, but when he disappeared a second time, producer Hopkins disgustedly decided to close the play. It had achieved eighty-four performances.

Hedda immediately began making pictures again, but she no longer limited herself to one type of role. She played leads, menaces, vamps, best friends and mothers. She wanted money. Whether or not she admitted it to herself, she seems to have reached a decision that she and her son could not rely on Hopper. At the beginning of 1918, she had persuaded him to rent a house in Great Neck, Long Island, claiming that their son could not be properly reared in a hotel. The oft-divorced Hopper adamantly refused to own property. So Hedda saved her film earnings toward the day when she would have accumulated enough money to make a down payment on a house in her name.

For some reason, however, she hesitated in May, 1919, about playing Norma Talmadge's mother in a picture known as both *Isle of Conquest* and *By Right of Conquest*. Yet it is indicative of her growing confidence that she could laughingly report her husband's estimate of her "lousy" acting to Louella. She had also tentatively begun to attempt to develop a panache. Contemplating an egg, she could unselfconsciously say to an interviewer: "Eggs. There is something simple about eggs. I adore the simple life. You see I haven't acquired temperament yet. Call around in a year or two. In the interval, I'll develop temperament and dig up a scandal or two."

III

Many things have been written about the way I
got my job with Hearst newspapers. Some of the
rumors are enough to make your hair stand on end.
—LOUELLA PARSONS
in *The Gay Illiterate*

EXAGGERATION, malice, distortion and misinforma-
tion encircle the name of every adventuress. Louella
Parsons was no exception. It is at least a part of the fascination of this unexceptional-looking, hardworking newspaperwoman that her career should have been explained
in terms of a lurid murder and a devious blackmail scheme.

If Louella's career is to be put in proper perspective,
it is necessary to jump from 1919 to 1924. All during
that fall rumors circulated that the distinguished producer-
director Thomas H. Ince and Hearst were about to arrive
at an agreement which would bring Ince into Hearst's
Cosmopolitan Pictures.

Ince was a former operator of a small-time stock company who had established himself as a topnotch director.
By 1924 he was the head of his own company and enjoyed
a reputation both as a "doctor of sick films" and as a man
who played as hard as he worked. Such a man was potentially invaluable to Hearst, who, despite his wealth and
the automatic paeans accorded his Cosmopolitan films by
Hearst writers, had not distinguished himself as a producer. He hoped that with Ince as part of Cosmopolitan's

operations, the company might be turned into a prestigious and profitable enterprise.

Shortly before November 16, 1924, Hearst spontaneously scheduled a weekend party on his yacht, the *Oneida,* to celebrate Ince's forty-third birthday. Mr. and Mrs. Ince were invited, but since they were attending a preview of *The Mirage* on Saturday night, they declined. The next day Ince went to San Diego alone. He boarded the *Oneida,* harbored south of the ferry landing, and joined a party that included actresses Marion Davies, Seena Owen, Margaret Livingston, Julanne Johnston; novelist Elinor Glyn; Dr. Daniel Carson Goodman, Cosmopolitan's head of West Coast production; and George H. Thomas, Ince's own general manager.

Once there, Ince so overindulged his appetites that during the night he suffered an alarming seizure. By Monday morning his condition was serious enough so that, accompanied by Dr. Goodman and an unidentified man, he left the yacht by tender. The three proceeded to the railroad station, where Ince and Goodman boarded the Santa Fe headed for Los Angeles.

When the train arrived in Del Mar, Ince and Goodman debarked. A porter commandeered an automobile, and the two men were driven to the Stratford Inn,* where Goodman summoned Dr. Truman Parker of La Jolla, who examined Ince and called Dr. Horace Lazelle for consultation.

At first Ince claimed that he was returning from a hunting trip in Mexico, apparently in a misguided attempt to keep his host's name out of the story. Then he admitted that he had "eaten heavily and smoked a good deal" while attending a yachting party. Only later did he mention that there had been "plenty of liquor, but that the man who supplied it could well afford the best." Since Prohibition was then in effect and some of the homes of leading screen personalities had recently been raided, it is understandable that Ince should have been reluctant to mention Hearst.

---

* Renamed the Del Mar Hotel, it became popular with the sporting crowd when the Del Mar racetrack opened. It closed in 1963 and was demolished in 1969.

But he also must have feared being blinded or poisoned by bad liquor.

Drs. Parker and Lazelle concluded Ince was suffering a severe gastric disorder or had had a mild heart seizure. Nurse Jessie Howard was hired to attend him, and several days' rest in bed was prescribed.

Later the same day Mrs. Ince, the Ince's fifteen-year-old son, William, and their family physician, Dr. Ida C. Glasgow, arrived in Del Mar and discharged the La Jolla doctors. They arranged for a private railroad car to be attached to the Santa Fe train the next day and, with nurse Howard in attendance, proceeded to Los Angeles. There an ambulance was waiting to take Ince to his Beverly Hills home.

They arrived at his Dias Dorados estate in Benedict Canyon late in the afternoon, and by five o'clock the following morning he was dead. Cause of death was listed as angina pectoris. At his side when he died were his wife, his three children and his two brothers.

There the matter might have ended, had the San Diego district attorney not begun investigating rumors that Ince had drunk some bad liquor on a yacht. The investigation which began on December 10 was abandoned on December 11. Then, almost two years later, on September 21, 1926, the Los Angeles *Times* published a story that the investigation was about to be reopened. This proved untrue.

At no time was there any mention of Louella. Possibly her name was later added by jealous rivals. Possibly readers, puzzled by her mind-boggling syntax and frequent inaccuracies, furnished a melodramatic explanation for her position. Numerous people around Hollywood still claim to have known someone who was on the yacht and saw Louella there, but these eyewitnesses always turn out to be dead, senile or unreachable.

One version of the story is that Hearst killed Ince during a business argument; Louella saw it. A variation had Hearst discovering Ince and Miss Davies in *flagrante delicto* and shooting the producer; Louella witnessed the shooting. By far the most popular version had Hearst bursting into a stateroom where Charlie Chaplin was making love to Miss Davies. She screamed. Hearst scrammed. Guests rushed to the stateroom. Hearst returned, shot at Chaplin but hit Ince. Louella and the other guests saw it all.*

Louella contented herself with the comment that rumors of how she kept her job ranged in style from Edgar Allan Poe to Boccaccio—but all implied she was guilty of perpetrating the cagiest of blackmail schemes. As a hard worker, she resented it. In this case, her version seems correct.

"I checked out the story when I came out here for the *Morning Telegraph,*" said Jerry Hoffman, who went to Hollywood to become vaudeville editor and general reporter for that paper. Subsequently he worked as a legman for Louella, produced films and was a public relations man. "I heard the story, and being a boy-hero vigilante, I wanted to know why somebody didn't print it. People said nobody would dare. I said I would.

"I spent six months off and on running down the things that were supposed to have happened. Finally, I checked George Thomas, who had an important job with Ince. If anybody had reason to hate Hearst he did. And he said, 'Jerry, I could have saved you all that work. I was on the yacht. It was a birthday party, and Mr. Hearst was going to give Ince a part of Cosmopolitan Pictures as a present. Ince made a pig of himself—overate and overdrank. That's all there was to it.' "

Hoffman went on to say that later a Hearst newspaperman claimed he saw the bullet holes in Ince's body when the producer was laid out in the San Diego morgue. "And I looked at him and said, 'You know, unfortunately, you've told that story so often, you believe it. But it's a goddamn lie.' "

A check of Louella's column datelines on, prior to and after November 19, 1924, the day Ince died, showed her

---

* If everyone rumored to have been in the stateroom had been there, it would have been more crowded than the one in *A Night at the Opera* and the conspiracy of silence would have made the conspiracies that supposedly surround John Wilkes Booth and Lee Harvey Oswald pale in comparison.

writing from New York. One item mentioned a letter from California. A second read: "Thomas H. Ince is more than signing contracts today. Word came yesterday that Jacqueline Logan signed a contract whereby she will make pictures for Thomas Ince for the next five and a half years. I asked why the half year and no óne seemed to know."

So much for Louella and the yacht. She was 3,000 miles away and was not to arrive in California for the first time until May, 1925.

There is a canard that Louella O. Parsons' career can be explained in one word: Hearst. Nonsense. Had Hearst never existed Louella would have wheedled, flattered, flirted, threatened, clouted, wept, bulldogged and done whatever else was necessary in order to succeed. In 1919, almost five years before she joined the Hearst newspapers, she had already established herself as a small but important cog in the motion-picture business.

"I first knew her when I was on the *Clipper*, the oldest theatrical paper in New York. She was the motion-picture editor of the *Telegraph*," Jerry Hoffman said. "By 1920 every motion-picture columnist who got a break would automatically start gunning for her. Her column meant something. But I'll say this for her, she never pulled a knife first. Only in self-defense. She was one of the most generous persons in most ways—unless it affected her column. It was like a schizophrenic personality."

It is pointless to speculate on whether or not Louella conducted the *best* motion-picture column in New York. One might as well debate whether the editorial content of the *Register* in Winslow, Illinois, was superior to that of the *Leader* in Lemmon, South Dakota. What is pertinent is that by 1920, in spite of the disruption of World War I, an abrupt change in movie fans' tastes and a postwar slump in the film industry, Louella's hard work had increased the size of the Sunday film supplement in the *Telegraph* to twenty-four pages. Editorial content included reviews, hard news, feature interviews, answers to questions and squibs of the "Items of Local Interest" type. Stylistically, she had not progressed beyond *"The Song of*

Songs is food for thought . . ." ". . . news am news," and "tempus does fugit."

Yet she had already made an impact on both the city and the industry. When Olga Petrova invited Louella to accompany her abroad, Louella accepted. In London she managed to make friends with Lord Northcliffe and through him to obtain a job writing a column for the *Picture Goer*. She also wangled a couple of stories about herself. If the tone of the interviews describing her as "Queen of the American publicity writers" and "probably the most prolific writer of fan stuff in the States—which is going some," is somewhat tinged with malice, she could still take comfort in asking how many other visiting reporters were interviewed.

From the first Louella assumed a proprietary air about the fledgling art form. In her eyes, she was not only "for it" but "with it." So fiercely protective were her feelings, that as a guest at the 1921 Authors League Fellowship Dinner, she misinterpreted novelist Cosmo Hamilton's satirical description of the distractions (including secretaries in transparent blouses) by a literary fellow employed in a film company. She publicly took him to task. "There may be no Art in newspaper work, but at least, all the men and women I know who write for the daily papers respect their work. It seems incredible that any man or woman could be cad enough to accept money from the motion picture industry and then turn around and tear it limb from limb."

Louella's bold solution: "Why not a blacklist in pictures?"

A few days later she printed an explanation from program chairman Gelett ("I Never Saw a Purple Cow") Burgess, who regretted that she had misinterpreted Hamilton's remarks, which had been "transparently" in the spirit of fun. Burgess assumed responsibility and added that if ever an evening was devoted to newspapers, he feared wit would have to be labeled—or reporters excluded.

Was Louella cowed? Not at all. "I agree with Mr. Burgess that a joke is often a risk," she wrote. "Why shouldn't wit be labeled?"

In relation to the films, Louella was trying for a "100%

Loyal" rating. When U.S. Senator Henry L. Myers called for film censorship on the grounds that Hollywood was riddled with "debauchery, drunkenness, ribaldry, dissipation and free love," citing three scandals in the past year, the intrepid Louella counterattacked. "He does not mention that there have been dozens of scandals on Wall Street and yet no one attempts to put the bridle on the financial world and put it under official censorship."

In an editorial she would defend pictures against the charge that they encouraged runaways, led innocent girls into lives of degradation, encouraged honest youths to become thieves and lowered the moral fiber of the nation. "Immature minds and ignorant folks whose only connection with the ways of the world are gleaned from photoplays are said to be so influenced by what they see in films that they model their lives after these make-believe situations. Such a contention is serious . . ." Louella wrote. But she ended with testimonial, fervent as those customarily given at revival meetings. She bore witness that Emil Jannings' masterful impersonation of the Russian czar in *Peter the Great* so stimulated her that she went home and "boned up on Russian history."

Producers, directors, featured players and even luminaries of the caliber of Mary Pickford responded to Louella's dedication by going to see her in the old streetcar barn that housed the *Morning Telegraph* and later at the New York *American* building. It was a custom that Louella lovingly perpetuated after she moved to Hollywood. Then promising newcomers were invited—or was it commanded?—to drop by the Villa Carlotta or her home on Maple Drive in Beverly Hills for an interview. Those who sought out the oracle and spoke the magic words were rewarded by frequent plugs in her column.

Miss Pickford, Theda Bara, Tom Mix, Pauline Frederick, Douglas Fairbanks and Charlie Chaplin were early favorites. Madge Kennedy achieved special distinction by rating three separate breaks in one column. But even Miss Kennedy was no competition for the extraordinary space lavished upon Marion Davies, the blond comedienne whom the "political" Louella realized could thrust her in Hearstian orbit. Of course, Louella told it another way.

She claimed she had been thrilled "by Davies" in *When Knighthood Was in Flower,* but that at that time—1922— it was fashionable for a critic to seem to earn his or her salary by carping about something. Louella chose to criticize Hearst for emphasizing the cost of the picture rather than his star's talent, charm and beauty. Hearst was amused and arranged for Miss Davies to introduce them. Eventually, he offered Louella a job, and to discourage him, she demanded $250 a week. He agreed at once. Then, according to Louella, she persuaded his own lawyer to draw up an outrageous contract that Hearst was sure to reject. He did. But when Louella remained firm, Hearst gave in. Making an unlikely story less likely, Louella contended that she stalled in signing, until Hearst called her in and forced the issue. As she was leaving, he confided he was disappointed in her. "Miss Parsons," she quoted him as saying, "you forgot to ask for hairpins."

Meanwhile, back to reality. Her criticism of Hearst's promotion of *Knighthood's* cost may have appeared in the *Telegraph,* but if it did, it is well buried in the gusher of Marion Davies items that began as a trickle in 1918 and by 1922 had developed into a deluge. With an unerring instinct, Louella devoted 100 words of praise to Miss Davies to every one for Hearst, even before meeting the star. Then in early March, 1919, after seeing *Cecilia of the Pink Roses,* Louella dined with Miss Davies, and in her first major interview with Miss P, published March 9, she was hardly able to contain herself. "To say that she has any conceit would be a prevarication. She was so ingenuous for 15 minutes I regarded her with suspicion— probably this was a new form of screen poise I had not yet encountered, but as we grew acquainted and I saw how hard she tried to please and what an effort she made to be interviewed, I made up my mind she was what she seemed —naïve and unspoiled."

Despite all evidence to the contrary, many writers hostile toward Louella continued to attribute her power with Hearst to the fact that she introduced him to Marion

Davies. Miss Davies finally spiked that rumor by announcing Louella hadn't introduced WR to her; she had introduced him to Louella.

Yet certainly Louella owed her swift rise to more than her flattery of Miss Davies. She worked longer and harder than any of her colleagues and so inextricably entwined her working and her social life that they were one and the same. The filmmakers recognized this; other reporters realized it. What did it matter that on July 12, 1923, she had to include the following: "Yesterday we carried an item in which we called Clara Bow, Clara Bows; J. G. Bachmann, J. H. Backman, and B. F. Schulberg, B. S. Schulberg. Aside from that the article was correct. Heat? No, old age." What, after all, was the difference whether it was B. P., B. F. or B. S.?

Nor was Louella shy about trumpeting her successes. On June 27, 1923, she patted herself and her department on their collective backs for having been chosen to supply the material for a nightly radio show. "We feel very much like the winner of some medal in having WOR pin the glory on the *Morning Telegraph*. To have our reviews chosen as being the most valuable, to have our opinion selected as carrying the most weight in the outside world is an event in the day's happenings." Although she was careful to share the honor with her staff, there was a hint of the imperial and imperious "we" in her item.

Thus, Louella had no need to know where any bodies were buried to join Hearst. On November 19, 1923, she became motion-picture editor of the New York *American*. On December 9, 250 representatives of the film industry, her former staff from the *Morning Telegraph* and members of the Hearst press gathered to honor her. Her "Persian Garden of Cats" presented her with a traveling case—and in Louella's mind there could have been no question that the direction she was headed was up.

On the surface, Louella would seem about as mysterious as a bowl of boiled potatoes. Yet her personal life poses an even more intriguing puzzle than does her career. Inquiry about McCaffrey caused a highly protective former associate to reply, "Not McCaffrey, Brady." Subsequent inquiry to other sources also brought forth Brady's name. Theatrical publicist Nat Dorfman, who in the early 1920's, as representative for the Sunrise Picture Corporation, had been friendly with Louella, was under the impression that McCaffrey had not played a significant role in her life at that time. Did he recall a Brady? Yes, Peter J. Brady, a well-known public figure of the 1920's.

When Louella met Brady, she, fourteen-year-old Harriet and Captain Jack were living in a three-bedroom apartment on 116th Street, presided over by their housekeeper from Chicago, Jennie Mattocks. Captain Jack, who was then piloting an excursion boat on the Hudson River, resented Louella's unrelenting pressure to elevate their standard of living, and although he was a well-educated man, he had the outdoorsman's contempt for adults who spent their days pretending to be someone else. Actors!

He enjoyed meeting Bat Masterson, the retired lawman from the West, Hearst, or a beauty such as Marion Davies, whose warmth and charm captivated almost everyone, but Tom Mix, for example, was a disappointment. "Gone Hollywood" was not yet a way of describing loss of perspective, but it fit what Captain Jack felt about Mix, as well as about Louella—who still had never set foot in that California village.

Louella later told her friend Mrs. Walter "Fieldsie" Lang that she quickly realized the marriage was a mistake. Why then didn't she end it? Friends say that for all her professional *chutzpah* Louella was extremely sensitive to personal criticism. Divorce was a terrifying step for her even when, as with John Parsons, she was the injured party. And to divorce a man for incompatability was unthinkable to a woman who, however ruthless professionally, was basically sentimental, kind and conventional.

How the inevitable break between Louella and Captain Jack occurred is impossible to uncover, but he afterward confided to his Burlington friend Adeline Churchill that he had been deeply hurt. Louella inflicted that hurt when she fell in love. In her autobiography, she included a short section in which she told of her involvement with an un-named man who was not free to marry. "There is no real happiness for a woman falling in love with a man who cannot get his freedom from another woman. I know that. There are two heartaches for every joy you know. . . . I wasn't happy. I couldn't be under the circumstances. But neither could I help being deeply in love."

The man whose name Louella omitted was, of course, Peter Brady, a New York labor leader, a banker and an associate of prominent political figures. He was a bluff, charming Irishman who had come up the hard way.

Born in Ireland in 1881, he was brought to the United States by his parents in 1890, only to have his schooling cut short a year and a half later when his father suddenly died. The ten-and-a-half-year-old Brady immediately went to work as a news boy, supplementing his earnings by running errands. At night he attended school in the best Horatio Alger tradition.

An engaging extrovert, who had known grinding poverty and loneliness, Brady was drawn into union activities for both the job protection and social activities they provided. Eventually, he became president of the New York State Printing Trades Council, and in 1920, he was appointed to the Mayor's Commission on Taxation and was spon-sored by Samuel Gompers to draft a constitution for the Central Trades Council in New York. In 1922, he at-tacked the governor's and the New York legislature's policy toward labor and on September 17 of the same year sent a letter to the Motion Picture Theater Owners of the state, coming out against film censorship. It was his con-tention that it had been used to remove examples of brutal conduct "by employers' hirelings and officers of the law against working people engaged in industrial disputes." He maintained that this action endangered "the Constitu-tional rights of the freedom of the people" and promised that labor would send committees to both the Democratic and the Republican conventions to demand a plank for the repeal of censorship laws.

Louella first mentioned Brady on August 23, 1923, when she ran a long item announcing that he had been invited to address one of the Theater Owners' Chamber of Commerce luncheons. "His subject will be 'Banks' and it is expected he will tell something of the purpose of the Federation Bank, which, by the way, now boasts more than $2,000,000 in deposits. This certainly speaks well for the bank, which only opened its doors May 19 last. It is expected that deposits will reach the $3,000,000 point by October 1." Any careful reader of Louella would have recognized her habit of promoting those who were loved by, related to or of professional use to her. Two weeks later Brady was again heralded as being about to speak on motion pictures and "the new Federation Bank of New York City" at the luncheon.

Thus began the relationship which was to bring Louella much personal suffering and guilt, since Brady was a married man, who, as a Roman Catholic, could not consider divorce. But since both worked closely with the film industry, they were able to manage their love affair with a great deal of discretion.

In innumerable ways Brady widened Louella's horizon. His varied interests brought him into contact with Franklin Delano Roosevelt, Herbert Lehman, Alfred E. Smith, James J. Walker, such athletes as Jack Dempsey and Benny Leonard, as well as bankers, aviation enthusiasts and labor leaders. When Louella attended the 1924 Democratic Convention, she remarked she'd had no idea it could be as entertaining as the *Ziegfeld Follies* but had to admit that after seeing "our own set * floating around day after day I knew that no first night ever inspired greater interest than this carefully staged drama. . . ." †

The Parsons-Brady relationship—marked by highs and lows—continued over a period of years and was broken

---

* Celebrities and newspaper people.

† Not surprisingly, she turned it all into a huge backdrop for Marion Davies, printing in her column a letter from one Morgan Marsh, who claimed that it was fitting the real inside story on the nomination of John W. Davis should come from Louella since

off only after Louella met and fell in love with Dr. Harry W. Martin. But even after her marriage to Martin, when news came that a low-winged private plane in which Brady was a passenger had crashed into a West New Brighton, Staten Island, housetop, killing him and a resident of the house, Louella was overwhelmed with grief.

The other joy in Louella's life during these years was Harriet, whose precocity delighted and amazed her. She clucked proudly when her thirteen-year-old published her first fan magazine piece, not foreseeing that it might fore-shadow a future in which Harriet's standards would rise higher than those Louella could meet, however sympa-thetic she might feel toward them. Nor was she bashful about proclaiming the senior class play at Horace Mann High School as "so good we are forced to admit that we have seen many plays produced on Broadway that were not in the same class. . . ." After many bouquets, the proud mother concluded: "And Harriet O. Parsons, of course, we cannot forget the latter. Her part was not as big as some of the others, but we think she did very well and we do not mind who knows it. . . ." Harriet might set Louella straight on the historical inaccuracies in *The Covered Wagon,* complain about the vulgarity of allowing

---

"Will Rogers and all these here other fellers thought they had the right dope, but they were all wrong. . . . The truth of the matter is that they nominated this feller Davis because they thought he was the father of Marion Davies and I can prove it." According to Marsh, only two things interested the American public—radio and movies, the latter interesting them more because they paid to see them. "Of course," he went on, "there are some folks that will say Davis does not spell his name like Marion Davies does, but then these here politicians ain't such good spellers like you and me so they just naturally went wild over the idea that here was the father of Marion Davies up for nomination. Wouldn't it be a great thing, said they, if their candidate should advocate free movies just like William Jennings Bryan advocated free silver? So you see, it was the movies and Marion Davies to which Mr. Davis has got to say thank you in case he happens to be elected president of these here United States. Yours for truth always, Morgan Marsh."

newspaper delivery trucks to carry her mother's photograph on their sides or dislike being referred to as "the little girl who lives at my house" when she was eighteen years old, but Louella regarded all these things as signs of progress.

Truth to tell, Louella juggled her family life, her secret love affair with Peter Brady and her career with a consummate skill, but by 1922—even before she joined Hearst—she was having health problems.

Later, in March, 1924, Louella caught a cold which developed into tonsillitis and kept her away from work, but when it became difficult for her to write her column from home, she defied her doctor and returned to the office. Complications developed. She was thought to be suffering from a severe chest cold, but she refused to remain in bed. Then, one day she suffered a hemorrhage at her desk, prompting her physician, Dr. Henry Cave, to prescribe a chest X ray. Considering that her father died from tuberculosis in his early thirties, the prospect can hardly have failed to alarm her. But in her column she treated the situation with bravado, announcing that she could never become a film actress because she did not have the patience to remain quiet long enough for an X ray.

Bravado proved not to be enough. By the middle of May Louella's condition had worsened, and she was sent to Roosevelt Hospital for two weeks with no visitors allowed. This did not prevent the appearance of an athletic gentleman and three of his friends one evening. He announced himself as Jack Dempsey to the nurse but turned out to be prizefighter Benny Leonard. The nurse allowed him in, to the annoyance of Dr. Cave but to the delight of Louella since it provided material for her Sunday column, which she wrote from her hospital bed.

On May 25 she was back on Broadway, announcing that her hospitalization had reinforced her conviction that films served an underrated function in the lives of people who worked under pressure. The nurses, she said, could endure the suffering and grief that was all around them much better because it was possible for them during their leisure to enjoy vicariously the adventures and romances of a Norma Talmadge or a Gloria Swanson.

Although warned to take it easy, Louella was unable to slow up. Almost at once she was off to Boston to address the convention of Motion Picture Theater Owners of America at the Copley Plaza Hotel, where one of the other speakers was Peter J. Brady.

For the remainder of 1924, Louella's health remained precarious, although she took great pains to keep it out of her column, which overflowed with enthusiasm and activities. Naturally, no enthusiasm for anyone else quite equaled that reserved for Marion Davies. On August 6, in reviewing *Janice Meredith,* Louella lamented that the man who wrote it "could not have lived to see Marion Davies play his character. He would have had a feeling of supreme contentment from her performance. It is a remarkable performance, given with the same charm that characterized her work in *Little Old New York* and made it one of the finest motion pictures ever produced on any screen. . . .

"Familiar as I am with her work, and I think I have seen every picture she ever made, she astonished me by her versatility and her ability to get across subtleties that would have fallen flat in less skilled hands."

Those were the kind of words designed to warm any actress' heart. It was the period when the friendship between Louella and Miss Davies was at its warmest, and two months later Louella uttered what has come to be regarded as the invention of a gag writer when, on October 8, 1924, she observed: "My second view of *Yolanda* at the Capitol Theater again convinces me that this is one of the most beautiful pictures ever produced. Marion Davies in the costumes of the English period has never looked lovelier. . . ."

"Marion Davies has never looked lovelier. . . ."

"never looked lovelier. . . ."

"never looked lovelier"

has echoed down the years, a standard line to be uttered

whenever a Louella Parsons impersonator was at work. And it is only fair that credit should be given where credit is due: Louella wrote it herself.

IV

I really didn't have a husband; I had legal
permission to live with a star.
—HEDDA HOPPER
in *From Under My Hat*

A DELICATE balance was sustained between the Hoppers during 1920. At sixty-two, DeWolf Hopper found
roles in new plays were scarce, but he could always as-
semble a season of Gilbert and Sullivan revivals. The
ambitious Hedda was weary of the condescension she
received not only from her husband, but also from his
friends and even her own agent. She realized bold, dramatic action was needed to earn their respect. Her method
of attack: *money*.

When she was offered what was known as "a meaty
role" in the film *The New York Idea,* she dressed modishly
and informed the producer and director that she'd be delighted to play the part for $1,000 a week. To her surprise,
they acquiesced without haggling. Hedda had doubled her
salary simply by asking. She went directly to the office of
her agent, Edward Small,* and announced her salary.

"That was a lot of money for a featured player," Edward Small recalled in 1970. "But Hedda got it. When

---

* "Small—that's the way he thought. What I needed was Eddie
Big," Hedda once told Elsa Maxwell—before the two began their
long-standing feud.

I was her agent, other actresses let me do what I could. Hedda had ideas of what I was to do and how I was to do it."

Hedda could hardly wait to leave Small and hurry back to Great Neck, Long Island, to impress her husband with her new financial success. Years later Bill Hopper still vividly recalled the scene that ensued. "I'll never forget the night she came home—I must have been five or six years old. Pop was making $1,000 a week on the stage which was good money in those days. And all of a sudden she comes home and she's making $1,000 a week in pictures. He blew his stack. He'd been on stage all his life, you know, and all of a sudden she's getting a grand in pictures."

Shortly Hedda took her savings and made a down payment on a house in Douglaston, Long Island. Her husband predicted she'd never be able to make the payments, warning her not to count on him for help.

As a man about town Hopper was noted for his beneficence. Any down-on-his-luck actor knew "Wolfie" was a soft touch. He automatically picked up tabs—as a matter of pride, but now he found himself an uneasy guest in the house of the show girl he had married. "I feel like a damned gigolo," he grumbled to John Barrymore. As a result, he began escaping to baseball games and bull sessions at the Lambs Club and seeking the company of more comfortable, less ambitious women. If Hedda discovered a stray hairpin or a bit of finery in his car, he claimed that one of her friends must have dropped it.

The relationship deteriorated at an accelerated pace, with Hopper spending more and more time in Manhattan. When Hedda suggested meeting his friends, he informed her that they wouldn't be interested. Hedda couldn't understand that—until she began discovering lipstick stains on his collars and handkerchiefs.

She undertook a new role, detective, when, in July, 1921, Hopper announced that he was going to attend a weekend yachting party and Hedda wanted to accompany him. Refusing to believe his explanation that the affair was strictly stag, she trailed him to Wading River, New

Jersey, and confronted him on a moonlight stroll with a singer from his touring company.

Her contrite husband was awaiting her in Douglaston to beg her forgiveness and promise to reform. He was terrified that yet another marital scandal would end his career. He promised that the young singer would not be included in his company when it reopened. Furthermore, he swore she had been only a casual friend.

Whether it was her Quaker upbringing or her feminine ego, Hedda agreed to give the marriage another chance. Then she embarked on a schedule that was staggering. With Bill away at school and Hopper on tour, Hedda began rehearsals of William Anthony McGuire's *Six-Cylinder Love,* a play that examined the devastating effects of automobile ownership upon family life. In it, Ernest Truex received what Alexander Woollcott, in his New York *Times* review, described as "the kind of ovation usually reserved for actors on their farewell tours."

Simultaneously she signed to support John Barrymore in a silent version of *Sherlock Holmes* in which William Powell made his screen debut. During the filming, Hedda was on the set at 9 A.M., worked all day, appeared at the Sam H. Harris Theater in the evening, staged a running cat fight with June Walker over a hat Hedda substituted and finally fell into bed exhausted.

This rigorous schedule not only brought in money but also rated her publicity breaks, including one in Louella Parsons' increasingly important movie column. In a long interview in the November 20, 1921, issue of the New York *Herald,* Hedda claimed to have worked nineteen pictures and two plays in the preceding four years. " 'And if anyone thinks 19 pictures in four years is a slight achievement, let them try it. I get so furious when people say to me, "Oh you just do pictures for the fun of it, don't you?" Fun! I've done some pictures I've loved and some pictures I've been ashamed to tell people I've been in. But I never did one that wasn't hard work. Nineteen pictures in four years!' She shrugged her slim shoulders. 'Is it any wonder I'm haggard and cross and old before my time?' "

A contributing factor to these feelings was the discovery

that Hopper's Wading River companion was once again with his company. Reluctantly, Hedda consulted a lawyer and on February 3, 1922, filed suit for divorce in Queens County Court. The following day Hopper agreed to pay $250 a week support for Bill, plus $5,000 counsel fees. He also consented to provide $250 a week alimony until she remarried.

On July 21, in Long Island City, Hedda began action for an absolute divorce on statutory grounds, naming no corespondent and asking full custody of Bill. Hopper, who was in the midst of a four-week engagement in Baltimore, did not contest the suit. The following day Louella wrote that the Selznick Company wouldn't think of publicizing it but Hedda had had experience in playing a troubled wife when she did that type part for them in *Conceit,* opposite William B. Davidson. Davidson, she said, played a boasting, overbearing husband, whose treatment of his spouse served as the foundation of a unique triangle. "This is all apropos of Mrs. Hopper's suit for divorce. She having filed against DeWolf Hopper, making the fifth—or is it the sixth?—wife to ask for her legal separation. And still Mr. Hopper doesn't believe marriage is a failure."

In Long Island City, Hedda called a press conference and made one of those statements that played down so many Hollywood marital disasters: "He is the grandest man in America, but we must part."

On August 1, Hedda went to court to obtain an order directing Hopper to pay $6,500 in back alimony and $5,000 in counsel fees. He was warned that he would be liable for contempt proceedings if he failed to comply. But Hedda soon learned that the law was no match for her ex-husband. He was unable to hold onto money long enough to pay her. Finally, she bitterly took out a policy on his life, paying the premiums herself. It (together with the policy she carried on herself) was the only protection their son would have in the event of both their deaths.

Despite her personal problems, Hedda stayed with *Six-Cylinder Love* for ten months. Then she turned in her notice and spent some time with Bill while accepting any available film work. That fall she played an "involuntary old maid" in Louis K. Anspacher's *That Day,* which opened to blistering pans. Of the cast, Hedda fared best, with the man from the New York *Commercial* calling her "easily the star" and saying she played "with grace and charm and real ability."

The play closed, and since Hedda had completed *What's Wrong with Women?,* starring Constance Bennett, and *Has the World Gone Mad?* * she impetuously decided to see Paris with Zabelle Hitchcock, wife of comedian Raymond Hitchcock. Zabelle was accompanying a cousin on a buying trip; Hedda was looking for diversion. Before leaving, she called Louella to tell of the trip and to get in a plug for *Has the World Gone Mad?* by saying she'd answer the question by studying "how the other half of the world is managing the foreign question."

While away, Hedda left her small son in charge of a hard-bitten Canadian guide whose tales of frontier life had fascinated her when she met him on location in Banff. Thinking her son would be equally fascinated, she sailed on the *Olympic* two days before the boy's eighth birthday, leaving behind a pile of beautifully wrapped gifts. It was a costly mistake. Well intentioned as her action may have been, it was interpreted by the child as rejection. Try as she would to reestablish a rapport upon her return, she was never able to recover the boy's trust.

In recalling his early life, Bill said, "Hedda never seemed to be around much. I was at various and sundry schools. Not that I blame her . . . what the hell, she was divorced. She had to work. Pop couldn't be counted on. He never paid her any alimony. I was shunted off. I didn't see him much. By the time he died, Pop was owed—he was the world's softest touch—he was owed a fortune. Maybe half a million. Hedda got the life insurance she'd paid for. I got a ring of his. . . .

"So you can't—I really can't—blame her. He never gave her a present. One birthday, she said, 'All right, Wolfie. You've never bought me a present. Never an anniversary present. I want a present for once!' He said, 'Fine,

---

* The Toledo *Blade* critic announced: "Hedda Hopper can say more with her eyebrows than any woman alive."

Fine!' Well, he runs into Tyrone Power, Sr., who was flat broke. There goes the 600 bucks. Pop did it . . . goddamn, he was something else. He was funny.*

"But I always thought Pop did more to color our lives than she would ever admit, than anybody ever knew. I think he clobbered her. Pop wasn't a stinker, but he was a big kid until he died at 76. I'll say this for Hedda. She did what she could for me."

Upon returning from Paris, Hedda left for a year in Hollywood. Before sailing for Europe, she had encountered Louis B. Mayer, whom she had kept shooing out of camera range during the filming of *Virtuous Wives*. Mayer twitted her about not bothering to respond to three offers he had made. She explained that it was because of family obligations. Now, with her marriage dissolved and her son enrolled in an Eastern prep school, she challenged him to make a new offer. He asked the minimum she'd accept. After some lightning calculation, she came up with $250 a week, a modest price for an experienced leading woman at that time. Hedda had yet to learn that Hollywood accepted one at his or her own valuation.

She later claimed that her professional reputation was permanently damaged at Metro-Goldwyn when news spread that director Reginald Barker had refused to accept her in a leading role. It was to have been her first picture under the new contract. He claimed that she photographed unattractively despite evidence to be seen in her twenty-odd New York and New Jersey films.

Gossips had another version. They claimed that when Mayer chased her around his office and Hedda outran him, she should have run right on out the gate—as far as her hopes of obtaining good roles were concerned.

When Hedda reported to Metro-Goldwyn, for reasons of economy the studio still rented space at the Selig Zoo,

---

* Years later when Tyrone Power, Jr., was at Twentieth Century-Fox, Hedda laughingly told him of the incident. The next day Ty's check for $600 plus interest arrived. He insisted on paying his father's debts.

one of whose lions became its trademark. It was there that Hedda worked with Carmel Myers in *Reno,* written and directed by Rupert Hughes; *Sinners in Silk,* with Eleanor Boardman, Adolphe Menjou and Conrad Nagel and the mysterious Miss Du Pont (who used no given name); and *The Snob,* starring Norma Shearer and John Gilbert. In view of Hedda's unconstrained ambition, it is easy to imagine her private despair at not rating a single mention—good or bad—in *Variety's* reviews of these films.

On her first trip to Hollywood in 1915, as the wife of a prestigious theater star, Hedda had regarded the scene from aloft. As a divorcée in 1923, she saw the town from quite a different point of view. At thirty-eight, she was just another moderately successful character actress, struggling along in a success-oriented industry, appearing in picture after picture—often in roles that turned out to be scarcely more than bits. Her expenses were increased by having to support her son and herself on a fraction of what her ex-husband had earned. Living by her wits was no longer an amusement—it was a necessity.

She registered at the Hollywood Hotel. In 1915 she had had a home in which to entertain lavishly. Now it became difficult to return invitations since ready cash was in short supply. To promote her career, she dressed in a tasteful, if somewhat flashy, manner. She cultivated a brittle exterior and made it her business to dig out the inside story on everyone in order to spice up her conversation. She resorted to all the popular tricks utilized by actresses past the flush of youth who had to earn a place on guest lists.

Where she differed from most was that she was totally respectable. It was traditional for women in her situation to take to drink, to drugs or to wealthy men. After her divorce, Hedda was admired by many men, but she never really loved any of them. She had, according to her own son and Frances Marion, no lovers, no love affairs. She claimed that she wanted to marry again but until she did was interested only in platonic relationships.

One of her staunchest allies was Louella, who was finding it increasingly difficult to cover an industry located

3,000 miles away. Hedda shrewdly took to writing her long, gossipy letters, and Louella reciprocated with column breaks.

Usefulness or no usefulness, Louella couldn't find much to say about Hedda's acting in *Dangerous Innocence* (with Laura La Plante) or *Déclassée* (with Corinne Griffith). But in reviewing *Raffles,* she wrote, "Hedda Hopper, charming and attractive, struggles along with the role of Clarice trying her best to get something out of her situations with the unmentional [*sic*] Miss Du Pont . . . whose film career will always remain one of the great unsolved problems of my art."

In *Zander, the Great* naturally most of Louella's enthusiasm was focused on Marion Davies—who else?—but she squeezed in the fact that Mrs. Caldwell won sympathy in "the capable hands of Hedda Hopper." * More important than the role she played in the movie was Hedda's good fortune in furthering her acquaintanceship with Marion Davies. It earned her numerous invitations to San Simeon and the chance to become friends with Hearst and Miss Davies.

Even though 1925 was a disappointment professionally, Hedda decided to remain on the West Coast, and like many semisuccessful entertainers before and after, she supplemented her income by dabbling in real estate. Then, in 1926, having already transferred Bill to Black Foxe Military Academy in Los Angeles, she sold the Long Island house, bought an automobile and hired a chauffeur to teach her to drive. (To the end of her life, friends facetiously called her "Hell on Wheels Hopper.") She also moved into an apartment with two other actresses, and by December she had managed to acquire a house. Louella soon was proclaiming that while no formal invitations were issued, half the film colony had taken to dropping in on Sunday afternoons.

In the same year Louella dubbed Hedda "Queen of the

---

* *Variety* said: "Hedda Hopper appears to advantage as a jealous woman." Freud's and Stanislavsky's followers can draw their own inferences.

Quickies" and begged her readers to excuse her for not thinking of a better term to describe the pace at which Hedda was going from part to part. She also credited Hedda with popularizing the society woman type.

Offstage, Hedda was very much on the fringe. She was, for instance, overlooked when invitations were issued for a huge gala reception at the Los Angeles Ambassador Hotel in 1927 honoring Charles Lindbergh for his solo flight of the Atlantic. When Bill was crushed that he was not to see "Lucky Lindy," the indomitable Hedda loaded him, a school chum of his, her maid and a friend of her maid into a car and drove to the hotel, where she made sure she attracted the attention of one of the hostesses, a woman who often dropped by on Sunday. The hostess shamefacedly crowded Hedda's party into the space at her table. "Imagine Elda Furry horning in on a party like that. . . . But we have to think fast to keep ourselves up to the mark now . . ." was her heads-up explanation.

The years of 1926 and 1927 were ones in which Hedda accepted whatever was offered whether at Metro-Goldwyn or on loan to another studio: *Dance Madness* (Conrad Nagel and Claire Windsor), *The Silver Treasure* (Lou Tellegen), *Fools of Fashion* (Mae Busch), *Diamond Handcuffs* (Mae Murray), *Orchids and Ermine* (Colleen Moore and Jack Mulhall), *Adam and Evil* (Aileen Pringle and Lew Cody), *Venus of Venice* (Constance Talmadge, Julanne Johnston) and *Wings* (Charles "Buddy" Rogers, Clara Bow, Richard Arlen, Gary Cooper). In *The Cave Man,* Myrna Loy was singled out by *Variety* as "one of the better vamp bets" while the rest of the cast was dismissed as "not mattering much." Hedda would have been less than human not to have reacted to the fact that younger women were progressing while she remained a relative nonentity. In *Don Juan,** which had a musical

* Although Louella regarded the movie as a triumph for John Barrymore, she said she must not forget the galaxy of beauties who contributed to its success. Among the supporting players, Hedda's name led all others, including Myrna Loy, Helene Costello and Phyllis Haver. She further described Hedda as the kind of woman any man would go wrong for.

score, sound effects and John Barrymore in the title role, she made it a point to appear on the set every day whether or not she had a scene. This eccentric behavior inspired gossip that she misguidedly hoped to snare the great matinee idol, leaving her to explain that, as a theater-oriented performer, she simply realized Barrymore would be inspired by an appreciative audience.

Shortly afterward her hopes skyrocketed when she was awarded the title role in *Mona Lisa,* one of a series of Technicolor shorts based on famous paintings, produced by Arthur Maude. With Hedda were Crauford Kent and Arthur Shaw, whose disappearance had closed *Be Calm, Camilla* almost a decade earlier. But nothing important came from this other than the promise from B. P. Schulberg that her role in *Children of Divorce** would be a big one and that she had his word that after the picture was edited, she would not find herself on the cutting-room floor.

Nevertheless, that was what happened in *Children of Divorce,* and it was repeated in *Harold Teen,* which a promising young director Mervyn LeRoy was handling.† Hedda's fate was summed up in two sentences in *Liberty* magazine's 1928 review: "In the process of cutting, *Harold Teen* has lost some of its characters. For instance, just a flash remains of the giddy widow Honora Hazzit, who was played by Hedda Hopper."

In August, 1928, the month that *Harold Teen* was released, Hedda accompanied Frances Marion and Miss Marion's niece Caroline Bishop to Europe for a six-week vacation on money she had made in the stock market. On August 17 the trio sailed on the *Île de France.* A few days

---

* Hedda recalled that Clara Bow, who was playing opposite cowboy Gary Cooper in his first "playboy" role, said Cooper certainly knew what to do with a horse. Then she added that the trouble was, "When he puts his arms around me, I feel like a horse."

† By the time Hedda had established herself as a powerful columnist she and LeRoy were feuding bitterly. One day she encountered him at the betting window of Santa Anita and brashly said, "Hi, Mervyn. Give me the name of a winner." "Louella Parsons," snapped LeRoy as he walked away.

later Hollywood's number one gossip received a menu upon which Hedda had collected messages from Dolores Del Rio, agent Paul Kohner, Miss Marion and other film figures. Hedda also reported on Lillian Gish's, Miss Marion's and her visit to Max Reinhardt's palace in Salzburg. In fact, during Hedda's absence, Louella kindly included her in no less than six items.

One aspect of Hedda's life was not reported to the columnist, however. For the first time since her divorce from Hopper, Hedda fell in love. Her only confidante was Frances Marion, who later recalled: "It was during our grand tour. You see Hedda came from Quaker stock, and underneath it all she remained a Quaker all her life. While the rest of us were throwing our petticoats over the windmill, she never would. Even Mary Pickford broke out of that Catholicism. I used to say to her, 'Hedda, for heaven's sake, throw your panties over the windmill.'

" 'Oh, Fan,' she'd say. 'You're awful.'

"But she met this man—unhappily married—whose wife wouldn't give him a divorce. They fell in love—and I never saw a more magnificent couple. He was dark, and she was fair. And they were madly in love, but she refused to sleep with him.

"I told her, 'Over here in Europe, nobody knows us. You owe it to yourself. You married an older man, you owe it to yourself. Don't be afraid of life. Of love! Throw yourself over the precipice. Look at me! I throw myself over the precipice and hope someone will catch me before I hit the bottom—and they always do.' But Hedda wouldn't do it—couldn't do it."

Hedda later said though she'd met a handsome painter on the ship and had fallen under his spell, it had never occurred to her to invite him on the tour. But when they returned to Paris, he was there and showed her Sacre-Coeur. Then, by chance, he obtained a commission to paint a ballroom and flew to London—so he happened to be on hand to guide her around that city too.

When Miss Marion was asked to identify the man, she refused. "He came to Hollywood to visit Hedda, but she wouldn't give in," she said. "That was the last time she saw him. The reason I can't reveal his name is he committed suicide. I'm not implying it was *only* because of Hedda— but I know she lived to look back and regret it."

V

LOUELLA left New York in May, 1925, to go to Hollywood as Marion Davies' house guest. Her response to that
initial visit furnishes an insight into her journalistic appeal,
for her chatty reports provided her readers with a fulfilling
fantasy life.

The adventure began when Louella and her hostess de-
parted from Grand Central—given a rousing send-off by
celebrities, reporters and, for some inscrutable reason,
seventy-five disabled war veterans. In her first glimpse of
the sunshine-drenched Los Angeles railroad station Louella found a veritable preview of the promised land. "The
first thing that met my gaze was the glitter of gold—I
thought I was seeing some brilliant reflection of the sun's
rays when about 15 young men stepped forward, each
bearing a gold key." The keys symbolized the open-door
policy of all studios.

In a wildly exhilarated state, Louella, ignoring Miss
Davies' entreaties to wash the grime off her face, insisted
on being driven through the fabled streets at once. Sys-
tematically thereafter, she began to visit one studio each
day. She watched Chaplin titling *The Gold Rush* and
dropped in at Metro-Goldwyn. At Fox, she saw Alma

Rubens portraying Lady Isabel's ultimate humiliation in *East Lynne*. At Warner's, she was personally escorted around the lot by Jack L. Warner.

In mid-July, determined to experience the "feel" of picture-making, Louella "anonymously" reported as a $7.50 a day extra for a crowd scene in Miss Davies' *The Lights of New York*. Vicariously Louella took her readers to the wardrobe department, where "Mother" Coulter offered a yellow dress which the star had rejected as "too frilly." Later, when Louella viewed the dailies, she wished that she had exercised Miss Davies' judgment. "That dress with all the ruffles, bustles and flounces would make a bean pole look fat," she complained—and Louella was no bean pole.

When Florence Lawrence (no relation to the Biograph Girl), drama editor of the *Examiner*, gave a luncheon for Miss Davies and Louella, it was almost a command performance for the silent film crowd. Both Norma and Constance Talmadge, still wearing greasepaint, came directly from their respective sets. Norma wore an elaborate white court dress from her picture; Constance, a modern sport suit, but she had young Ronald Colman in tow. The Talmadges and Colman could linger only long enough "to eat a sandwich" before returning to work, but Elinor Glyn,* Seena Owen, Ann Pennington (of the dimpled knees) and Hedda stayed on.

The next evening, actor Wilfred Lucas and his wife, scenarist Bess Meredyth, who was just back from Rome where she'd been struggling with the script for *Ben Hur*, staged a Spanish fiesta complete with sweeping colored lights and 150 guests, including Mabel Normand, Blanche Sweet, Ramon Novarro and Beverly Bayne, who danced on the greensward to music provided by a *genuine* Spanish orchestra. In quick succession, Mack Sennett had a small dinner for thirty in Louella's honor; Prince Avazzanae, a supper dance; Gloria Swanson, a Bastille Day party for her current consort, the Marquis de la Falaïse, *and* Lou-

---

* Louella described her as: "Redheaded, green-eyed, definitely regal in bearing and far more intelligent than her literary classic, *Three Weeks,* would indicate. . . ."

ella. Madame Glyn, as well as Natacha and Rudolph Valentino, hosted dances at The Sixty Club in the Biltmore Hotel ballroom. Meantime, Louella squeezed in her first Hollywood premieres, *Don Q: Son of Zorro* and *The Gold Rush,* a visit to Mrs. Thomas Ince and trips to San Francisco and Santa Barbara.

The healthful rest she had planned to take had been forgotten, but clearly Louella had been captivated by Hollywood's life-style. "I came West with the conviction too many pictures were being produced in Hollywood," she admitted, "and that not enough imagination was employed in their making. I know now that Hollywood is the legitimate home of the movies. I have also learned that any lack of imagination is not the fault of the geography, but the individual."

One of her more mystifying observations was that Los Angeles was a "planned city" and that . . . "one can see it day by day taking on the splendor of the builder's dreams." If she had a reservation about California, it was the limited amount of theater and opera available. But she said she was no longer one of those snobs who insisted that a frock or a hat come from Fifth Avenue or the Rue de la Paix. In fact, she felt tempted to copy California fashions. Entraining for New York on July 28, she regretted waiting so long to take Horace Greeley's advice and promised she would soon return.

As it happened, Louella did go West again in mid-November for what the New York *American* euphemistically described as a few weeks' vacation. This time she went as a thoroughly frightened woman whose destination was not Hollywood, but Colton, California. Recurring hemorrhages, the loss of eleven pounds and other symptoms of the lung ailment that had killed her father haunted her.

Until election day, 1925, Louella had never been sick. That day she awoke with chills and fever but was determined to vote, write her column and attend a party at Hearst's that night. At her desk she suffered a slight hemorrhage, then another at the doctor's office. He sent her for X rays, but she insisted upon being home when Harriet arrived from school and upon attending the party.

There, when Louella ran upstairs to speak to Marion Davies, who had phoned from California, she hemorrhaged again. Honeymooners Frances and Samuel Goldwyn drove her home, where she paced the floor all night. The next morning Hearst called and fired her—at full salary until she recovered.

In Colton, she found life so depressing that she soon had herself moved to Nellie Coffman's Desert Inn in Palm Springs. Palm Springs, which had had its first permanent white settler in 1854, was still a tiny desert community in 1925. There were four hotels, one general store and a school, but no newspaper.

In February, Louella discovered that English novelist John Galsworthy was wintering there and could not resist the opportunity to score one of her beloved "scoops." She sought the author out, and in early February her by-line appeared over an interview. Galsworthy surprised her on at least two counts. He claimed no interest in screenwriting and he used a pencil instead of a typewriter. "How can anyone do creative work on a machine?" he asked. Louella countered that typing was quicker, but Galsworthy told her time meant nothing to him. "Oh shades of all the newspaper articles written on one's favorite portable," Louella wrote. Then she elicited a testimonial about Palm Springs from the novelist and added her own prediction that Palm Springs would become "the best winter resort in the entire world."

Hedda, with an eye for the main chance, visited Louella and, as Louella informed readers, looked over desert properties since she was supplementing her picture income with real estate sales commissions.

Louella's only real complaint against the Springs was that the once-a-week movie was often five years old. Sydney Chaplin heeded her and changed the situation—at least one Friday. The way Louella told it in 1944 was that he sent down a print of *Charley's Aunt* to cheer her up and that hotel guests and deadpan Indians made up the audience. In 1926 she said the picture was *Oh! What a Nurse* and described the evening as a gala occasion despite the fact that "swarthy-skinned Mexicans" and Indians arrived early and took all "the white folks' seats," adding that not even a rich New York debutante protested when she found "a nice fat squaw" occupying her chair. "The desert," Louella philosophized, "has a disarming way of making one forget social standing. . . ."

In the early years, Louella's column reflected many subconscious prejudices. In addition to the "swarthy Mexicans," she blithely announced that the black *Our Gang* star Farina (a favorite of hers) was back from a week of eating watermelons. In a review, she observed that "there are several other pickaninnies,* who all but stole the show." At another time, she designated Benito Mussolini as her favorite hero. Nevertheless, Louella was an essentially well-meaning, if somewhat unthinking, member of the Establishment who had climbed a rung or two up the ladder and was bent upon reaching the top.

Publisher Hearst was more than willing to help her. In fact, when she returned from Palm Springs to Los Angeles near the end of March, 1926, he insisted that she settle in California to cover the motion-picture industry's activities. "Nobody had to push Louella with him. He knew what he had," said Mac St. John, ex-newspaper and magazine writer and a public relations man. "You know this is a funny town. When anyone makes a success, everyone goes around trying to find out why. 'What do you suppose it really means?' they ask. Well, in this case, it meant Louella was the best at covering the Hollywood scene. She had faults; but she sold papers, and that's why Hearst hired her and kept her on. He was not given to keeping people on who didn't sell papers. . . ."

Casey Shawhan, who worked as a reporter, a city editor and a public relations man, stated: "There are a hell of a lot of guys in Hollywood, as you well know, who would double cross you for a headline. And one of Louella's great sources of power was that she sold Hearst on the idea that everybody else was a liar or a thief or worse. Scandals broke, and she convinced him his other people were covering up. And then, of course, the covering up

* When a reader took her to task for using this derogatory term in 1931, Louella apologized and pleaded ignorance. Then on November 8, 1932, she used it again!

she did for Marion—that was an unbeatable combination."

Personally, for Louella, the offer to remain in the West produced deep conflict. Not only was Harriet attending Wellesley, but also the move placed 3,000 miles between her and her married lover, Peter Brady. Discreet meetings would be difficult to manage, and Louella was one of those marshmallow romantics who believe "every girl has a right to have a fella"—even if the girl happens to be a mature forty-five. Yet from the first, there was little doubt about her decision. "After you knew her a very short time, she let you know business came first, family and friends second," said her friend Mrs. Walter Lang.

So Louella accepted Hearst's offer to become motion-picture editor for his Universal News Service, which meant that she not only would be read in the New York *American,* but would write for the Los Angeles *Examiner* and be syndicated in the *American,* the Denver *Post,* the Seattle *Post-Intelligencer,* the Portland (Oregon) *Journal* and the Indianapolis *Star.* Once Louella had made her decision and was ensconced in Hollywood, it succeeded New York, as New York had succeeded Chicago as the center of her universe. She trumpeted the fact that film production ranked first among California's thirty-five leading industries and that $175,000,000 was spent on production in 1925. Did that sound as if the public was tiring of films? Certainly Louella wasn't. Rumors that the silent-film industry was in trouble were obviously false.

Temporarily, she moved in with Maggie Ettinger, her cousin, who was now a successful public relations woman. Since Miss Ettinger privately was a wife and mother, it might have seemed a crowded household. But Louella, ignoring her recent illness, was too eager to make the most of her new opportunity to spend much time there. When she was better organized, she rented an apartment at the Villa Carlotta.

She ate her luncheons at the Montmart Café, making her way around greeting stars, directors and producers. "Any news, dear?" she'd ask repeatedly, giving the subject a vague, slightly unfocused look—consciously cultivating the half-zombie air. It was a clever ploy. By developing a reputation for absentmindedness and eccentricity, she enjoyed the freedom to abandon abruptly anyone with whom she was conversing if a more newsworthy subject heaved into view.

Louella was as relentless as she was tireless. She produced the daily column, reviewed pictures and wrote a full page for the Sunday paper. In fact, she dwelt so exclusively upon material about films that legitimate theater owners protested that she was neglecting major advertisers of the spoken drama for non-advertisers of motion pictures. Yet publisher Hearst gave her free rein. Early on, she established her credentials as a full-fledged, card-carrying Hollywoodophile. Film people, according to her, refused to get excited about European royalty. Too many such people were working as extras. As for Eastern writers, Hollywood wasn't impressed. After people got to know Dorothy Parker and enjoy her "merry quips," they discovered she was a "charming young person" and "the fact that she was a part of that circle of intellectual snobs" * was not held against her. Louella was not so pleased later when the politically oriented Miss Parker observed the only "ism" Hollywood believed in was plagiarism. "People who fail in our town invariably attack it," Louella rationalized.

She further built loyalties in the film industry by withholding stories, thus putting producers or important stars in her debt. But she also violated what she considered outmoded taboos. For example, studios consistently suppressed the marital status of romantic stars, fearing a fate similar to the one that befell Francis X. Bushman when it was revealed he was married and a father. Louella claimed times had changed and told her readers that cowboy Tom Mix was no bachelor, but a married man with five children. She said that the children had been coached to deny the relationship. When a writer pointed to Mrs. Mix and asked one of the boys if that was his mother, the boy said it was. The writer then indicated the star and inquired, "Is that your father?" "Oh, no," the boy answered.

* The Algonquin Round Table.

When pressed for an explanation, the child responded: "You see, my mother and father aren't married."

Mild as that revelation may seem today, it created a furor at the time and resulted in increased candor in the industry. Asked to explain her success as a reporter, Louella may have been thinking of the Mix incident when she said: "You have to have a nose for news and an eye for stories to run a daily column. You have to have a good disposition and the hide of a rhinoceros. How do I know? Just try writing something that press agents do not think is according to Hoyle or the producers believe interferes with the plans they have for their pet stars. . . . I am getting so that I now consider a day lost when I do not have at least a dozen people come to me with some grievance."

Public tastes were changing, and Hearst sensed that masses of people hungered for a departure from the conventional hard news approach. Thus, Louella, vicariously identifying with the triumps of film stars and consciously or unconsciously aping them privately, did indeed sell papers. She was thrilled to count among her friends such top executives as L. B. Mayer, B. P. Schulberg and Adolph Zukor, to say nothing of the struggling Warners, Harry Cohn and Carl Laemmle.

Criticism of Louella's work did not then unduly disturb her. In the 1926 volume containing her columns and stories mentioning her, Louella included a critique from an unidentified publication in which the writer complained about the reverent treatment accorded the Hearst film *The Flaming Forest* by reviewers in Hearst papers, adding, "I have nothing against Hearst papers. I like them because they reflect Hearst himself, who is the greatest dramatist in the newspaper business. But I wish he would issue an order to Louella Parsons and others that they could tell the truth without losing their jobs. I would like to see him do it before the next Marion Davies picture is released."

Obviously, Louella subscribed to the old chorus girl theory that it's not important what they say about you— so long as they spell your name correctly.*

---

* Which Louella (and I) know is no easy thing to do.

She also saved a 1927 interview with a reporter from *Editor and Publisher* in which she said she had never intended to specialize. She claimed she had yearned to be a general reporter and was confident that she would have been a good one. In fact, she occasionally tried her hand at subjects outside the entertainment beat, including sports, politics and crime.

What Louella did not go into was that as a woman who required a rich emotional life she was undoubtedly constantly tormented by her separation from Peter Brady. Although she was reconciled to the fact that his religion made marriage out of the question, she was both unwilling and unable to break off the alliance.

A psychic masochist might have endured the situation and found some gratification in it, but Louella took steps to solve the impasse, at least temporarily, by wangling an assignment to cover the Dempsey-Tunney fight in Philadelphia "from the woman's angle," noting that Dempsey and Tunney might be heavyweight pugilists, but to her this was a battle between film stars. On September 16, 1926, she left for the East Coast—and a reunion with her beloved.

On the way, she stopped off in Chicago long enough to confide to a Hearst reporter that Dempsey's wife, Estelle Taylor, had given her a note to be delivered just before Dempsey stepped into the ring—"If that terrible Kearns† will let you. . . . Promise me that you will hand the letter to him [Dempsey] yourself so that I will know he has direct word from me," Miss Taylor was quoted as saying. "If I send it by telegraph or telephone I cannot be sure it will not be intercepted." From Philadelphia, Louella herself told readers that she had asked Dempsey not to "hurt Gene too much, for actually, you film actors ought to stick together."

After Dempsey's defeat on September 23, Louella went from Philadelphia to New York and Brady. Her excuse was that she needed to reconnoiter the Broadway scene after a ten-month absence. As weeks passed, Louella, who was relying upon a small staff and friends (including

† Jack Kearns, Dempsey's manager.

Hedda) to cover her Hollywood beat, realized she ought to return to California but she was reluctant to bid Brady good-bye. Resourcefully she persuaded Hearst to allow her to cover the Hall-Mills murder trial in New Jersey, thereby gaining additional time on the Atlantic coast.

Louella's approach to crime reporting was to write her stories in the metaphor of filmdom. Inhabitants of New Brunswick, New Jersey, were described as "extras in this drama of real life." According to her, the whole town was aware of the triangle and was now watching the trial * of the accused Mrs. Hall "with the same interest that a motion picture audience would give a situation of this kind, unreeled on the silver screen. . . . Mrs. Hall, now on trial for the murder of her husband and his inamorata, presents the most unfathomable angle of the mystery. Hers is an unsympathetic role and she plays it with a realism few actresses on the screen could duplicate. Her mask of indifference, her absence of emotionalism and her sphinx-like expression must be termed Hallesque." Among her more exotic speculations, Louella theorized that if Mrs. Hall had learned to smile more and earlier, perhaps the tragedy would have been averted.

One of the few times in Louella's career that she was forced to admit that any movie would seem dull by comparison was after a day in the Somerville court. "If some scenario writer should invent a tale where an Episcopal clergyman and his sweetheart were murdered under the circumstances that surround this lurid, yet highly romantic tale, we all would be asking for more realism and less romance. I hate to be bromidic and say that truth is stranger than fiction, yet that is exactly the case. What an adventure to report a case like this and what a chance for drama." *

* In *Tell It to Louella,* she embellished the story. Reviewing the book in the Newark *Evening News,* E. S. Hipp noted: "Miss Parsons may have been the greatest of newspaper women, but it was 'Carpender' not Carpenter, the trial was held in Somerville, not New Brunswick and the murder victims' bodies were not found in a cemetery as the columnist twice states. . . ."

* In covering a less celebrated murder trial, Louella "reviewed" it, complaining that the defendant William Edward "The Fox"

From December, 1926, when she returned to Hollywood, until June 1, 1927, Louella alternately sniped at and praised Garbo; criticized the studios for giving carte blanche to "Eastern scribblers" (such as Herman Mankiewicz and George S. Kaufman) who had never proved

they knew anything about the "tricky essentials" of screenwriting; deified Marion Davies for having the courage to appear on screen in pigtails and without makeup while wearing an unflattering costume to "hide her blonde loveliness" in *The Red Mill;* and informed readers that Mary Pickford had received a letter from Mussolini, whom Louella lauded as "one of our most picturesque statesmen."

Then suddenly, on June 1, her readers found her dashing out to Clover Field in Los Angeles, donning mechanic's overalls, having a 25-pound parachute strapped to her back and climbing into a Fokker Army plane to fly to San Francisco. Those who knew her only through her writing must have wondered why she had been chosen for an assignment to stimulate interest in aviation. Buried in the story lay the explanation: "I looked around. Captain Ervin has gone to sleep. Porter Adams is playing parchesi. Peter J. Brady, the banker, is reading a profound-looking volume. I alone seem to have qualms about this descent to earth."

On August 30 Louella went to New York. Within a week, she was telling her readers that Peter J. Brady, the labor bank president, thought the League of Nations would provide the setting for a good comedy. Silent, of course, because neither Louella nor anyone else suspected that something called talkies by friends—and squawkies by adversaries—was lurking nearby.

After three weeks in Manhattan with Brady, Louella

Hickman would never be cast as an archvillain in a film. The trial, she said, lacked suspense. The motive of revenge had been destroyed, and his "sordid greed" lacked drama because the sum was so paltry. "The whole affair," she concluded, "is devoid of imagination and color. If it were dramatized, the movies would be criticized for exaggeration and bad taste."

went to Chicago to cover the Dempsey-Tunney rematch, refusing to make any predictions on the outcome. That practice struck her as being as foolish and unfair as trying to predict whether the unproduced films of Douglas Fairbanks would outgross those of Harold Lloyd. In fact, Louella even refused to divulge for whom she was rooting, although she observed Hollywood was her hometown and "also the home of Jack and Estelle Taylor. . . ." She added the sidebar that Estelle confided to her that she intended to "think" Jack to victory. In another sidebar, she claimed that Gene Tunney was not the least interested in women and would one day be the only ex-prizefighter-priest in the world.

At ringside on the night of the fight, Louella was filled with wonder at the thought of what her puritanical grandmother would have said if she could have seen her favorite grandchild "there alone, if you please, sitting in the seats of the mighty.

"I have met these fighters under other circumstances and it is hard to believe they are the same affable men who talked so lightly on this and that subject. Gene Tunney, with whom I conversed at some length at a dinner party one evening, bears no resemblance to this fighting demon. Jack, whose eyes were filled with love and tenderness when I saw him bid his wife, Estelle Taylor, a fond adieu, has a brow as black as a thundercloud. . . ."

This time she attempted a round-by-round analysis. Samples:

Round 1: "Gene Fowler said it belonged to his namesake. I thought both fighters seemed equally furious. I shouldn't have liked to be in either man's shoes."

Round 7: "Jack Dempsey stages a most spectacular comeback. He knocked Tunney down and the crowd went wild. I couldn't write."

Round 10: "The judges have declared that Gene Tunney is the champion of the world, but he never fought a harder battle. . . . I always thought a fight could not be decided unless by a knockout. I think I have learned a lot tonight and I think I will return to the movies. I know more about them, and just between you and me and nobody else, reporting fights is no job for a lady."

By 1927 there were eight first-run theaters in Los Angeles, and even the indefatigable Louella needed additional assistance. Her cousin and general factotum Jimmy De Tarr recommended a young reporter named Jerry Hoffman. De Tarr was impressed with Hoffman's untiring presence at vaudeville theaters, film houses and studios. Louella offered Hoffman $40 a week on a part-time basis. As a prospective father, Hoffman welcomed the extra money, and the arrangement seemed to work to everyone's advantage. Then, in June, while Louella was in Chicago covering the Dempsey-Tunney fight, the publisher of the *Motion Picture News,* where Hoffman was then an editor, suddenly demanded that Hoffman quit the Parsons staff. Hoffman argued that it added prestige for the trade paper to have a reporter good enough to work for the highly regarded Hearst film department since the *News* concentrated on production items while Louella printed gossip. Given an ultimatum, Hoffman resigned and continued to work for Louella.

When Louella returned and learned of the incident, she went directly to Hearst, presented Hoffman's case and arranged for him to receive full-time pay retroactive to the time of his discharge from the *News* four weeks earlier. In speaking about Louella in 1969, Hoffman said: "Everything I say about Louella is not done through misplaced loyalty. Because God knows, there were times when I hated her guts. You don't work for someone for ten years without getting to love or hate them. For me, love overcame hate. She was a mass of contradictions, but she was the most generous person in the world—unless it affected her column. She was like Harry Cohn and Columbia."

At the time Hoffman joined Louella's staff, a semirecession and rumors of several new sound processes had the film industry off-balance. At first, Louella was a defender of the golden silence, although she admitted that hearing Marshal Foch's voice on Fox Movietone filled her with awe. Still, she did not believe producers would be stupid enough to destroy the international language of pantomime. Less than a month later, on November 29, 1927, in reviewing *The Jazz Singer,* she did an about-face and said that what distinguished the picture was the Vitaphone sound, although she added that the producers had wisely limited it to one scene of spoken dialogue plus the Jolson songs. "The combination excelled this reviewer's best expectations," she wrote.

In April, 1928, Louella reported that studios were in a state of confusion. Samuel Goldwyn predicted that 20 percent of the established stars faced extinction by the end of the year, but Louella still refused to believe films would try to compete with the legitimate stage. A month later, in another about-face, she was trumpeting the news that Hollywood had gone talking picture mad. Elocution teachers were opening classes everywhere. Louella was adept at running with the tide.

VI

Could Caesar's wife have remained above suspicion
if suspicion were elevated to print in each issue of
the *Acta diurnal?* For that matter, could Caesar?
                                        —LEO ROSTEN
                                        in *Hollywood*

HEDDA could. Her name was untarnished by scandal,
but if she was, with one exception, indifferent toward
suitors, she was ambivalent toward her son. In handling
him, she veered erratically from excessive devotion to
seeming disapproval. For his part Bill found his mother be-
wildering. Yet in her often misguided way, Hedda was
doing everything possible.

In an interview with Jerry Hoffman, Hedda stated:
"Men are my hobby and pastime, but I don't mean it in
the popular way those words could be applied. I should
specify young men, because I'm the mother of a 16-year-
old boy myself. Bill is the grandest fellow on earth. When
I see nice, clean young chaps out here, away from home
for the first time, I picture my boy in their place. I know
I'd like someone near him to advise him properly, to see
that he meets the right people and doesn't get enmeshed
with bad company. So I make it my hobby to meet such
youngsters and try to do for them what I'd like someone
to do for mine. I think the good we may do for others we
may get back in our own children."

While others might seek her out for advice, Bill seldom
did. Thinking back over their relationship, Bill mused:

"It's funny how hard it was for Hedda and me. Before she had her column, she was kind of the 'Dear Abby' of Hollywood."

He cited a few examples:

Adrian came directly to Hedda to tell her that he had proposed to and been accepted by Janet Gaynor.

Lee Tracy called her from Mexico for advice after drunkenly relieving himself from the balcony of his hotel onto the heads of members of the Mexican Army.

Gary Cooper asked her what he should do about an impending scandal. "Go home and tell your wife before it breaks," Hedda advised. Cooper did—and was saved.

Bill was never able to establish that kind of relationship with his mother. He felt almost from the beginning that he was a disappointment. "To her achievement was everything," he said. "With me, it never was. If something happened, fine. But I wasn't going to break my neck. I couldn't care less. And she couldn't see that."

After the two of them moved to Hollywood, Hedda eventually decided that it was an absolute necessity to send him to the Catalina Island school. "It cost two grand a year in the middle of the damned Depression," he said. "To do it, she lived in a little basement apartment. Apartment, hell—a room. You should have seen parents' day. Good God, other mothers came on their yachts. But Hedda thought the contacts were valuable. Then too, it had a scholastic rating comparable to a couple of years of college—which I never had."

Hedda adored the powerful and celebrated; Bill shied away from them. She complained, explained and nagged and couldn't understand why her handsome son was so perverse that he refused to take advantage of the opportunities she provided. Unable to attend a parents' day function, she sent every girl at the dance a corsage—to her son's chagrin.

One enthusiasm they shared was Hearst's San Simeon —the ranch.* Bill was truly happy surrounded by its

---

* She took such interest in its history W.R. sometimes designated her to show new guests around, saying she knew it as well as he did.

swimming pools, tennis courts, riding horses and private zoo. "Mr. Hearst—this was—to me—I'm not talking about his business or anything like that. I don't know about that. But he always had time for me. This was a very sweet, quiet, shy sort of guy. They'd have big parties, and he'd be like a big kid, seeing everybody had fun."

During Bill's boyhood, Hedda never lacked for escorts, but most were more interested in films, the party circuit or trying on Hedda's hats than in discussing hunting and fishing with a child. Almost the single exception was Dick Richards, a handsome architect who was married to a hopeless cripple whom he would never divorce. "I think he loved Hedda," Bill said. "But he never touched her. Never. That suited her. She liked him, but she didn't love him. They were great friends. That strict Quaker upbringing and Pop ruined her—and it's a damned shame because, let's face it, she had an awful lot to give—beneath the façade."

Richards treated the boy as an adult, and in return the boy idolized him. Even as a middle-aged man, Bill became enthusiastic as he told how Richards had solved in ten days a racetrack problem that had stymied engineers for months. Richards also designed and built the Los Angeles County Hospital, using a controversial material, for which he was indicted and brought to trial. During the trial a severe earthquake occurred and not a window was broken in the County Hospital. "Charges dismissed," Bill recalled. "He was so brilliant! When Roosevelt took office, he outlined what would happen if the new President's program were carried out—and he hasn't been wrong more than a couple of times in thirty years." When the Einstein theory began to be discussed, Bill was fascinated but unable to understand the concept. Richards patiently translated it into terms a young man could comprehend.*

* When Bill was on a stock contract at Warner's, Bette Davis, James Cagney and several others began discussing the theory and confessed their inability to grasp it. "Maybe I can help," Bill offered. They looked skeptical and when he proceeded to do what he promised—startled. "For several days I walked tall around the lot," he recalled.

Hedda became fully aware of Bill's need for a father when she accidentally heard him boasting of the Paul Bunyan-like achievements of DeWolf Hopper, whom he barely knew. So in 1929, when Hopper came to Hollywood to appear in an MGM revue, Hedda called and insisted that he get together with their son when the boy came from Catalina for Christmas vacation. Hopper arrived, and Bill was captivated as he saw his father take over the house to tell stories that made everyone laugh until they cried.

Hopper also promised to take his son to the Rose Bowl game. Hedda, wise to her ex-husband's vagaries, went out the next day and paid $30 for two tickets. But Hopper remembered his promise, and on New Year's Day Bill was bedazzled by the affectionate and widespread response that greeted his father as they made their way to their seats. As they parted, Hopper made Bill a present of a $20 gold piece.

When Bill was about to return to school, he asked Hedda for spending money. She mentioned the gold piece, but Bill responded he couldn't spend *that*. His father had given it to him. Then Hedda undid much of her good work, bitterly rendering him an ultimatum—spend it or go without. Bill went to his room, thought it over and surrendered.

As an adult Bill reflected upon his childhood. "I always felt . . . I never talked to Hedda about Pop," he said somewhat haltingly, "that it was . . . she was very understanding about it. She always tried to get us together when he came out here. But I was a kid and he was an old man. Then one summer, she sent me to New York.

"I remember Pop, my half-brother, Jack, and me walking down the street. I was in my teens, Jack was in his forties, and my father was about seventy. But Hedda's ploy worked. I got to know my father very well the last few years of his life. Also, I got close to Hedda the last few years of her life. But when I was young . . . there was not a closeness. There was like a—well, sort of like a wall between the two of us. We were close, but not like a mother, definitely not like a mother-son relationship. I mean like we wanted it."

* * *

Upon her return from Europe in late 1928, Hedda signed for *Tomorrow*—a play with almost no future. By December she was back in Hollywood to spend the holidays with Bill and to thank God every night—as she had since the premiere of *The Jazz Singer* with its spoken dialogue—for her stage training. In silent pictures, she had been regarded as competent, if unexciting. Director Allan Dwan evaluated her as "a good actress, but inclined to be stiff." Aileen Pringle felt she gave stock performances because she distrusted her ability. Madge Kennedy described her as a "lovely actress." When told that not many felt that, Miss Kennedy paused, then remarked: "Well, standards weren't as high in those days."

With the emergence of sound, Hedda hoped for a chance to score more heavily. During 1929 and 1930 she had roles of varying size and richness in numerous pictures including Fox's *Girls Gone Wild*; American General's *The Divorcee*; MGM's *The Last of Mrs. Cheyney*, with Norma Shearer and Basil Rathbone. These were followed by RKO's *Half Marriage* and MGM's *His Glorious Night*. In the latter, she played John Gilbert's gushing mother. Legend has it that Gilbert's high voice ruined his career. From what Hedda saw, she was prone to blame the debacle on Lionel Barrymore's haphazard directing.* Then there were *Hurricane*, with Hobart Bosworth and Johnny Mack Brown, Fox's *High Society Blues* and *Such Men Are Dangerous*, with Billie Dove and Warner Baxter; the Pathé version of *Holiday*, starring Ann Harding, and MGM's *War Nurse*.

As a result of her work, Hedda was able to renegotiate her contract at MGM when option time came. "Real estate can go hang so far as Hedda Hopper is concerned," † wrote Louella on July 11, 1930. "She doesn't spend a

---

* Ina Claire, Gilbert's ex-wife, agreed. She said, "Jack didn't have a high or effeminate voice. He had a light baritone." *Variety* said: "Gilbert presents a passable voice when it does not have to work into a crescendo."

† Early in 1929, Hedda sold Frances Marion's home for $450,000, earning herself a $7,500 commission. She deposited the money in a bank which failed before she could spend any of it.

moment on it anymore. . . . No wonder Hedda has all the new clothes one sees her wearing at the Embassy and other places where stars congregate. A woman with a steady job can afford to buy herself a becoming frock now and then."

Hedda's credits for 1931 included MGM's *Flying High, A Tailor-Made Man* and *Up for Murder*; Fox's *Good Sport*; Pathé's *Common Law* and *Rebound*. In 1932 there was *The Man Who Played God* at Warner's starring George Arliss. Hedda claimed that the dour Arliss was kindness itself to Bette Davis, and Miss Davis flowered. When it came to Hedda, she said he coldly demanded to see what she could do and so terrified her that she was unable to relax enough to act. She never forgave him.

She was also in Universal's *Speakeasily,* attempting Polly Moran-type broad comedy. At MGM, she did *West of Broadway, Skyscraper Souls* and *As You Desire Me,* in which she played Garbo's sister. Kindly Paul Bern, the ill-fated husband-to-be of Jean Harlow, gave Hedda the role, knowing that if she didn't have an important credit, the studio would drop her.

Although the number of pictures in which she appeared seems impressive, Hedda admitted that she realized she was on the same old treadmill. Her duties at the studio were more social than creative. She helped plan parties to entertain such visitors as the VIP's attending the 1932 Olympics—and ended up at the "tail end of the table." She helped plant a microphone in the table decoration for a luncheon at which W. R. Hearst entertained Winston Churchill in Marion Davies' bungalow at MGM. Churchill assumed he was speaking off the record and was horrified to have his speech blasted throughout the sound stages and subsequently printed in the Hearst press.

Undoubtedly one of the reasons Hedda was chosen for these roles, in addition to her poise, was that L. B. Mayer's assistant, Ida Koverman, a large, forthright woman who had been Herbert Hoover's secretary when she met the actress in 1921, admired Hedda's brand of Americanism, her staunch Republicanism and her juicy gossip about film stars. An intense, lasting friendship existed between the two, and when Hedda's career seemed to be grinding to a halt, Miss Koverman did what she could to help. She encouraged Hedda to run for political office in August, 1932, and Hedda announced as one of twenty-seven candidates seeking one of the seven seats on the County Central Committee of the 57th Assembly District.

Louella was also giving Hedda whatever aid possible. On August 14, Louella included Hedda in a feature asking "six reigning favorites" what new type of role each preferred, and on August 26, Louella, then a Democrat, wished Hedda well in her bid for public office, adding, "Even if we differ with her in politics, we can't help but hope that Hedda will be elected."

Hedda lost both the election and her contract, but she gallantly persisted. She sold real estate again, even tried her hand at writing a play, *She Might Have Seen Better Days.* She thought perhaps stage acting would revitalize her career and at various times appeared in West Coast companies of *The Second Man* and *Dinner at Eight.* MGM bought the latter, and Hedda was outraged when Billie Burke was cast in the part she wanted.

Her savings had gone with the crash, but she still managed to present a chic appearance through a natural instinct for striking clothes and the generosity of Marion Davies, who quietly saw to it that her hard-pressed friends were taken on impromptu shopping parties. Poor though Hedda might be, she put up a brave front. While rehearsing *Dinner at Eight,* she told Florence Lawrence, who interviewed her, that she was meeting with groups to solve the industry's Depression problems and in helping the needy—although naturally she hid the fact that this included her. "Well," she said, "perhaps we all needed to learn something of effort and hard work. Perhaps films have spoiled us, and we needed to face reduced incomes and mental suffering to teach us fortitude."

That statement came from a woman who had only five brief jobs in 1933: MGM's *Men Must Fight, The Barbarian, Beauty for Sale*; Majestic's *The Unwritten Law*; and Fox's *Pilgrimage,* directed by John Ford.* Nor were

---

* The two were good friends, but once, in a fury, she called Ford "an Irish son of a bitch"—and he reprimanded her for being redundant.

her prospects any brighter. As it turned out, her film credits in 1934 were limited to Universal's *Bombay Mail, Let's Be Ritzy, Little Man, What Now?* and Liberty's *No Ransom.*

In addition to her financial problems, Bill was becoming rebellious. He was tired of having his clothes chosen for him and of having Hedda meddle in every decision right down to having to give her approval if he took Isabel Jewell nightclubbing, thereby providing Louella with another Hedda item. So when Hedda suggested that he become an actor, he refused, and when she decided that he was a born lawyer, he perversely took up acting.

Bill later claimed that he chose acting as the easiest way to make a living. Hedda naturally decided to lend a hand, wiring "Wolfie" to give their son a place in his company. The wire was ignored. Hedda was outraged. (Long after, she learned her husband was playing one-nighters in a cut-down company and didn't want his son to see him in reduced circumstances.)

In looking for new ways of earning money, Hedda lasted for one day with Major Zanft's talent agency. She hated being crowded into an office with two secretaries, and although she swore like a longshoreman, she claimed his language offended her. But she was not too proud, after joining the Rebecca and Silton Agency, to meet the incoming train when a client, the famed singer Helen Morgan, arrived to begin rehearsals for a play.

Being an agent was not conducive to peace of mind, happiness or prosperity, so Hedda proceeded to New York, having obtained a summer job for Bill at the Ogunquit (Maine) Playhouse. Upon being asked by a reporter what she was doing in the East, Hedda tactlessly responded that she was with Bill, who, she said, "is darned good-looking but needs experience." By October Bill had a small part in *Orders, Please,* and both Hedda and "Wolfie" were complaining about his deplorable diction, although the play hardly lasted long enough for anyone else to notice.

As for Hedda, an MGM lawyer brought her and Elizabeth Arden together with the suggestion that Hedda would be an asset to the cosmetics company. Hedda had almost made up her mind to accept Miss Arden's offer when producer-director Guthrie McClintic cast her as the "cynical, sensible sister from Paris" in a play called *Divided by Three* which had been written by Margaret Leech and Beatrice (Mrs. George S.) Kaufman.

As Hedda told it, the star, Judith Anderson, took an immediate dislike to her at the first reading of the play. During rehearsals Miss Anderson never spoke to her, and on opening night the star took her solo curtain call, ignoring the frenzied cries of "Hopper! Hopper!" from friends of Hedda's in the audience. In fact, Hedda claimed to have been physically restrained from taking a bow at Miss Anderson's express instructions.

"There was a bit of trouble," Dame Judith recalled in 1970. "But, oh, dear, it was so long ago. It was about shoes or something. She never liked me. As for her acting —I never gave it any thought."

Another acquaintance of Hedda's analyzed the situation, saying, "Hedda was shrewd in picking fights with people who were more important than she was. It increased her stature." In the light of her feud with Anita Stewart over the wardrobe in *Virtuous Wives* and her stand-off battle with June Walker over the substitution of one hat for another in *Six-Cylinder Love,* the observation seems pertinent.

In any case, *Divided by Three,* which opened at the Ethel Barrymore Theater in New York on October 2, 1934, ran for thirty-one performances and was distinguished only by the fact that the juvenile in the company so impressed Hedda that when she returned to Hollywood in February, 1935, she recommended to Rufus LeMaire that MGM put Jimmy Stewart under contract forthwith.

Before returning to Hollywood, however, Hedda spent a couple of months working for Miss Arden. Although soon convinced that this was no business for her, whatever the possible profits, she stuck it out and was at the traditional Christmas party given by the employees for the boss. When Miss Arden breezed in and found a bedraggled Hedda, who hadn't had time to freshen up, she took one look and blurted out, "You look terrible!"

Hedda sought a mirror, left the party, returned to her

hotel and sent Miss Arden a telegram—wishing her a Merry Christmas and tendering her resignation.

After noting Hedda's return on February 2, 1935, Louella did not mention her again until mid-May. What had happened was that at a social gathering someone speculated on Hedda's age and she quipped, "I'm one year younger than Louella admits to."

A false friend repeated the remark to Louella. Recalling all her kindness in Hedda's behalf, Louella was crushed. Hedda, who was never able to resist a wisecrack, was astonished at Louella's response. Eventually, she sent flowers accompanied by a note of apology—and Louella forgave her. It was a game the two of them played many times over the years.

By June 4 Louella had forgotten the incident and was bubbling with enthusiasm at the prospect that the public would see all the chic clothes Hedda had brought back from New York. Hedda was to wear her wardrobe in *Alice Adams.* "Hedda hasn't been working in the movies for a long time and I wonder why, because she is an excellent actress," Louella wrote. Now at last she had a job. Two days later Louella was further elated that Londoners were to be treated to the sight of the wardrobe. Hedda was accompanying Frances Marion to England in hopes of doing films there. Hedda's British picture work failed to materialize, and in September she brought her companion's two sons back to California to attend school.

With no acting jobs in sight—even though Hedda's price had fallen from a high of $1,000 a week in 1917 to $1,000 per picture in 1935—Hedda eked out an existence as best she could. She attempted to help Jan Kiepura unscramble his Polish accent for films. She talked of, but finally decided against, managing Ted Peckham's escort service for lonely women.

At about the time she was considering that desperate step, Wolfie died at seventy-seven in Kansas City, Missouri, and Hedda collected benefits on the life insurance policy she had prudently taken out in her own name many years before. She was fifty—and a failure.

Then because Hedda talked so vividly, she received an

offer from her friend Cissy Patterson to write a weekly letter for Cissy's newspaper. The arrangement was reached at the Hearst ranch, where Marion Davies saw to it that Hedda was often invited. In fact, it has been said, although not by Hedda or Cissy Patterson, that the newsletter was Miss Davies' idea. Louella, who was present, thought so little of the plan that she included it in the run-on items at the bottom of her column. There in the catchall was: "Hedda Hopper engaged to do a weekly Hollywood fashion article for Eleanor Patterson of the Washington *Post*; . . ." That a washed-up, middle-aged actress represented a potential challenge to the uncrowned queen of Hollywood was beyond anyone's wildest dreams that October 5, 1935. Little more than a year later, however, it became apparent that Hedda's perpetual thrashing had finally been given direction.

VII

According to the movies, love is the be-all
and end-all of existence.
    —HORTENSE POWDERMAKER
      in *Hollywood, the Dream Factory*

IN THE late 1920's and early 1930's romantic figures
in films were never casually introduced to their future
mates. Writers racked their brains so that their characters
could "meet cute." For example, the hero might parachute
through an open skylight into the middle of the heroine's
bridge table, or she might crash her beat-up old Ford
into the hero's shiny new Packard convertible. But in
whatever way they met, they married.

Louella always said that she and press agent Beulah
Livingston were breathlessly racing along the Los Angeles
station platform to catch a Chicago-bound train when
Maggie Ettinger introduced her to another passenger. Suddenly Louella felt a strong arm propelling her up the steps
of the railroad car, and in the vestibule she found herself
staring into an attractive Irish face and two of the bluest
eyes she had ever seen. When their owner spoke, he had
a husky voice of the type she'd always found particularly
attractive. Louella liked Dr. Harry Watson Martin immediately, but she claimed it never entered her mind that he
might be *the* man in her life.

During the journey to Chicago, Louella, Miss Livingston
and Martin ate together, laughed together and played cards

endlessly, but Louella's real joy lay in anticipating meeting Peter Brady at the end of the trip. Then, at one of the stops, she received a sarcastic telegram from Brady saying that because of her delay in departing, it was impossible for him to be in Chicago, but that he would try to meet her train in New York. Louella was crushed. "Docky," as she generally called Martin, asked what was wrong. Impulsively, she handed him the telegram.

He advised Louella to tarry in Chicago to teach Brady a lesson. When she protested that she had reservations, Martin volunteered to change them. He also sent a telegram to Jack Dempsey. It read: "I have just met the woman I am going to marry. You know her. Her name is Louella Parsons!"

Louella remained in Chicago for two days before proceeding to New York and Brady. Having managed to lose not only her railroad tickets but also her identification for admission to the Democratic Convention, which she was to cover for the Hearst press from the woman's angle, Louella appealed to Docky* for help. The result was a barrage of telephone calls from her new admirer that infuriated Brady.

Following a side trip to attend Harriet's graduation from Wellesley on June 17, Louella returned to New York and proceeded to the convention in Houston, Texas, as the only female member of the entourage on James J. Walker's chartered railroad car. As with all her so-called special assignments, Louella reported the convention from a movie commentator's point of view, lamenting that there was no crew on hand to shoot crowd scenes since the delegates would have made picturesque extras.

After Alfred E. Smith's nomination, Walker decided to visit California with his party. In Los Angeles, at the Breakfast Club, Louella was seated between Walker and Brady when Docky appeared. Louella was terrified that Brady would discover the doctor's identity and cause a

---

* Freudians can draw their own conclusions on how she happened to lose the passes and why, of all the people she knew in Chicago, she sought Dr. Martin's assistance in locating them.

scene, but Docky bided his time and, after Brady returned East, asked Louella to give up the labor leader and marry him. If she decided in Brady's favor, he said, he would accept her decision regretfully but gracefully. "I knew then—if I had not suspected it in my heart before—that I loved Harry," Louella wrote in her autobiography. All Docky needed now was to receive William Randolph Hearst's approval.

Louella, in the four years since her return from Palm Springs, had set up offices in the Los Angeles railroad building, catercorner from the *Examiner,* and had increased her power enormously. Through her own initiative and the connections of the Hearst newspapers, Louella had become the legwoman supreme. Critics might cavil at her style, her spelling and her casual scrambling of facts; but she did invest trivia with excitement, and as a result, she had established a unique rapport with film tycoons and celebrities.

"She'd get on the phone," Jerry Hoffman said, "and she'd whine, 'Things are so terrible. Don't you know any news? Gosh, I need a good strong lead.' She'd call anybody —Mayer, Goldwyn, the Warners—direct." Nor did she hesitate to call a star who was in the midst of a scene or a producer who was at home asleep. Louella recognized her power and utilized it in any manner feasible, taking full advantage of the far-reaching Hearst press to accomplish her ends.

Among the string of assistants and secretaries who passed through in the early years by far the most valuable was Hoffman, who was both ingenious and persistent. Louella recognized this and went out of her way to show her appreciation. For instance, although the Hearst organization allowed employees only a two-week vacation, Louella insisted that Hoffman take three, saying that it took one week to unwind enough to be on vacation. During the extra week, Louella covered for him.

"She couldn't get me a raise," Hoffman recalled. "She'd got me ninety dollars a week, which was high for a noneditor in those days. But she wanted me to have more.

The boss said no. But Universal Services gave her thirty dollars a week for office expenses, and she turned that whole check over to me in lieu of a raise."

Of course, Louella's kindness was not unrelated to her need for Hoffman's help in handling her growing work load. In March, 1929, Hearst placed her in charge of the entertainment pages of all his papers with instructions to improve the quality. To institute the program, Louella spent three months, visiting twenty-five states. Preceding her, a letter from Hearst arrived. "Louella Parsons puts out a wonderful moving picture page and also a wonderful movie department. She did it on the New York *American* and she is doing it on the Los Angeles *Examiner*. Her page is readable and well made-up and clean and clear pictorially. She does not have lazy group layouts that I detest and I am sure that readers detest. . . .

"The average picture department is sloppy, more or less confused and more or less worthless, poorly edited and poorly selected. I want Miss Parsons to improve not only the appearance of the pages but the contents and not only the contents but the methods."

In each city Louella spent the time required analyzing the existing practices and criticizing both the selection of material and, as the Atlanta *Georgian* phrased it, "the technical details of type, its beauty and its symmetry."

When she returned from her tour, she received the same reception accorded a star. The seven-piece Montmart restaurant orchestra, decked out in circus-band costumes, serenaded her, and a sizable contingent from the film colony and Hearst papers assembled to greet her as she made her prebreakfast descent from the Union Pacific Limited.

If Louella had once needed Marion Davies to intercede for her with Hearst, that day was long past. In fact, Miss Davies mischievously sponsored a parade of would-be Hearst columnists, including Regina Carewe, Lloyd Pantages and ex-silent star Eileen Percy. Although Louella and Miss Davies remained good friends, as Louella's power increased, their personal intimacy diminished slightly. She still accorded the actress mind-boggling critical deference,* but she was fully aware that her value to Hearst was based on her performance, not Marion's. Things were going so well, in fact, that increased amusement advertising revenue made it possible to expand entertainment coverage in the Los Angeles *Examiner* from two to three pages in October, 1930, in spite of the Depression.

There can be little doubt that Louella's copy was marked MG—meaning "must go as is." For often in a single column two items would begin in the same way —*i.e.* "Now I've heard everything . . ." or "Count the day lost that . . ." or, as of old, "Tempus sure do fugit!" The MG came about after Louella's review of Cecil B. De-Mille's *Ten Commandments* was mysteriously changed from favorable to unfavorable. She flew into a rage, wrote a letter of resignation which she rescinded only when WRH promised that the culprit would be punished and that Louella's power was absolute—subject to his approval. (Years later she discovered Hearst himself had rewritten the review because he was feuding with De-Mille.)

Louella had always been—and continued to be—pro-Hollywood in attitude. Whether the problem was drug addiction among stars (Mabel Normand, Alma Rubens, Wallace Reid), manslaughter or murder (Fatty Arbuckle, Paul Kelly) or guilt by association (Mary Miles Minter), Louella was sympathetic, and the industry welcomed her public relations work.

On the other hand, Louella had also begun to "put her two cents' worth in" on internal matters, and since she was far from consistent, producers found it irritating. Besides alternately praising golden silence, and blasting silent films as "old-fashioned," she would offhandedly pronounce

---

* In reviewing *Dulcy* (retitled *Not So Dumb* for the movies) on January 31, 1930, Louella wrote: "Lynn Fontanne, now prominent Theater Guild actress, made her first success in *Dulcy*. I hope I am not prejudiced when I say, even with all her experience, I did not like her Dulcy as well as the one Marion Davies presents on the screen. You feel sorry for Marion's Dulcy and you wish you could help her. You didn't care what happened to Miss Fontanne's Dulcy—in fact, you felt you could help assassinate her."

on what was and what was not fit screen fare. For instance, she rebuked producers for their insistence on filming plays of Eugene O'Neill. According to Louella, *Desire Under the Elms* had raised a few eyebrows in New York as a play. If it were brought to the screen with Pola Negri, Louella predicted it would increase the danger of censorship.

For standards she substituted prejudice. Announcement of any story dealing with newspapers brought a warning that reporters had better not be portrayed as common drunks. She also became the self-appointed defender of the film industry against literary inroads. Producers Jack Warner and Howard Hughes were lectured for buying *Once in a Lifetime* by Moss Hart and George S. Kaufman, and *Queer People* by Carroll and Garrett Graham. Louella later softened her attitude toward *Lifetime,* but before seeing the play (perhaps because she had heard she was lampooned as Prunella Parsnips), she commented: "It seems all anybody need do is to present Hollywood in a bad light to get a play or book purchased." However, she remained adamant about *Queer People*. "The young authors, now in New York, are reported to have laughed merrily when their book was purchased and to have said: 'If you slap Hollywood in the face, she turns the other cheek.' Of course, the authors did say this to their close friends, so they probably had no idea it would reach their former hometown."

When Lillian Gish defected to the legitimate stage, Louella accused her of going highbrow after falling under the influence of drama critic George Jean Nathan. In her column, she bitterly informed her partisan readers that Lillian now held "plebeian" motion pictures in contempt. The materialistic Louella dragged out one of her favorite phrases and thought that now she had heard everything when she learned that Charles Laughton would forgo a four-figure salary to do Shakespearean plays "at the unpretentious sum of $100 a week."

Ironically, although bored by financial reports, business transactions and any statistics more complicated than the comparative number of fan letters received by Joan Crawford, Norma Shearer and Greta Garbo, Louella helped create an atmosphere in which art was scorned and most of the industry's output was designed to appeal on the most primitive widespread level.

She was prone, too, to interfere with casting decisions —or nondecisions. She reprimanded Howard Hawks for wasting so much time filling the leads in *The Cradle Snatchers*. Why couldn't he see that Hedda Hopper was perfect for one of the wives?

Blanche Sweet, according to her, was a more logical Diane in Fox's *Seventh Heaven* than Janet Gaynor, who seemed altogether too young and inexperienced to trust with such a fine property. (When she saw Miss Gaynor's performance, she apologized in her column.)

Why, she asked her millions of readers, didn't L. B. Mayer and Irving Thalberg allow Greta Garbo to go home? Who needed her tantrums? She was certain that Jeanne Eagels would be as good in *Anna Karenina*. (A few days later, she attended a new Garbo film and ecstatically praised the star, venturing that "no other temptress on the screen lured her victims with the subtlety of Miss Garbo.")

She campaigned for the once-popular Clara Bow in the leading role of *The Red Headed Woman,* even though Miss Bow wasn't in the least interested and refused to test for the part. When Irving Thalberg cast platinum blond Jean Harlow, who was to wear a red wig, Louella sniffed that she doubted Thalberg would have accepted Miss Harlow "if he could have gotten a red-headed woman."

She lamented that Harriet Lake had given up a perfectly good name to become Ann Sothern and bemoaned the fact that Archie Leach had been "burdened with the name Cary Grant. When Cary and Gary Cooper are at a party, you get tongue tied trying to differentiate," she complained.

Supersensitive to the slightest criticism of her own physical imperfections, Louella could be blunt in describing the defects of others. Although she was often reduced to tears by printed hints that her figure was not sylphlike, she observed that it would take a lot of reducing to get Sylvia Sidney "to be the right size to play *Madame Butter-*

fly." And Jeanette MacDonald was warned that it was time for her to diet. "Too bad with her looks and voice, she continues to ignore her figure for Metro-Goldwyn-Mayer has a big idea for her," Louella told her readers.*

Announcing "little Bette Davis, blonde, young and with ability" was being groomed by Warner's, Louella added: "Bette has a great chance if she will put herself in the hands of a capable make-up man. She gave a good performance in *Seed,* and I was not disturbed by over-beaded eyelashes and an over-rouged mouth. . . ."

She granted that Judith Anderson was one of the stage's finest actresses but couldn't resist adding: "Miss Anderson fascinates with her sheer ugliness."

As for Katharine Hepburn: "Extra! Extra!" Louella began. "Katharine Hepburn has proved that she is not all snobbery and self-satisfaction. Miss Hepburn forgot to be arrogant when she had a chance to take Adalyn Doyle under her wing to develop into a motion picture actress. . . . Adalyn is prettier than Katharine Hepburn, who by no stretch of the imagination can lay claim to beauty; but then Sarah Bernhardt never won a beauty prize."

Later she relented in her attitude toward Miss Hepburn —just as she did toward Mae West. When Miss West first appeared in Hollywood, Louella's claws were fully exposed. "The buxom, blonde Mae West, fat, fair and I don't know how near forty has come to Hollywood . . ." she led off.

Recalling the relationship with Louella, Miss West said she felt the columnist never liked her very much. "She kinda like t' find somebody 'n' give 'em the big buildup," Miss West observed. "Y' might say, I arrived ready-made. We didn't exactly feud, y' know. But the way she started off, that put doubt in my mind. She come to my bungalow at Paramount 'n the first thing she says to me is: 'How d'ya think you'll do with picture audiences?'

"So I says, 'Whadaya mean?'

---

* Louella was forever dieting—or talking of it—but when she saw a tempting morsel that someone else was enjoying, she always begged "a little taste." As Ben Lyon said, "Everybody else's plate was Louella's smorgasbord."

" 'How d'ya think they'll lika ya? Movies are a lot different from theater,' she says.

" 'I'll tell ya, I'll either be sensashunal or nothin',' " Miss West drawled. " 'But bein' an optimist I'm sure I'll be sensashunal. Why shouldn't they like me? Wouldn't you like it if y' were gettin' a Cadillac for the price of a Ford?' "

When Miss West scored in *She Done Him Wrong,* Louella found her thinner and more attractive on the screen. As the siren's popularity increased, Louella decided Miss West was one of her "favorite actresses" and later hailed her as "one of the greatest showwomen who ever visited Hollywood" as well as an actress "who can be vulgar and make everybody like it." But when Will Hays clamped down with censorship, Louella's enthusiasm dwindled.

One of Louella's favorite targets was vaudevillian Benny Rubin. Rubin had deserted two-a-day in 1928, expecting to work as emcee at the State Theater on a fifty-two-week contract. His opening went well, but Louella attacked his comedy and suggested he return to his fiddle. The result: He was canceled. This happened twice more, but when Rubin began getting and keeping jobs despite Louella's diatribes, he decided she was helping more than hurting him. Then, in mid-1929, Rubin was cast in Marion Davies' *Marianne.* When Hearst visited the set, Miss Davies told Rubin to explain what had been happening. "I said, Louella'd printed I was drunk and broke a violin over my wife's head," Rubin recalled. Hearst suggested stepping in. " 'Oh, please don't! I can't buy better than you're giving me all over the country," Rubin said, having decided the jabs were keeping his name before the public.

Prior to Louella's first visit to the set, Miss Davies had a microphone attached to Rubin's chair so that she and Hearst could overhear the exchange. When Louella arrived, the star pointed toward Rubin, and shortly Louella approached, saying, "Well! What have you to say?"

"I rose and said, 'I don't know who I am speaking with.' So then she says, 'Then sit down or you'll fall down. My name is Louella O. Parsons.' " Rubin asked whether she was in the picture, pretending he wasn't aware of her. When Louella said she was in the *Examiner,* he replied he only read the *Times*. Whereupon Louella attacked him for drinking and hitting women with violins. When she finished, Rubin said, "Look, I never drink. And I never hit a woman with a fiddle because I don't play one."

And then, he said, "She started, 'Oh, my God! How can I. . . . It was Jan *Rubini*! Oh, how can I make it up to you?' So I said, 'Just keep printing my name. Make it a mock feud.'"

It is as easy to make a case out of Louella's errors as out of her syntax. In 1931, for instance, she noted: "Helen Gahagan with new husband Douglas Melvyn is visiting Hollywood. Not so long ago Miss Gahagan was married to John Cromwell. . . ." Six days later she noted: "I owe two apologies, one to Helen Gahagan and one to John Cromwell.* I don't know how I happened to make the mistake, only I was under the impression that Helen Gahagan was in the W. A. Brady plays which John Cromwell directed. I'm sorry to make this error as it is embarrassing to be given an added husband, especially when one is happily married. The first Mrs. Cromwell was Alice Lindahl and Miss Gahagan's husband is Melvyn Douglas, who will play opposite Gloria Swanson. This is her first marriage."

Louella once explained her numerous errors by observing, "I use the old bean." While this may at first seem a *non sequitur,* it is a valid explanation. She preferred to rely on her faulty memory rather than to look a fact up. If she admired a long-run Broadway play, she assumed that it had won a Pulitzer Prize, and if it turned out not to be Helen Gahagan who had appeared in William Brady's productions, it was someone like her. Louella's enthusiasm for running down a story did not extend to the tedium of cross-checking. For Hearst, the bulldogging of a story was what counted, and for Louella that was part of the romance of being a newspaperwoman.

In 1915, before she began working for Hearst, she had slipped in a side door of a Chicago theater to see the local pre-preview of *The Birth of a Nation,* and again in 1930,

* Apparently Melvyn Douglas didn't rate an apology for transposing his name.

despite Howard Hughes' ban on any outsiders* at a private screening, Louella and her secretary used the same method to enter Grauman's Chinese Theater to view *Hell's Angels,* refusing to budge when Hughes ordered them out.

Her tenacity certainly made her errors easier for Hearst to tolerate, but the errata became increasingly annoying to studio heads and publicity chiefs. Especially since, with her large syndicate, she demanded forty-eight-hours' protection from the studios on items she consented to run. Finally, the representatives of major studios met and decided that henceforth there would be no preferential treatment. News would be released to all reporters simultaneously.

Louella interpreted this as a challenge. Together with Hoffman, she devised a plan that held enormous potential. As Hoffman later recalled it: "I started to contact Hollywood talent agents I knew had deals pending. One of my closest friends was the head of the biggest actor's agency of its day, the Joyce-Selznick Agency: Frank Joyce and Myron Selznick. They had the biggest stars in the business.

"I talked with Frank and told him the problem. So I began to check the agency every morning for news. It was to their advantage, too. They could release information that was helpful in contract negotiations. They even let me use an office and they gave me carbons from their subagents. They [the subagents] reported on deals that were being worked on or had been made by other agencies. The only thing that had to be promised—which Louella lived up to—was that we would never break a story until Frank said it was okay.

"Well, all hell broke loose. Nobody could figure out where Louella was getting those stories. The worst or best —it was in the early 1930's—was when Connie Bennett made a deal with Warner's to make two pictures in ten weeks for three hundred thousand dollars. Louella played it up as thirty thousand dollars a week, which was the highest salary yet paid a picture star. In fact, when people talk about big salaries, it's still mentioned because it was before the days of percentage deals.

* This included the owner of the theater, Sid Grauman.

"So when the story broke, the poor publicity man at Warner's got his ass eaten out by J.L. The studios were going crazy. Louella was breaking stories while deals were still pending. They couldn't figure out how she was doing it. Finally, the publicity directors formed a committee and came to Louella. They wanted to go back to the old system of giving her a forty-eight-hour exclusive. She didn't want that. She wasn't vindictive, but she was doing better under the new system. She wasn't dependent on publicity departments. 'I'm paid to supply exclusive news and I have it,' she told them. 'Otherwise, the paper can get anybody from cityside to do a rewrite, and they don't need me.' What she said made good sense."

Louella had exposed the iron fist within the velvet glove and the studios respected her for it. In a town where so much was based on connections, tenacity and public image, she had established herself as a power.

Professionally successful, Louella was also ecstatic that WRH approved of her bridegroom-to-be. Later Hearst wrote her a facetious letter, which she preserved in her 1929 scrapbook (these scrapbooks, along with others containing her columns, personal publicity and other memorabilia, are now at the library of the Academy of Motion Picture Arts and Sciences). Written in a childish scrawl, the letter reads:

San Francisco, 1929

Dear Miss Parsons:
I am so glad to hear of your approaching marriage. Now that you are going to wear the ball and chain maybe it will make you kinder to some of your movie friends who have done likewise. Who lets the world know of the private heartaches? Why not let Cholly Knickerbocker keep his job? You never bother about Marion Davies????

Always your friend,
WRH

Improbable is the most fitting word for Harry Watson Martin. He might easily have wandered out of a Ben-Hecht-Charles MacArthur farce. To all but a few intimates, he seemed to lack the shading of a living, breathing man. He went beyond the stock character into caricature. The stories about the man are legion.

Costume designer Orry-Kelly told of attending a party at which Dr. Martin drank excessively and eventually fell to the floor in a stupor. When someone tactfully called Louella's attention to this state of affairs, she brushed it aside, saying, "Leave Docky alone. He has to operate in the morning."

Producer William Dozier recounted the same incident at a different party. Buster and Stevie Collier claimed it happened at their home. Frances Marion said she witnessed it at a fancy dress ball in the 1930's and added that Docky was wearing a Roman toga.*

The story seemed apocryphal until Hunt Stromberg, Jr., offered a plausible explanation by saying this happened at his parents' home more than once. He said a favorite drink of Dr. Martin's was the silver fizz. When he and Louella were coming to dinner, Mrs. Stromberg always ordered extra eggs, because Docky would drink between ten and fifteen silver fizzes during an evening. The drinking didn't astound Martin's hostess in the least—only that he could consume all those raw eggs, since each drink contained one.

The name of Harry Watson Martin still evokes strong response. Many people maintain that he was brilliant. An equal number will tell you that he was nothing more than an affable buffoon. A minority found him not only foolish, but cruel and dangerous.

Among the facts not in dispute are that Harry Martin was born in Redfield, South Dakota, on January 16, 1890; that he attended the University of Illinois College of Medicine from October 8, 1908, to June 4, 1912, and was awarded a degree as Doctor of Medicine. His specialty eventually was to be urology.

After graduation, Martin remained in Illinois for a time, and contemporaries predicted a bright future for him as a

---

* A variation on the story had Dr. Martin's penis exposed, which caused wit Wilson Mizner to quip: "There's Louella Parsons' column."

diagnostician. But Martin was always more interested in promoting his reputation as a two-fisted barroom fighter than as a doctor. He told his close friend Joseph Schenck, the Twentieth Century-Fox mogul, that he had once "knocked Jack Dempsey on his ass." Schenck told the former champion of Martin's claims and suggested that Dempsey pretend to recall the incident. Once, when the three were together, talk turned to fighting, and Martin expanded on what a barroom brawler he had been. Schenck interjected that Martin claimed he had once knocked Dempsey down. "It's true," Dempsey said. "He decked me." Martin was beside himself with glee. "See!" he crowed. "Didn't I tell you?"

When Martin intended to drink, he customarily hired a man named Bob Perry to drive for him. Perry, who had been a fearsome street fighter, walked into a bar with Martin one evening where they encountered Prince Mdivani. An angry exchange between the prince and Martin ensued. Martin swung, missed and fell on his face. The prince went after him, but Perry knocked the prince out. When the latter came to, Martin, brushing off his hands, said, "Let that be a lesson to you, you SOB."

This high-spirited Irishman arrived in Los Angeles in 1919 and soon established a reputation as a raconteur, practical joker and a good drinking companion. In 1920, after a particularly liquid evening, he retired to the Bimini Turkish bath where, after spending some time in the steam room, he staggered out and dived into an empty swimming pool, breaking his neck. This sobered him enough so that he held it in place until it could be set.

The event so impressed itself upon show business cronies that in 1924, in reporting that Martin was to wed actress Sylvia Breamer, *Variety* added: "Four years ago, Dr. Martin broke his neck in a dive at a turkish bathhouse. He startled the medical world by setting the bones himself and recovering."

Discussing the incident, Madeline Fields "Fieldsie" Lang, who knew Martin from the time she was a child, said, "It's true he held his neck in place after he broke it diving into an empty pool. He just couldn't drink. A few drinks and he was practically out. I guess it was something in his system. He got in more scrapes. After the second drink, he had to prove he loved you and he wanted to beat you up if you didn't believe it. 'I love you,' he'd say. 'You're the greatest friend I have in the whole world, and if you don't believe it, I'll knock your block off.' "

Another of the Doc Martin stories concerns a *Cosmopolitan* magazine editor from New York who stayed at the Villa Carlotta while in Los Angeles scouting writers. Late one evening, the editor suddenly developed severe abdominal pains which turned out to be appendicitis. Fearing the worst, he struggled off his bed, opened the door to the hallway and telephoned the desk to ask whether there was a doctor in the house. Shortly Doc Martin appeared at the editor's door to find him gasping on the bed. Doc, who had been drinking, approached the bed, pulled up the editor's shirt, poked at his right side—and unceremoniously passed out on top of his patient. Summoning all his strength, the sick man managed to shove the unconscious doctor aside, get to the phone and ask, "Is there another doctor in the house?"

Despite such stories, many people insist Dr. Martin could have had the biggest practice in town if he had wanted to. "He was brilliant," said one of the claimants, "but he was a party guy. He started out as a urologist, but then in plain words, he got to be known as a clap doctor, and that was the end of promise."

Sometime in the 1920's he encountered Lee Frances, Hollywood's most successful madam, and unofficially became her house doctor. Long after he married Louella, his reputation as a venereal disease specialist followed him. In the 1930's it was fashionable for everyone to attend prizefights on Saturday night. One evening, when a reporter fainted, a doctor in the audience rushed over, loosened the unconscious man's tie and opened his shirt. He came to. The next day when radio announcer-actor Paul Douglas heard of the incident, he quipped: "It's a good thing it wasn't Doc Martin or he'd have opened his fly."

"Doc never took himself seriously," said one of his

drinking companions. "Later Louella took him seriously. She tried to build his ego. But he didn't need to build his ego. All he wanted was to have fun. And he really loved Louella, and she loved him. She was a demonstrative woman who wore her heart on her sleeve and she believed wholeheartedly in the romantic items—some real, some pure bullshit—that were a part of Hollywood's stock-in-trade. And when she gave her heart to Doc, that was it. She made no secret of it. To some people, the sight of this woman who was pushing fifty and Doc—well, he was a few years younger—but neither one was young, the sight of these two necking at a party after a few drinks struck some people as funny. But it was a real love affair, a passionate love affair."

Although the Depression had already begun to cut into Hollywood production in 1930, Louella rented an extra apartment in the Villa Carlotta, where she lived, to hold the avalanche of wedding presents that descended upon her and her bridegroom. At dusk on January 5, 1930, with her daughter Harriet, then a writer for *Photoplay,* as maid of honor, Louella became Mrs. Harry Martin in a service performed by Dr. James Lash of the Hollywood Congregational Church. Immediately after the ceremony, there was a wedding dinner at the Chateau Elysee for "60 of the newlyweds' relatives and closest friends." This was followed by a wedding reception at the Villa Carlotta between 8:30 and 10:30 P.M., after which the bride and groom left to honeymoon at W. R. Hearst's San Simeon.

Honeymoon or no honeymoon, Louella and her staff continued to turn out the column. After returning briefly to Hollywood, the couple made a quick trip to New York in February, and Louella alone flew to San Francisco to promote herself professionally in the same month. In mid-May, in addition to her other activities, she appeared with Hearst before the University of Southern California's class in photoplay appreciation—where Louella concurred with the Chief that the problem with most critics was that they were too critical.

Noting Louella's obvious happiness when she visited San Francisco, financier Louis Lurie twitted her that her husband must be something in the bedroom to which Louella replied, "You must have been peeking!" *

Perennially busy and totally happy in her personal life, Louella would hardly have been aware of the Depression had not news about studio and theatrical-chain crises been fed to her and had an increasing number of friends— ex-stars, out-of-work newspapermen and press agents— not been forced to ask her to lend them something from the weekly checks she was drawing from her various activities. Louella, whose monetary generosity has seldom been questioned, gave willingly and in her column urged support for destitute actors and applauded executives for accepting 50 percent cuts in salaries—say, from $2,500 to $1,250 per week.

Her own income increased at this time. For early in February, 1931, she made a second attempt to break into radio. When her first Hollywood-based program had been canceled in 1928, she had attributed its failure to the fact that some of her guests couldn't speak English, adding that she was not referring to foreign imports.

This new CBS network show, which the Los Angeles *Times* labeled "chitty-chatty gossip," was broadcast on Wednesday evenings, featuring top film stars. The first guest was Wallace Beery. They exchanged nostalgic anecdotes about Chicago days. Constance Bennett not only gossiped but sang. Among others who agreed to work for Louella for oranges and lemons, donated by the California Citrus Growers who sponsored the show, were Charles "Buddy" Rogers, Marie Dressler, Lew Ayres and Mary Pickford, who had turned down an offer of $5,000 a week to be mistress of ceremonies on a similar show. As with everything in which Louella was interested, radio now became an obsession with her, and she bragged about hearing from people she hadn't seen or thought of since

* At a party Benny Rubin, who had been in the men's room when Doc was, was asked if Martin was really well endowed. Rubin, affecting an Irish accent, replied: "All I can say is—it looked like a baby's arm with an apple in its hand." The remark got back to Louella, who said: "You SOB—a baby's arm!" "Well, what do you call it?" Rubin asked. The furious Louella turned and stomped off, refusing to speak to Rubin for several months.

leaving Essanay. Although her show drew an average of 800 letters a week, the sponsors inexplicably decided to drop it after sixteen weeks.

Busy as Louella was with her own career, she saw to it that Doc's also progressed. During the first years of their marriage, he frequently was hired as technical adviser on such films as *Doctors' Wives* and *Life Begins.* Of the former, Louella observed: "My favorite physician, Dr. Harry Martin, is credited with the technical direction. I hope I'm not prejudiced when I say I think the technical details are pretty good too."

Some jobs came to Docky because members of the industry understood that when pleased, Louella paid off in publicity breaks. Other positions were given him at Louella's instigation. For instance, Louis Lurie received a call from Louis B. Mayer informing him that Louella was eager for her new husband to be appointed to the California State Boxing Commission. "You claim you have power. Now show it," Mayer challenged. Lurie contacted Governor Clement C. Young and urged him to call Mayer and assure him that he was appointing Martin only as a personal favor.

The governor, who was agreeable to the appointment, balked, but Lurie persisted. "Damn it, Governor. Call him. You may need him sometime!" The governor asked for what reason. "Haven't you Presidential aspirations?" Lurie asked. "He can be of help with all MGM's resources . . . stars . . . money. . . ." And under those conditions the governor called Mayer, who called Louella O. Parsons to tell her that on January 1, 1931, her husband would be appointed to the commission. "That," said Lurie, "was just one of the ways the power was connected."

In the fall of 1931 Louella accompanied her husband to New York, where, by some not so strange coincidence considering the power of Hearst and his newspapers, on October 16, Dr. Martin was awarded an honorary degree at a meeting of the American College of Surgeons.*

---

* On the last day of the visit, Louella witnessed a television experiment which reminded her of the infancy of the film industry

In addition to Dr. Martin, Harriet benefited from Louella's growing success. Earlier that year when Louella and Doc went to Honolulu on vacation with their friends Bebe Daniels and Ben Lyon, Harriet substituted for Louella, turning in what seemed to her mother such a superb performance that there was hardly anything for her to report upon her return. Soon Harriet, billed as Parsons Jr. in the Hearst press, was turning out regular features for the *Examiner* as a member of its staff. And when Louella and Doc spent six weeks visiting Berlin, Vienna, Budapest, Paris and London during September and October, 1932 (Louella was visiting film studios; Doc purportedly surveying hospital conditions), Harriet again wrote the column and looked after Louella's pet Boston bull, Pansy Parsons. (To digress a bit, Louella was inordinately fond of Pansy, and when the animal died, Dorothy Parker happened to be a dinner guest. During the evening Louella went on and on and on about her loss, causing Miss Parker to murmur, "Next time wouldn't it be simpler just to adopt one?")

The column was now appearing in 372 newspapers throughout the world, and Louella's fame was such that she rated a major interview in the September 18, 1932, edition of the London *Express,* which awarded her "eight valve ears and [a] news-seeking nose . . ." The reporter who met the columnist at Waterloo Station found she was loaded down with thirteen newspapers, eight magazines and four books of memoirs, which, Louella explained, helped her keep in touch. "Her personality is fascinating," the writer observed, "because it is propped up against such a glamorous background. She doesn't talk much, probably because it would be foolish to be indiscreet. She never mentions the power she wields over the fates of Hollywood celluloid puppets. There is no need to boast about power when you have a monopoly on it.

" 'What I *could* tell!' " Louella said, casting her eyes heavenward and recalling for the interviewer the dim past

---

and led her to predict that one day it would become the entertainment of the future.

when the unknown Norma Shearer had accompanied her to a party and vowed that one day she would know as many stars as Louella. (At the time of the London interview, Miss Shearer was queen of the MGM lot.) Louella recalled Mary Pickford struggling along on $15 a week and recent suicide Paul Bern guiding the platinum-haired Jean Harlow toward stardom.

Nineteen thirty-two was a year of traumatic changes in the industry. Jesse L. Lasky and B. P. Schulberg were thrown out of Paramount. David O. Selznick left Radio Pictures. Scores of lesser figures were fired or resigned. Stages were empty. Cameras ground to a halt, but Louella lauded *42d Street,* promoted Hearst's "Buy American" plan, applauded Marion Davies for throwing a "Keep Smiling" party and prospered as never before. She was steadily increasing her power with Hearst, and when anyone attacked her or her work, she gave the Chief to understand that that person was trying to cover up something or was being spiteful toward her.

She also scored some clean victories over rivals in securing the kind of gossip movie fans in general and Hearst readers in particular relished, although she experienced some close calls. For instance, on March 18, 1933, a young woman sued Douglas Fairbanks, Jr., for $5,000 in a heart-balm suit. Louella, concerned about protecting Fairbanks' career and seeing an opportunity to give his wife, Joan Crawford, a sympathetic real-life role, was prepared to write a sob-sister story of a woman's determination to stand by her husband. Luckily, however, she reached Miss Crawford to confirm the story and found her evasive. Finally, the star requested a meeting, at which she told Louella that the marriage had foundered long before the heart-balm suit was filed, that fan magazine writer Katherine Albert had managed to get the facts and that the story was now on the fan magazine's presses. Louella managed to "scoop" Miss Albert, but only escaped by a few days the humiliation of being outreported by a writer with a two-month deadline. No matter. Louella had been the first to tell.

Then, on March 27, while England's greatest living playwright George Bernard Shaw was a guest at San

Simeon, Marion Davies prevailed upon him to grant Louella an interview. He agreed—provided he was allowed to approve the finished product. Louella acquiesced. When Shaw read her effort, he reorganized and rewrote it almost completely—but it went out under the Parsons by-line.

Euphoric over her two successes, Louella was further buoyed up by the confidence FDR, who had replaced Mussolini as her public hero, had provided the film industry and the country in general. The worst of the crisis was over, she was certain.

For her, lucky breaks continued to pyramid. She was first to announce the impending divorce of the Richard Dixes, and in July she "shook the United States" with the news that Mary Pickford and Douglas Fairbanks, Sr., the uncrowned king and queen of Hollywood, were breaking up their marriage. Soon after, she announced that Carole Lombard and William Powell were parting, the combined effects of these revelations earning her the sobriquet "Love's Undertaker."

In her 1944 autobiography, Louella rated the Pickford-Fairbanks divorce as her biggest scoop, attributing it to news sense, accident and black magic. Miss Pickford in *her* autobiography, *Shadow and Sunshine,* viewed the incident as personal betrayal.

What is indisputable is that Louella got the story during a luncheon at the Vendome. According to Louella, four people were present; according to Miss Pickford, three. Both agree that Miss Pickford had confided to Frances Marion that she had received a cable from Fairbanks informing her of his intentions to remain abroad and never to return to Pickfair.

Miss Pickford's version is that at luncheon the next day Miss Marion brought Louella, whom Miss Pickford identifies only as "a newspaper columnist I had known for many years. . . ." The columnist, *she* says, demanded: "What about this other woman, Mary?"

Miss Pickford, wanting to keep the matter private, claims she said she knew nothing of her. Then, as in all good movies, since there had to be a villain, she casts Miss Marion in the role, claiming that the writer insisted she show Louella the cable, which she did, pouring out her heart and speaking as one might to "two friends who were trying to help." In any case, she wanted no notoriety and "counted trustingly upon the columnist's discretion" to protect her "against sensation."

In her version, Louella, a woman who always put her profession even before her family, casts herself as a dog-faithful friend ready to sacrifice anything in the name of friendship—even a "big scoop." As she tells it, Miss Marion turned to Miss Pickford and said, "Tell Louella, Mary. Confession is good for the soul." And Miss Pickford played the scene simply and calmly, saying, "Douglas and I are separating. It's just—over."

Louella claims she urged the star not to be rash—even though breaking the news would have given her the biggest divorce story yet to come out of Hollywood. But no, Miss Pickford is quoted as saying, "Louella, you are an old friend. You may write the story."

Finally, Louella says she agreed to write it, then to telephone the actress: ". . . if you change your mind, I won't print it." But Miss Pickford didn't change her mind—and Louella printed it, shrewdly holding up its release for the final Saturday edition of the Los Angeles *Examiner* in order to score a clean beat on wire services and other newspapers.

Louella's story brought headlines. Other reporters tracked down Miss Pickford at church. In her autobiography she says that when she emerged from services, she was met by her press agent, showing her the headline. She was stunned, speechless, sick: "Where there had been only heartbreak and hope, a full-sized scandal stared me in the face."

Louella claimed that the reporters followed Miss Pickford from church to Pickfair, where the beleaguered woman phoned Louella in despair. Louella urged her to say that she had been forced to give out the story, adding that Miss Pickford "told them no fibs." Louella relates that the disgruntled press agent accused her of tattling on Douglas Fairbanks and Sylvia Ashley to Miss Pickford, but she denies it, observing she knew nothing, that getting the story was only "Parsons luck" and that no scoop is worth breaking a woman's heart.

Frances Marion's version of the incident is that "Mary was going to give the break to the Los Angeles *Times*. I said to her—'If you're going to give it out, give it to Hearst. Make it a national story.' " And that, says the pragmatic Miss Marion, is exactly what Mary Pickford did.

On July 24, 1933, Louella announced she was packing up her typewriter, giving her brain a month's rest and leaving the column in Parsons Jr.'s "capable hands," but a week later she was filing an exclusive report of her visit with Carole Lombard in Reno, where Miss Lombard was divorcing William Powell.

When it came to running down a story, Louella felt secure in her reign, and she was often disarmingly honest about her writing ability. Speaking of Harriet, she told a reporter: "She writes better than I do. She has more background, more education. It is as it should be."

To the world, Louella and Harriet presented a perfect mother-daughter relationship. There were column items about their backgammon games and other homey evenings. When Harriet took over, there were complaints about the unpaid bills her mother had left, and when Louella returned there were comments about the disappearance of paper and pencils—all in good fun. But beneath the façade, the real relationship was no more satisfactory than was the one between Hedda and Bill Hopper.

Louella had educated Harriet beyond the chitchat she purveyed so successfully. In addition, Harriet was by nature of a precise turn of mind, while her mother was vague and changeable. Harriet loved making budgets and working with figures, while Louella was often overdrawn and financially distressed despite her earnings. Harriet was a straightforward, no-nonsense girl, who might have found real happiness teaching English classics at a college or university. Louella was fluttery, vague, dithering and— unless aroused at being double-crossed or double-planted —affectionately sentimental.

Although Harriet always denied it, several friends maintain that she was secretly embarassed by her mother's gaucheries. In addition, the two often quarreled. Several times in moments of confidence, Harriet told friends that a mistake had been made: She should have been Phyllis Daniels' daughter, while Bebe Daniels should have had Louella for a mother.

The Parsons-Parsons Jr. relationship was made up of a series of quarrels, reconciliations, further quarrels and further reconciliations, all complicated by the fact that while Harriet and Louella's second husband, Captain Jack McCaffrey, had been fond of each other, she and Harry Martin shared a mutual dislike. Devoted as she was to Docky, however, Louella did protect her offspring when Martin, with more than a couple of drinks in him, became obstreperous toward Harriet.

In February, 1934, Louella, bursting with pride—she, like Hedda, subscribed to the theory that achievement was everything—announced that Parsons Jr. had made her debut as a director of Columbia's *Screen Snapshots*. In her column, she admitted that it might be put down to maternal pride, but that she felt Parsons Jr. had done a "swell, elegant job." Thereafter she frequently found space in her column to single out the dialogue, the pace or the subject matter of one of Harriet's short subjects, which, she announced, were the first documentaries (although she called them newsreels) on Hollywood to play first-run theaters.

In 1934 Louella increased her schedule by once more assaulting radio—undeterred by her previous failures. This time she served as a kind of mistress of ceremonies of a peculiar mélange—part variety show, part dramatic hour and part interview stint. Campbell's Soup sponsored this stew and called it *Hollywood Hotel*.

In the beginning Ted Fio Rito's Orchestra played in the mythical Orchid Room, Dick Powell and Jane Williams sang, and Louella wandered about doing interviews and dispensing gossip. When the program was in the planning stage, Louella confided to Powell that she was nervous about appearing and asked him what she could do to prepare herself. Powell innocently responded that since she wouldn't be seen and few people knew her voice, she should allow a professional actress to play her part. "You," he said, "can just sit home and collect the money." Louella was outraged and hardly spoke to him for a month.

The entire program cost between $12,500 and $15,000 a week because Louella persuaded what might conservatively be estimated as hundreds of thousands of dollars worth of talent, including Clark Gable, Marion Davies, Dolores Del Rio, Jean Arthur—in fact, almost all Hollywood luminaries except Garbo, Hepburn and Ginger Rogers, to do scenes to promote their latest films. Louella received $1,500 per show (a third of which by contractual agreement had to be turned over to Hearst Enterprises), while guests were presented with a case of soup, to say nothing of Louella's goodwill and frequent columnar mentions. Wags claimed that stars who appeared more than once were allowed to specify the flavor of the soup.

In her witty memoir of soap operas, *Tune In Tomorrow,* Mary Jane Higby recalls her experiences as one of the "gay ad-libbers" on *Hollywood Hotel.* It was their job to provide background gabble ("Isn't that Lupe Velez and Johnny Weissmuller?" "Look! Rochelle Hudson!") during Louella's appearances in the lobby prior to interviewing a guest star. The interviews presented a particularly difficult problem, according to one radio writer. Since Louella prided herself on knowing what was happening before it happened, she'd tell guests what they'd done, were doing and were about to do in posing questions—leaving them with little to say except—yes, no, uh-huh, unh-unh and maybe.

Unlike the stars, the gay ad-libbers were paid—$20 a performance. On one program radio actress Barbara Luddy appeared opposite guest star Francis Lederer and was thrilled to hear her name mentioned along with his. When she inquired how much she was being paid, she was told nothing since she was receiving billing. Miss Luddy announced that she was a radio actress, not a star, and on principle must be paid. She was paid—but her billing was deleted.

Problems developed in January, 1935. At that point the J. Wallace Armstrong Agency sent out a troubleshooting executive whose assignment, according to *Variety,* was to keep Louella "under wraps" because in her zealousness for a scoop, she had interrupted a lively musical number to announce: "Friends, I want to tell you Lowell

Sherman died just a few moments ago." This eagerness to give out the news not only cast a pall over the remainder of that particular broadcast, but endangered the program's existence. *Variety* called it "the most flagrant case of bad judgment ever launched over the air"; the *Daily Californian* castigated it as "unforgivable"; Paul Kennedy, one of the Scripps-Howard newspaper chain's more widely read radio critics, nominated Louella as the season's worst performer. In a review of the preceding twelve months, the Hearst *Examiner*'s radio columnist solved the dilemma of what to say about Louella by ignoring the program.

The crowning blow was that her contract, which was due to expire on April 1, 1936, was rumored not to be scheduled for renewal. But when the program rose from twenty-ninth to tenth in the popularity ratings, the sponsor decided to stick with Louella and her high, nasal whine. In fact, her ingenuous line readings became almost as recognizable as Walter Winchell's staccato delivery.*

In her quest for success, Louella was as ruthless with radio competition as with rival columnists.† In the wake of the first success of *Hollywood Hotel,* Mary Pickford, the former First Lady of the Screen, reconsidered her earlier decision about having her own radio show and

---

* Her voice subsequently became a standard in the repertory of mimics. In the late 1940's Jean Meegan was assigned to write a profile on Louella for *Modern Screen.* She was invited to listen to the radio broadcast of Louella's show at Maggie Ettinger's. Later Louella arrived, and Miss Meegan politely congratulated her; but Louella persisted in wanting to know whether the writer had any reservations—any criticism. Finally, Miss Meegan asked whether she had ever thought of diction lessons. "Oh, I had my voice placed many years ago!" Louella whined. "I wouldn't fool around with it now. People might think I was phony."

† When columnist Sidney Skolsky was fired by Hearst, word spread that Louella had instigated his dismissal. She denied it, but years afterward Skolsky stated that he went to the publisher and Hearst said Louella had claimed Skolsky was a Communist. "Are you sure she didn't say columnist?" Skolsky asked. Hearst said, "No. She must be pretty mad at you." Then, later when Skolsky encountered Louella in Chasen's, she rushed over to offer her commiserations. By his own admission, the enraged Skolsky responded by biting her on the arm.

undertook *Parties at Pickfair*. The format was to consist of musical numbers, interviews and sketches, just as Louella's did. Guest stars were not to be compensated, but unbilled party guests (of which Miss Higby was one) were to receive $50. Everything was proceeding smoothly when suddenly, a few days before the first broadcast, a guest canceled, then another and another. Suspicion grew that Louella was threatening to boycott stars who appeared on this rival show. Hoping to outwit the columnist, the producers invited her to go on with Miss Pickford—and she accepted.

The producers proceeded to have the script rewritten to include Louella. It had just been finished and a break called. Dress rehearsal was scheduled for half an hour later. Then suddenly, Miss Higby heard writer Jerry Cady explode: "You mean I have to throw out all that stuff I wrote for Parsons?" And that was what he had to do. Louella had reneged on her promise to appear and was protecting her job by casually slitting the throat of her "dear friend" Mary.

But in reaching the level of success she now enjoyed, Louella had become fair game. She and Dr. Martin occupied a large home at 619 North Maple Drive in Beverly Hills. She covered her ample frame with Parisian and Orry-Kelly gowns. She rode in a chauffeur-driven Rolls-Royce limousine, promoted her family through personal connections, earned several large salaries—and succeeded, so far as her contemporaries could tell, not because she was enormously talented but because she had the right connections to make her hard work pay off. One anonymous writer estimated that at least 50 percent of her items were fictitious or erroneous. Others set the percentage even higher.

In its August, 1935, issue the leftist-oriented magazine *New Theater* published an attack on Louella entitled "Hearst's Hollywood Stooge." The article was signed by Joel Faith, a pseudonym. Faith was rumored to be almost everyone in Hollywood except Jane Withers, Shirley Temple and Farina.

The charges—that she was Hearst's hatchet woman; that she was Marion Davies' press agent; that she promoted her family through threats; that her wedding gifts had amounted to $250,000* and were given on demand; and that she had consistently encouraged film companies to produce capitalist pictures—were hardly sensational or new, but for some unfathomable reason they greatly upset Louella.

The rumors about Louella's responses were almost as long as the list of charges—that she seriously claimed that the art director of the magazine had administered the ultimate indignity by pasting her head on a fat woman's body; that she was perturbed that after some not-so-loyal Hearst employees were allowed to read the story, they had aided the financially troubled magazine by contributing cuts for the cover and the inside illustrations of the piece; and that, at Louella's behest, representatives of the Hearst chain bought up all available newsstand issues, thereby driving up the price per copy to $10 each. What wounded her deeply was that many of her friends among the stars allegedly paid that sum to obtain the story. What wounded her most of all were the sneers that Louella O. Parsons was a woman who could dish it out but couldn't take it.

The *New Theater* article had hardly been forgotten when on October 27, 1935, Joseph Alsop, Jr., of all people, published a long New York *Herald Tribune* interview with Louella, who was staying at the Warwick Hotel in New York. Louella's meaning was neatly summed up by Alsop: "Unless her audience is in substantial agreement with her point of view, no critic can be so potent as Miss Parsons. Therefore, quite aside from their esthetic weight, Miss Parsons' opinions on the cinema have a sort of sociological value, for they provide a fair map of the minds of a large class of patrons of the screen's enchantments."

He went on to quote her on films: "A successful photoplay should, she feels, be entertaining, 'because, after all, you go to the theater to be entertained,' be pictorial 'because, after all, motion pictures are pictorial,' and be ornamental 'with a little heart value, because after all, we like a little human appeal.' "

Having taken care of defining her esthetics, Alsop finally

* WRH contributed "a $25,000 bauble."

ferreted out the secret of his subject's success according to the lady herself: "I've just been lucky," Louella confessed to him, "and I've worked hard, and I still do! That's my little secret. I found that my attitude toward my job doesn't change a bit except that I grow more tolerant. I'm old enough to be tolerant, you know. You see, I'm not a little girl anymore."

Louella was at that time fifty-one years, two months and twenty-one days old.

VIII

This is a business of youth. No room for has-beens.
                    —A Radio Network Executive

NO JOB was too menial for Hedda Hopper. She posed for fashion illustrations, accepting the smart clothes as compensation so that any extra money could be used to provide her son with a car and wardrobe at a time when he was beginning his picture career. She delivered occasional lectures and was delighted to collect even a small fee. She endured the humiliation of appearing as little more than an extra in a short subject promoting pictures to be released by Metro-Goldwyn-Mayer, the studio where she had once been a featured player. And she was casting about unsuccessfully trying to discover an opportunity to break into radio.

Her first attempts at the medium were made through a San Francisco friend who happened to be an agent. Hedda later claimed the friend had almost succeeded in placing her as mistress of ceremonies on *Hollywood Hotel,* but the deal fell through because the sponsor was persuaded to accept Louella upon the assumption that the columnist could persuade major stars to appear gratis for the publicity she would give them.* Hedda claimed that when her

* It seems unlikely that Hedda was seriously considered for the

friend was unable to find radio work for her, she suggested that Hedda meet the powerful Dema Harshbarger, head of the Artists Bureau of NBC. After several delays, the friend said Miss Harshbarger wasn't interested in representing her. So Hedda went barging over to the Harshbarger office on Melrose Avenue and caused such an uproar with Honor "Suzie" Traynor, the agent's secretary, that Miss Harshbarger suddenly appeared to find out what all the fuss was about. Hedda explained and was asked what she had to offer radio. When she had finished, she quoted Miss Harshbarger as saying, "You've told me more about this town in five minutes than I've learned in a year." She added she'd see what she could do for Hedda.

Mrs. Traynor recalls the incident less dramatically, saying that Hedda called for an appointment and was told that one might not be available. When Hedda protested, the amiable Suzie managed to squeeze her in. "From the first a great friendship was established, and Miss Harshbarger persuaded Miss Hopper that her way of running her business and career were most unbusinesslike."

Both Hedda and Suzie agree that when Dema Harshbarger submitted Hedda's name to NBC in New York, a sarcastic reply was received reminding everyone: "This is a business of youth. No room for 'has-beens.' " That gratuitous insult only made Hedda more determined than ever to prove her detractors wrong-headed. In Dema Harshbarger, she had a powerful ally.

Dema Harshbarger was in appearance a comic strip character set down in the midst of real life. At the time Hedda met her, Dema was fifty-two. Five feet four inches tall and weighing 210 pounds, she looked as imposing as a bulldozer in her severely tailored tweed suits. Her personality combined masculine bluntness with feminine intuition and tenacity. She was just the type of overpowering personality who could order the volatile, boisterous Hedda about and get away with it.

---

program. Probably she later told the story merely to annoy Louella, with whom she was by that time in the midst of a full-fledged feud.

Dema was a businesswoman-promoter, who had early on adopted the attitude that since life is a cruel, unfair game in which there are no actual rules, you stack the cards in your own favor. As a child she had been stricken with polio, which had made it necessary for her to wear braces. While playing with other children, she had to stand and fight when trouble arose. She *couldn't* run away. So instead of playing, she spent most days accompanying her horse-trader father. After a time, Dema and her parent developed a routine. Little Dema followed the trading transaction closely. If the opposition proved stubborn, Dema would begin crying, begging to go home, and her father would threaten to cancel the deal to look after his little cripple. At that point, his opponent would usually give in and the trade would be consummated.

Afterward as an adult Dema operated on the principles of a horse trader. In the 1920's in Chicago she conceived the idea of selling preseason memberships to Lyceum performances. It was an original and appealing concept, but what Dema needed to put it into operation was substantial capitalization. She studied the situation, secured a number of contracts with sponsors for classical performers to appear in a number of cities and then approached Chicago tycoon Samuel Insull for an appointment. When the time came, Dema's friend, Jessie Christian, a former opera singer, accompanied her to the Edison Building, in which Insull's offices were located. While Dema was upstairs, Miss Christian waited in the lobby, transmitting positive thought waves to the meeting.

Upon her arrival, Dema discovered that she had been allotted only fifteen minutes in which to explain the plan, detail commitments already made and secure the promise of capitalization. Terrified, she plunged in and worked so swiftly that she was already emerging from the elevator on the ground floor when her allotted time finally elapsed. Miss Christian cried dramatically, "All is lost!" only to have the jubilant Dema whip out Insull's check for $50,000 and wave it in her face.

Dema and Samuel Insull became lifelong friends, as well as temporary business associates. The professional relationship was dissolved when Alexander Haas, of the

NBC Artists Bureau, decided the Lyceum with its small-town circuit would be a valuable new outlet for such NBC clients as Sergei Rachmaninoff and Fritz Kreisler. At his suggestion, NBC bought 50 percent of the business, then during the Depression acquired the other 50 percent. Dema was transferred from Chicago to the West Coast to represent the bureau there, accompanied by her secretary, Suzie. Thus, in 1936 Dema and Suzie determined to assist Hedda in a program that would allow her to exploit fully the salable qualities she possessed.

Hedda, never noted for her patience, tired of waiting for a job and in 1936 once again accompanied Frances Marion and Frances' children to England where Frances was to work on a script. Hedda's hopes to obtain film work proved unfulfilled, but upon her return in early 1937, she claimed that she had learned something from the British: "that your mental attitude—good or bad—added or subtracted from your bank account." She often repeated this idea in various versions, and when she made her New Year's resolutions a few years later, she strengthened it to: "Maybe this is showing a boastful spirit, but here [Hollywood], those who yell the loudest get the most. So my resolution for 1940 is to see all, hear all and tell all, and let the chips fall where they may."

Upon her return from London, one of Hedda's first stops was Dema's office to learn whether any progress had been made in her behalf. It had. Dema had a prospective radio sponsor in Maro-Oil shampoo, and together she and Hedda shouted—under the misapprehension that the account executive was the deaf Mr. Maro himself—and charmed their way into a commitment. It was the first of Hedda's many gossip programs, and it was a flop. Hedda's recently acquired British accent came across as affectation, and she was fired.

But Hedda had a new attitude—and she had Dema to work out strategy. At this point it was brought home to Hedda that her method of operation was ruinous. "You see," Suzie Traynor said, "Miss Hopper operated in a personal manner. She would try to book herself into films without consulting an agent. A producer would say, 'Oh, Hedda, I have a part for you in my picture,' and Miss

Hopper would say, 'Oh, I'd love to do it.' No mention of money. Well, that's fine as a friendly gesture, but it doesn't build up one's bank account or career. I was asked to handle Miss Hopper's bookkeeping, both personal and professional, so I saw how Miss Harshbarger straightened out Miss Hopper financially."

Hedda, according to her onetime legman David S. "Spec" McClure, for many years occasionally forgot to clear offers with Dema. "I remember Dema put a flat thousand-dollar* fee for Hopper to go on anything. Then somebody offered her a Mixmaster to appear. And when Dema found out, she said, 'For Christ sake, you could have taken the money and bought all kinds of Mixmasters.' Hopper wanted Dema to get her out of it, but Dema said, 'No, you go on the show. Get your Mixmaster. Maybe it'll teach you to do what I say.' "

Hedda learned Dema's methods slowly, but it eventually was to pay off for both of them. When Dema was eased out at NBC, she devoted herself entirely to Hedda's career. Later she confided to Alexander Haas that the 10 percent she received as Hedda's business manager, plus a new Cadillac which Hedda provided her with every other year, more than equaled what she had earned at NBC's Artists Bureau.

As Hedda learned to operate in a more businesslike way, she not only increased her financial position, but also was able to acquire at least a tiny portion of the power for which she had yearned. Eventually it would no longer be necessary to accept roles in *Artists and Models* (with Jack Benny and Ida Lupino), *You Can't Buy Luck* and *Tarzan's Revenge*. She was able to pick films that offered some personal gratification. For instance, *Midnight*, starring Claudette Colbert, gave her a chance to appear in the same cast as her son. *What a Life* and the Hardy series associated her with the wholesome Norman Rockwell view of the American scene that her Quaker upbringing approved of. And she fought to be cast in *The Women* because it was a Broadway success. Written by Clare Boothe Luce, produced by MGM with a star-laden cast

* Hedda claimed it was $1,500.

and directed by the distinguished George Cukor, it reeked of prestige.

In *The Women,* Hedda played the small part of the society columnist. Director Cukor was not impressed, and of her film acting in general, he said she was inclined to do "everything a little too much." In front of the camera she resorted to the tricks of a second-rate stock company character woman.

But Hedda no longer confined her efforts to films. Blessed with seemingly inexhaustible energy, she pursued radio with varying success. Undeterred by the failure of her first series, she tackled the assignment of a hardworking lawyer, a widow with two children to support, in *Brenthouse,* a dramatic serial in which Dema placed her, hoping to rid Hedda of the bogus British accent. Whether it was the role or merely experience with a microphone, Hedda improved enormously.

In January, 1939, *Variety* reported Hollywood had gone radio mad. Louella was presiding over *Hollywood Hotel,* Mary Pickford headed the *Motion Picture Relief Fund Hour,* Jesse L. Lasky emceed *Gateway to Hollywood,** while Hedda appeared regularly on *Brenthouse* and did a gossip stint twice weekly.

All this activity made it possible for her to purchase an unpretentious little house on Fairfax Avenue. She decorated it in her favorite colors—red and yellow—and boasted that now she owned a small garden and the tiniest living room in Hollywood. Even so, it became a gathering place for many of the film colony, including Louella (occasionally), on Sunday afternoons.

In the tiny living room she hung a painting of herself wearing the tea gown that had caused all the trouble with Anita Stewart in *Virtuous Wives* so many years before. Living with her was Bill (before he took an apartment of his own), a young German girl who served as cook and her dachshund, Wolfie.†

But neither films nor radio provided the escape from

---

* From it, Gale Storm emerged.

† So named, Hedda claimed, because like her ex-husband, the dog had only one thing on his mind: sex.

the snubs, humiliations and relative poverty which Hedda had hidden but endured. In the early 1920's a fortune-teller had advised Hedda to write. Hedda had later tried the weekly newsletter to Cissy Patterson's Washington *Herald* but quit in a snit when Cissy attempted to economize by cutting Hedda's salary from $50 to $35 a week. Nevertheless, Hedda wasn't through as a writer—although to the end of her days she never considered herself one.

The way Hedda told it was that in 1937 a representative of the Esquire Feature Syndicate, Howard Denby, approached her for a talk, saying that for a year he had been looking for a columnist who could write about Hollywood. Andy Hervey, of MGM's publicity department, had told Denby that he didn't know whether or not Hedda could write, but that whenever he wanted the lowdown on anyone, he went to her. Hedda protested that she couldn't spell, but Denby simply told her to submit sample pieces. The syndicate signed her and sold her column to thirteen newspapers.

Although Hedda could not be expected to have agreed, there would have been no columnist named Hopper had there not been one named Parsons. Even though Louella was pro-Hollywood, like any star, she began believing her own publicity. Personal friends such as Joseph Schenck, Harry Brand and Howard Strickling were willing to indulge her whims. Others, among them L. B. Mayer, found her increasing demands disruptive, and along with several other titans, he set about creating a rival who would be strong enough to curb Louella's power.

When Mayer's assistant Ida Koverman heard of the plan, she suggested her old ally, Hedda. Despite Hedda's rebuff of his amatory advances, Mayer had gradually come to regard her as an amusing, none-too-successful actress who was always grateful for work. He must have envisioned her as a wonderful antidote for Louella and have reasoned that she would be easy to control.

Hedda's new endeavor could hardly have disturbed Louella, who had seen competition come and go. Certainly Hedda's appointment was unlikely to be taken seriously. After all, Hedda was a fifty-three-year-old woman, with little formal education and no real newspaper experience. True, on her radio shows she had a segment "Just to Keep the Record Straight," which contradicted reports carried by Louella, Walter Winchell, Jimmie Fidler and other commentators. Since Louella, as reigning Hollywood gossip, had made it her royal prerogative to air some stories and suppress others, she resented the segment. It decreased the powerful leverage she held in bargaining with the studios by threatening to "tell all." But to most, Louella's and Hedda's relative impact must symbolically have seemed comparable to an elephant's and a gnat's.

Luckily for Hedda, one of the first papers to subscribe to her column was the Los Angeles *Times,* beginning February 14, 1938. "Simply because of this," said a longtime observer of the Hollywood scene, "Hedda became important. You don't make it in this town to the same degree unless you have a local outlet. Hedda had the best. Every producer read the *Times.* This meant that she'd be read and listened to."

Hedda initially set out to follow her friend Frances Marion's advice: "Don't bite the hand that feeds you caviar." * The prose was first cousin to fan-magazine copy. "I shall not set myself up as a judge or critic, but I'd like you to know the people of Hollywood as I do," she wrote. Hollywood was "mad, gay, heart-breakingly silly," and then she added a dash of cynicism by observing, "but you can't satirize a satire and that's Hollywood." The same column contained Hedda's first errors: (1) in *fact*: the prediction that Garbo would marry conductor Leopold Stokowski and was visiting his Philadelphia relatives (who turned out to be nonexistent) and (2) in *judgment:* she described Bob Hope as "the American Noel Coward."

Three-quarters of the second column was devoted to fashion notes. Two items in her third berated Twentieth

---

* Louella mistakenly suspected Miss Marion of ghosting Hedda's column, and their friendship cooled. "Although as long as I sat at Mr. Hearst's right, she was nice to me," Miss Marion recalled.

Century-Fox for hiring Annabella, whose French accent got in the way in *The Baroness and the Butler,* and Paramount for paying for Isa Miranda's English lessons. Like Louella, Hedda backed Hearst's "Buy American" campaign.

When a friend chided her for a "grammatical error," Hedda said in her column that she agreed with "Wolfie's theory that if it was grammatical, it wasn't an error. Why, I wouldn't recognize a split infinitive, if it came right up and shook me by the hand and I'm too old a dog to go back through life's vista. . . ."

This was hardly the stuff popular columns are made of, and odds were it wouldn't last three months. Ida Koverman, deciding Hedda needed a helping hand, gave a party in her honor, inviting Los Angeles' most popular actresses and celebrated newspaperwomen. When guests reached the front door, there was a sign: "No Cats Allowed Here." Hedda claimed she almost turned back. Afterward, in explaining Louella's absence, she said the sign had undoubtedly scared her away. But despite the wisecrack, she was hurt by Louella's refusal to acknowledge her professional existence. Later, Hedda privately admitted embarrassment that Louella swept out of a room as soon as she entered it. "The woman's a fool," Hedda told a close friend. "What's the reason? There is none!"

After the Koverman party, the column took on a slight edge—directed at unnamed individuals and groups. "For those who consider Hollywood a prison, I've discovered from my private research department that there are 48 trains, 20 boats, 75 buses and 24 planes leaving daily. And for those condescending to travel in a minor way, there are automobiles, bicycles and kiddie cars."

She criticized Los Angeles for its indifference to opera; criticized women for being more interested in golf and cards than politics; took anti-Semites to task; feuded with Constance Bennett; and, as a mother, worried about the stand she would take in relation to Hitler's youth movement, which seemed to her begging for death.

She was still objective enough to admit that Charlie

Chaplin* was one of the two authentic geniuses to emerge from films. Her other choice was Walt Disney.

But it is a devastating comment upon our society that not until Hedda resorted to bare-nailed bitchery was she able to put her career into orbit. "The minute I started to trot out the juicy stuff, my phone started to ring," was the way she put it. David O. Selznick, for instance, let Hedda know how incensed he was when he attacked Vivien Leigh's casting as Scarlett and Leslie Howard's as Ashley in *Gone with the Wind*. Hedda wondered why he had had his press agent call her instead of the House of Parliament, telling them they'd "won again." Helen Hayes, she conceded, had played Queen Victoria, but Helen Hayes represented the finest U.S. stage talent while Vivien Leigh was a comparative nobody. She accused Selznick of insulting every American actress with his selection.†

If Hollywood moguls had counted on her gratitude for the bone that had been thrown her and had thought she would stick to studio-dictated stories, they were destined for a major surprise. If anything, she proved more difficult to control than Louella. When Madeline Carroll attempted to avoid Hedda, Hedda was as ruthless as Louella in noting that the actress had gained "12 unflattering pounds." After that Miss Carroll was careful to acknowledge her. Hedda cackled with delight when Secretary of the Interior Harold Ickes couldn't find cooperation to produce a "propaganda film" about dams since he had charged studios from $50 to $500 a day for the use of national parks as locations. When Mary Livingstone (Mrs. Jack Benny) underwent cosmetic surgery on her nose, Hedda com-

* As late as 1939 she was printing friendly squibs about Chaplin in her column. For instance, she said his financial backer for *The Great Dictator* was none other than the distinguished scientist Albert Einstein. Another time she noted that Chaplin had founded the first commercial airline in America. It opened July 14, 1919, with a Curtiss two-seater flying from Los Angeles to Santa Catalina Island.

† When she saw *Gone with the Wind,* Hedda admitted in her column that she had been stupid to interfere with the casting and in attacking Miss Leigh, who she now predicted would be the star sensation of 1940.

mented that Mary had become selfconscious, "but her new nose is—to say the least—classy. . . ." She revealed that when "phonies" tried to crash Mike Romanoff's party, the "Prince" had turned them away at the door. Among the "phonies," only Kay Francis, with whom Hedda had had a run-in, was named. After a brief reconciliation with Victor Mature, she grew annoyed at him once more: "I expressed hope that Victor Mature might eventually live up to his name, but I'm beginning to despair. . . ." And she was malicious and inaccurate when she commented: "Noel Coward and Cary Grant took up where they left off about a month ago—I mean Noel was Cary's houseguest."

But yellow journalism aside, Hedda scored a clean beat on October 29, 1939, by scooping the seasoned opposition on James Roosevelt's divorce. Only his sister, Anna, among the President's children, had previously been divorced, and ferreting out the news was a coup. It is unclear how she stumbled onto the information that Roosevelt, who was employed by Samuel Goldwyn, had persuaded the studio to hire the sister of Romelle Schneider, the nurse who had cared for Roosevelt during his hospitalization at the Mayo Clinic. Suspecting romance, Hedda confronted him, and he admitted she was correct but begged her not to break the story. She held it until October 28, when other reporters began closing in.

At that point Hedda and a new associate, Hy Gardner, who was simultaneously writing his own column for eight newspapers, as well as working for her, rushed to the Roosevelt residence at 10 P.M. Gardner rang the bell, and when a servant tried to turn them away, Hedda stuck her foot in the door and yelled so loudly that Roosevelt appeared, wearing a robe and one bedroom slipper. After some persuasion, he agreed to release the story, provided Mrs. Schneider was not mentioned. Hedda later claimed that she called the *Times* and excitedly told them: "Stop the presses! Whatever that means!"

Her information was greeted with skepticism. But after Gardner produced Roosevelt's phone number, which he'd jotted down while Hedda did the interview, Roosevelt was called and confirmed the story.

A problem arose when the *Times* picture library came up with a photo of Roosevelt flanked by his current wife, Betsy, and Romelle Schneider. Honoring her promise that Mrs. Schneider would not be named, Hedda resisted. The brouhaha was settled when the photo mysteriously disappeared. Fifteen years later it turned up in Gardner's mementos.

Thus, on October 29, 1939, "Love's Undertaker," as Louella enjoyed being called, was clearly outreported. The next day in her column—for one edition—Louella blasted the Roosevelts, and thereafter Hedda's devils became Louella's angels and vice versa.

Perhaps not coincidentally, Hedda had made several moves immediately before her coup. On September 16 she sued NBC for release from *Brenthouse,* and on October 10 she moved her office from the makeshift bedroom setup in her home to a professional building near Hollywood and Vine.

Hedda obviously had found a profession suited to her talents.

IX

I have been sniped at by experts. And why not?
Almost everyone who has attained any kind of
public stature in his or her profession can expect sometimes to see a reflection in a cracked
mirror.

—LOUELLA PARSONS
in *Tell It to Louella*

THE year 1936 brought forth the announcement that
"cold figures" proved Louella was "far and away" the
United States' most popular "motion picture columnist,
critic and feature writer." The survey, commissioned by
Hearst's New York *American,* was conducted by the Mc-
Cann-Erickson advertising agency and was limited to
149,704 persons in the New York area who had bought
a new automobile in the preceding nine months. The results claimed Louella had no close rival in her field.

She was praised for her "sparkling style." Examples:
"Clap hands! Clap hands! Sam Briskin is about to descend
upon New York in one of the most sensational raids of
the current year . . ." or "I've been cogitating, if you'll
pardon the use of the word in this hot weather . . ." She
was lauded for her "treasury of interesting information."
Example: "Interesting is the news that Harry Rosen is
making overtures to Bridget Hitler, sister-in-law to the
Nazi dictator, who is in this country to act as technical
adviser on *The Mad Dog of Europe.* Hitler's brother, 'tis
said, is a bartender in Germany and the report is that

Bridget is on the outs with her in-laws." * She was saluted for her "knowledge of every phase of motion picture production." Example: "Shh! Don't tell I told you, on account of it's all supposed to be a beeg secret! But I understand while in London Jack Warner went hammer and tongs after Charles Laughton to play the role of Danton. Laughton, 'tis said, is greatly intrigued at the idea of working with producer Max Reinhardt, but other commitments may stand in the way." All these strengths grew out of "her long association with the industry." Example: "Hollywood lost its greatest creative artist and I have lost my greatest friend. Irving Thalberg, who at 37 had achieved fame seldom won by men twice his age, passed away. . . . I first knew Irving when he was an office boy for Carl Laemmle in New York. . . . Then suddenly, he was appointed Western manager of Universal City in Hollywood. I was asked to meet the new boss. We met in a tearoom on 48th Street in New York. I thought Universal was trying to kid me, for it didn't seem possible this boy could be elected to hold such a responsible position. . . . Our friendship started from that day and has continued through the years."

But Louella was not content to rest upon her laurels. Her eyes were on the stars, and she intended to join them. In September, 1936, she begged her readers' forgiveness for her excitement over the possibility that her radio program was to be turned into a Warner Brothers musical. Six months passed, and Louella nudged Warner's by noting in her column that there had been endless inquiries from fans all over the country wanting to know when they could expect the film version of *Hollywood Hotel*.† The

---

* This item did not appear until 1939 but is included not only because it illustrates so brilliantly Louella's treasury of interesting information, but also demonstrates her genius at translating fantasy into folksy gossip. In handling it, she truly exhibits her unequaled ability to invest any item with the common touch.

† While pressing for this froth, which would line her purse, Louella exerted her influence to discourage more ambitious projects. Upon hearing that *They Shoot Horses, Don't They?* had been bought, she remarked that she recalled it as a sordid book and

final week in May she explained to her readers that a re-write to include extra dance sequences for Ginger Rogers was causing the delay. But in July when Louella left for a European vacation, entrusting the column, as well as the *Hollywood Hotel* radio stint, to Parsons Jr., there was no progress to report on the film.

The situation remained the same when she returned on September 2, but on September 14 she positively bubbled with enthusiasm over the signing of a contract for her movie "debut." Warner's executive Hal Wallis reportedly said, "Who can play Louella Parsons better than Louella Parsons?" Actually, she was given a test, provided with Warner's best makeup man and its top designer, Orry-Kelly, who created a simple black dress to make her appear slim and then borrowed $165,000 worth of jewels to glamorize her.*

Before filming began, the neophyte actress called rehearsals at her home. There the professional actors ran through scenes with Louella while she pedaled away on her exercycle, trying to lose weight and perfect her acting technique at the same time.

On September 20, 1937, the film went into production. Ginger Rogers was absent, but the cast included Dick Powell, Lola and Rosemary Lane, Benny Goodman, Hugh Herbert, Glenda Farrell, Ted Healey and such regulars from the radio show (in addition to Powell) as Frances Langford, announcer Ken Niles and Raymond Paige and his orchestra. The direction was entrusted to Busby Berkeley. During the filming, Louella had Warner's provide her

---

insisted many changes would have to be made if it were to become fit for family consumption. It took almost thirty-five years before the film version of the book finally reached the screen.

* During the filming, when Louella saw Lola Lane's splashy movie-queen gown, she found her simple black too drab. When Orry-Kelly refused to give her another, Louella screamed, swore, threatened and threw a full-fledged tantrum. Finally, the temperamental Kelly, who was accustomed to having his way—even with top stars—pretended to give in. The result: He designed a gown for Louella that made her look like a large floating island.

with a private office so that she could turn out her column between takes.

In her report to her readers, Louella confessed harboring doubts and speculated that this ordeal might be retribution for the years she'd spent criticizing others. "I know that only a limited few can be actors and I'm not one of the select few," she admitted. Despite her long association with Marion Davies and other stars, she realized she'd never understood the difficulties and confessed she was terrified despite Busby Berkeley's "saintlike patience."

Berkeley expected little from Louella—but got less. For all her bravado, Louella was intensely insecure in her new undertaking. Innumerable takes were ruined when, in the midst of doing something relatively well, she would turn her large brown eyes toward him like a small child begging parental approval.

In a scene with Lola Lane and Mabel Todd, Lola delivered a long intricate speech which Louella was to interrupt with "But Mona!" the name of the character Miss Lane played. The nervous Louella invariably came in on cue with "But Lola!"— forcing Miss Lane to repeat the scene for almost a half day. After a few outbursts, Berkeley learned to keep his frustrations hidden and hope for the best.

Not everyone was so controlled. In one scene, Louella interviewed Lola-Mona, who had several dogs. "Lola was supposed to be getting measured or something while Louella interviewed her," Berkeley recalled. "During the starts and stops, the dogs got nervous and relieved themselves on the furniture. There was a lot of confusion, but the property man finally got things under control. After we wrapped up the scene, my property man, Buddy Friend, came up to me. He pointed to a wet spot on the seat of the chair Louella'd sat in and said, 'Buz, I'm sorry. I can walk the dogs, but what am I supposed to do about Louella?' "

Louella's constant plugging of the film caused ratings of her radio show to zoom, giving it an estimated 20,000,000 listeners—more than at any previous time.

In her autobiography—contrary to what she'd written in her column—Louella claimed that Berkeley was distracted by the strain of a trial arising out of an automobile accident in which several people were killed. Therefore, she was not helped sufficiently and was nervous when she arrived at the preview. She fled the theater when she thought she heard a local critic guffaw upon her first appearance.

Actually it was not a lone critic; it was a majority of the preview audience. Had it not been for their response, Louella's sobs would have been audible before the distraught columnist had to be helped out of the theater. There was no opposition from her when much of her footage ended on the cutting-room floor.

The *Examiner* hedged its bet by having Mary Pickford review the film, saying it was only fair since Louella had reviewed Mary's first. Mary found the movie "fun" which she thought was just what the world needed. As for Louella, Mary stretched the truth a bit to describe her as "a very pretty and slender Louella."

Frank Nugent in the New York *Times* rated the film as a fairly good entertainment which probably "deserves being called the best Warner musical in recent history." Of Louella? "Miss Parsons plays herself better than anyone else could hope to or want to."

Time reported Hollywood insiders got a chuckle out of the realization that the writers and the director "had just let Lolly be herself."

Louella, who often warded off criticism by getting in her own licks first, assessed her work by remarking: "As an actress, we are a good columnist and not even so bad on the radio." She later bragged that the picture had grossed $32,000 at the Strand in New York and had been held over in 150 theaters.

She also repeated some of the not-so-flattering out-of-town reviews, including one from a Vermont paper: "Louella Parsons looks just like she writes. Boy, am I sick to my stomach!" and one from an upstate New York critic, who noted: "Louella gives nothing to the film, but who'd expect her to?"

Nevertheless, the venture had proved a monetary bonanza for a woman who was noted for her extravagant ways. Warner's had paid her $40,000 or $50,000 (depending on which report you believe). And in November she signed a new radio contract which increased her weekly broadcasting earnings to $2,250 (less one-third to Hearst Enterprises) until October, 1938. Coincidentally, she was asked to contribute the major article on motion pictures to the prestigious *Encyclopaedia Britannica*. Lest anyone jump to the conclusion that Louella had developed a scholarly approach, a glance at her column will quickly prove otherwise.

For instance, she breathlessly reported that Norma Shearer would attempt to solve the "problem of Scarlett" by asking David O. Selznick to change the final half of *Gone with the Wind* to make the "Southern vixen more sympathetic." On another day, she confided that fantastic as it seemed, Hal Wallis had telephoned London to see if Dr. Sigmund Freud, whom she described as "probably the greatest psychoanalyst alive," would come to Hollywood to act as technical adviser to Bette Davis on *Dark Victory*, and Louella was confident Freud would accept.

Meanwhile, in 1937, Louella had indirectly secured a highly remunerative, if somewhat undemanding, job for Docky in the medical department at Twentieth Century-Fox. For $30,000 a year he dropped into the studio three or four times a week to treat those who needed his services.

One oft-repeated story is that he read about a Yale professor who had come up with a synthetic testosterone. Dr. Martin got in touch with the professor, who said that it was available at $25 a shot. Realizing that it would be of value to many of his studio friends who were past the first flush of youth, the doctor ordered a supply and was soon shooting many of the top executives in the third cheek. One eager fellow, who agreed to try it, asked somewhat plaintively, "Will it help me at home? Away from home, I don't need any help." When Dr. Martin approached another producer, he was sent off. The fellow was busy conducting interviews—and besides, he was a respectable married man. As Martin retreated, he spied a particularly stunning young lady entering the producer's suite. When he arrived at his own office, a telephoned question awaited him: "Will that new tonic work right away?"

Another widely circulated story was that while he served as studio physician, some Fox employees wore cards around their necks reading: "In case of fainting or accident, please keep Doc Martin away." Yet Producer Walter Lang and his wife considered Martin a brilliant physician, and Mrs. Lang believes that he saved her life.

"Louella was warmhearted, and she loved fun more than anything," Fieldsie Lang observed. "The most delightful times that I remember were the dinners she used to give. You'd have your cocktails and go in to dinner which would go on for three or four hours. She loved to make speeches—and never tell the truth about anything. Her childhood—Maggie Ettinger was there and knew she was fibbing. And Docky would lead her into it. And it wasn't only her—Jack Warner was at his most delightful. Everyone laughed so hard. What evenings!"

Weekends were spent at Marsons Farm, located in the San Fernando Valley near Northridge, California. In retrospect, Louella felt this was the scene of her happiest memories (quiet evenings with Lombard and Gable, preparations for Harriet's wedding) and her saddest moment (the night when Docky, ill with pneumonia, seemed unlikely to survive).

When Docky had first proposed acquiring a weekend retreat, she had been so opposed that she refused to consider looking at places. Undeterred, he bought land and began building the ranch house while she stubbornly refused to visit the site. But after she relented and went to take a look, she fell in love with it at once—so in love that she even agreed there would not be a single telephone installed on the premises. They would isolate themselves.

Each Friday, once the house was finished, Louella would rush through in-town tasks to get to the farm, while her husband spent Friday mornings at the Farmers' Market on Fairfax Avenue, making her personal selection of the fresh vegetables and fruits for the weekend. Far from becoming the Martins' Walden, Marsons Farm soon became a mecca where friends and acquaintances felt perfectly free to drop in—and Louella loved it.

It was an inevitable development. "You know, Louella didn't ever want to be alone. I don't know what it stemmed from, but she had to have people around her. Of course, Bebe Daniels was her closest friend. Then there were Carole and Clark, Joe Schenck, Harry Brand, Howard Strickling, Dorothy Manners, Mecca Graham, Ruth Waterbury and George Leigh—with new ones added as they came along," Mrs. Lang said. "Louella just loved people."

Louella could no more live without a telephone than without friends, and soon there were several lines into the house. When Rosalind Russell and Frederick Brisson were arrested for speeding on their way to their wedding, the arresting officer called to tip off the *Examiner,* and someone there telephoned Louella—at Marsons Farm. She would never have forgiven herself for losing an exclusive for lack of a telephone.

Far more completely than the big house on Maple Drive in Beverly Hills, the ranch house reflected Louella's personality—a combination of early American and modern. It easily accommodated everything from her girlhood bedroom furniture to a blond kitchen table which could suddenly be transformed into a poker table (a housewarming gift from Lombard and Gable). There was an etching done especially for Louella by Lionel Barrymore, a pair of china roosters from Sid Grauman, some pot holders from Jack La Rue, a collection of dainty English figurines and cups from Bebe Daniels and Ben Lyon, the original manuscript of Eugene Fields' sentimental "Little Boy Blue" from director Joseph von Sternberg and other treasures from the thousands of dollars' worth of gifts that poured in on special occasions from her friends in the industry.*

All this is not meant to imply that the Martins' relationship was a smooth one—far from it. Louella's devotion to newspaper work and Hollywood irritated Martin. Once,

---

* Refuting the rumor that she made the studios replace her Christmas gifts when they were stolen from her automobile one year, Louella said her detractors underestimated her. She'd never have gone to pick up her presents—she'd have insisted upon having them sent.

Yours DeWolf Hopper 1912

(Above right) DeWolf Hopper, Hedda's stage-star husband, was five years older than her father, had bluish-tinted skin and no hair on his body. Because of his marriages, wags dubbed him "The Husband of His Country." Although their relationship was stormy, Hedda was devoted to her son, DeWolf, Jr.—better known as Bill—who eventually achieved success as Paul Drake on the Perry Mason television series. (Above left) Hedda with Bill as a baby, (below) as a young man.

Bill as he appeared on the Perry Mason Show.

Granddaughter Joan rides with Hedda in <u>The Music Man</u> parade at the Mason City, Iowa, premiere of the film.

Louella's complicated love life included an unacknowledged husband, Captain Jack McCaffrey, a riverboat captain (top right as the gentleman on the right); a long attachment to Peter Brady, union leader and banker (above left); and the love of her life Harry W. "Docky" Martin (below)—shown here with Louella and Harriet in 1931.

Looking robust, Louella had fully recovered from tuberculosis when she posed with her typewriter in Palm Springs early in 1926.

In <u>The Battle of Hearts</u> (top opposite page), Hedda's first film, she was cast as a lady sea captain. In 1926 she appeared in <u>Don Juan</u> (far right, opposite page), which had music, sound effects and John Barrymore. In 1927 she played the title role in <u>Mona Lisa</u>, a color short film. And in 1939 (lower left, opposite page) Hedda played the leading role in <u>Brenthouse</u>, the first sustained transcontinental dramatic radio show to originate in Hollywood.

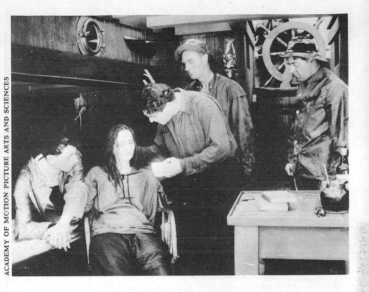

Hedda in a glamorous publicity pose.

Louella joined stars Conrad Nagel, Marion "Never Looked Lovelier" Davies, director Monta Bell, and Ramon Novarro for a publicity photo of her own on her first Hollywood visit in 1925.

Louella as she wished to look.

In the latter part of her life, Marion Davies and Hedda became closer than Marion and Louella. Here Hedda and Miss Davies pose after the star appeared on the television special <u>Hedda Hopper's Hollywood</u>.

Hedda's Hollywood included promising newcomers. Here she and "Prince" Mike Romanoff gather around Harry Revel's piano with Mark Stevens, Betty Garrett, Guy Madison, Peter Lawford, Barbara Hale (leaning on piano), Lizabeth Scott, Gail Russell, Marilyn Maxwell (in front of Peter Lawford), June Haver, Bill Williams and Johnny Coy.

Louella and her troupe of upcoming stars broke records with their personal appearances at theaters across the country. Members included Joy Hodges, Ronald Reagan, Jane Wyman, June Preisser, Arleen Whelan, Mecca Graham, and Susan Hayward.

Louella took great interest in the career of her producer-writer daughter, Harriet (top, opposite page), child of her marriage to John Parsons. Louella visits writer DeWitt Bodeen, director John Cromwell and her daughter on the set of RKO's The Enchanted Cottage. Harriet and director Fritz Lang (below, opposite page) on location in Monterey, California, during the filming of Clash by Night.

CBN-Pub-A7

After Doc Martin's marriage to Louella, their association with the film colony brought Martin a position at Twentieth Century-Fox and temporary jobs as technical director on medical films. They appear with Dan Dailey and Eleanor Powell.

Louella with Hearst columnist Harry Crocker.

Louella thoroughly enjoyed the trappings of stardom—whether clowning with Stu Erwin and Ken Murray (below) or going over a radio script with Bob Hope (above). Although she had no illusions about her performing abilities, she recognized the value of her name in the ratings game.

After Dr. Martin's death, songwriter Jimmy McHugh became Louella's escort. They remained friends until his death.

Comedian Robert Q. Lewis was one of Hedda's many escorts during her later years. Here, Lewis escorted the elegant Hedda to the final Academy Awards ceremonies that she attended before her death.

when she was entertaining a group that he thought was exploiting her, he arrived home to stand in the doorway silently surveying the crowd for several minutes before malevolently roaring: "Not a goddamned ounce of sincerity in the room. Out!"—and that ended the party despite Louella's tears.

Under less explicit circumstances, Louella was capable of ignoring his behavior. Once, when she had friends in to tea, her husband emarged from his automobile, visibly weaving. Louella smiled and noted, "Oh, Docky's had a beer." When a dinner for a staid group of San Franciscan financiers required additional help, Martin sequestered a young female impersonator, dressed in a maid's costume, among them. During the evening, whenever one of the San Franciscans entered the bathroom, the "maid" would follow him in, offer him a towel and inquire in insinuating tones whether there was anything else he needed. Responses were so erratic that the bathroom carpet had to be replaced the following day. Louella was furious, but then she always said, "People who don't fight don't really love one another."

San Francisco attorney Jake Ehrlich said, "At least once a week at exactly three o'clock in the morning—not at two thirty and not at three fifteen—I'd get a phone call from Doc saying, 'I'm going to divorce that damn woman.' He and Louella would be tipping a few, and the discussion would begin about nine thirty. By three o'clock he would be on the phone ready to divorce her. Next day the fight would be forgotten, and the call was never referred to."

"Yes, they used to fight, but it never meant much," Fieldsie Lang said. "It all became dinner conversation. Louella would tell the stories, and they'd laugh about it. I remember when she and Doc went to the Gloria Vanderbilt-Pat DiCicco wedding in Santa Barbara. It was a long drive, and somewhere along the way Louella had to stop. So Docky pulled up alongside the highway, and she walked down on the beach on the sand.

"He sat there for a while and kind of let the car roll ahead. Finally, he said to himself that he'd better back up and get her. He started backing and backed about a mile. No Louella. He drove forward. No Louella. He got panicky and went to the Malibu police station. He said he'd lost her. She'd washed out to sea or something. They wanted to know what she was wearing, and he couldn't remember. So they called the house to find out—and Louella answered the phone. She'd come up from the beach and, seeing no Docky, assumed he'd forgotten her. When a truck came along, she hailed it and hitched a ride home."

If Louella's blithe assumption her husband had forgotten her seems strange, it must be remembered that she, too, had a reputation for absentmindedness. Once when Charles Gentry, editor of the Detroit *Times,* visited Hollywood, he gave Louella a courtesy telephone call only to have her insist that he must spend Sunday at Marsons Farm. Since he had already accepted an invitation from Gary Cooper, he demurred, but Louella insisted. When he arrived on Sunday afternoon, his hostess was absent, but he fell into conversation with Dr. Martin. When Louella returned, she was on horseback and engaged her husband in a long conversation about the horse. Then, finally noticing Gentry, she said hello in a slightly puzzled manner, adding that he must stay to dinner because she was giving a party for Charles Gentry of the Detroit *Times.*

Throughout 1938, she was kept off-balance—by exhaustion, by an unexpected illness of Docky's and by a minor revolt against her exploitation of stars on the *Hollywood Hotel* program. The film business was obviously changing, and try as she might, Louella couldn't help feeling a faint nostalgia for an earlier day. "I am not one to say the old days were best. I do think the older stars had more color; but there are exceptions," she remarked to an interviewer. That statement was made when Garbo, Gable, Joan Crawford, Mae West, Joan Blondell, Myrna Loy, Humphrey Bogart, Katharine Hepburn, Bette Davis, Spencer Tracy, Gary Cooper, Cary Grant, Charles Laughton, Claudette Colbert, Merle Oberon, Carole Lombard, Norma Shearer, Irene Dunne, Ginger Rogers, Barbara Stanwyck, Robert Taylor, Bob Hope, Paulette Goddard, Bing Crosby, Ann Sothern and W. C. Fields—to name a few—were reigning over Hollywood.

Louella received three severe jolts in 1939. On October 29, Hedda scooped her on the Roosevelt divorce, on July 15 the *Saturday Evening Post* published a scathing profile of her, and on March 30, she failed to be the first to know about the Gable-Lombard nuptials. Since she considered the couple close personal friends, she was devastated that they waited until she was in San Francisco to drive to Arizona to wed. Not only was she denied an exclusive, but the news was given to the entire press simultaneously. Louella considered it a major betrayal. She, of course, claimed that she was the only writer whom they telephoned after the ceremony, but it was apparent that she was hurt professionally and personally.

In recalling the period, Mrs. Walter Lang said, "Getting those scoops—somebody's engagement or marriage, somebody having a baby—that was her whole life. I was there when Carole promised she'd give her the scoop when they were getting married. Louella turned to me after they'd walked out of the room and said, 'They're not going to tell me. I know it.'

"She was angry with Clark and Carole for a while, but eventually she forgave them." Mrs. Lang paused thoughtfully, then added, "I'm sure Louella forgave both Carole and Clark, but I don't think Docky ever did."

Whatever her eventual feelings toward Gable may have been, Louella spitefully gave him short shrift when she chose her favorite performers of 1939. Gable as Rhett Butler in *Gone with the Wind* was conspicuously missing.*

After losing the Gable exclusive in March, Louella suddenly committed a series of journalistic gaffes. The first, which occurred on April 7, evoked a wry little essay by Richard Watts in the April 16 edition of the New York *Herald Tribune*:

Miss Louella Parsons is not only the most powerful of motion picture critics, but also the most influential of Hollywood journalists. As such she has been widely and justly acclaimed by the press, public and the hierarchy of the

* He was given fulsome praise when he reappeared on her 1940 list.

cinema, and I had imagined that all the laurels becoming to her had already been bestowed. Yet, I find that in at least one way Miss Parsons has been seriously underrated. No one has made her the official spokesman for that august school of critical thought that would keep a reasonably dramatic outside world from intruding upon the loftier world of art and letters. This, I maintain, is an injustice, since never has the viewpoint of the exclusionist theory of criticism been more eloquently put than by Miss Parsons in her column one day just about a week ago. It was at the close of the period marked by, among other things, the sack of Albania by the valiant hordes of Fascism that Miss Parsons led off her daily communique from Hollywood thus: "The deadly dullness of the last week was lifted today when Darryl Zanuck admitted he had bought all rights to Maurice Maeterlinck's *The Bluebird* for Shirley Temple."

This ringing dismissal of all that is not the gilded tower of dramatic art should, I am sure, be a great lesson to me. Now that my friends at *The New Yorker* have so sterling an ally in their war for the purity of dramatic criticism, I can see that my days are numbered, and so, passing over my liking for the tragic little country of Albania where I once spent several pleasant days, I had better say a quick word again about China while I can. . . .

That summer Louella reported a fan recommended *How I Lost My Girlish Figure* by Norman Harrington. Two days later she apologized. It should have read: *How I Lost My Boyish Figure.*

On July 7 the industry was surprised to read: "Conrad Nagel's latest heartbeat is Clare Olmstead. They were a devoted twosome the other eve at the Brown Derby." * Next day Louella beat out having competitors ridicule her error by writing: "Imagine my embarrassment to accuse Conrad Nagel of lunching tete-a-tete with Clare Olmsted [*sic*]. Clare is a he and not a glamorous female as we were told by a gossipy friend. My apologies to them both and I'll laugh at myself before someone else does it. . . ."

* Since the Brown Derby's publicity was handled by Louella's cousin Maggie Ettinger, the popular restaurant received at least its fair share of publicity in the Parsons column.

While *Liberty* magazine in its article "Queen Louella" commented: "With so much cooperation, it is hard to understand how she can be wrong so often unless it can be that the tops of the industry are a little gummed up too," the *Saturday Evening Post* was not so generous. Among other things, the author of the *Post* article, Tom Wood, pointed out that Louella attributed *Peter Ibbetson* to Henrik Ibsen; recommended Mary Pickford's *Why Not Try God?* as *Why Try God?*; cited the "tender romance" between Gabriele D'Annunzio and a lovely creature called "Il Duse"; and referred to Walter Wanger's *The President Vanishes* as *The Vanishing American* and *The President Disappears*.

Louella could forgive the Gables, and she was never sure how she and Hedda really felt about each other; but Tom Wood's by-line never failed to raise her hackles. She claimed what irritated her was that Wood pretended to be friendly and wrote the piece for the *New Yorker,* but that it was so inept that magazine rejected it and the *Post* published it only after screen-writer Nunnally Johnson rewrote it.

In point of fact, Wood allowed her 25 plus syndication outlets, made her nine years younger than she was and said that while she might be inaccurate, she "got her story." Wood's account of what transpired illustrates what an implacable enemy Louella could be. "I called up Louella and told her I'd like to interview her for a possible profile. I laid the cards right on the table. I didn't say it was a set deal, and she was delighted. I gave the thing to the *New Yorker,* and after holding it several weeks, they didn't buy it. Bob Benchley suggested I give it to the *Post.* They bought it.

"They eventually sent it to Nunnally Johnson for checking. And Johnson, who was a screenwriter, treated the manuscript like screenwriters treated other material. He started to fiddle around with it. He showed it to some columnists, and the first thing I knew everyone was under the impression he was the author. My name was on it, but the impression was that what I'd written wasn't good enough to be published and Johnson had come in and saved it.

"It didn't take long to know that no matter who wrote it, I was in trouble. My wife's [Lee Patrick] career was also in trouble, so we went back to New York. Then she got a call from Warner's and was given a contract. So I came back out here, and it was impossible to get a job at a studio. Screenwriter. Publicity. Anything.

"I know the finger was on me because Gene Herrick from *Look* called and asked me to do a piece on Bette Davis. Then about two weeks later he said the word is out that you didn't write the Louella Parsons piece, that Johnson did and we want the man who wrote the Parsons piece. I told him I wrote it and the only way I could prove it was to write the Davis piece, which they bought and never ran. However, Herrick gave me a job on the magazine.

"The only reaction we had from Louella was that she had that little lawyer—Geisler—threaten to sue the *Post* for a million dollars. The *Post* sent me a letter saying because I wrote the story I was co-liable. So the *Post* must have thought I had written the piece. But I was caught right in the middle. In the strange position of having to fight for the honor of having slugged a woman—which was kind of silly.

"When I left *Look,* I contacted Eddie Lawrence at MGM and he said, 'Come over here; we'd like to have you try it for two months.' I accepted; then he called and said he hated to tell me, but the offer had been withdrawn. I realized that there was this thing going.

"Paramount was desperate for people who could write. I called George Brown, and he said to speak to Teete Carle. So I called Teete, and he said to speak to George Brown. So I said, "What the hell is this, a runaround?' They finally offered me a job. I did features. And I'm sure somebody reported it to Louella. She used my stuff, but the planter asked me not to do it under my name or Louella wouldn't use it. It didn't matter to me. I was working anonymously anyway.

"Over the years things kept happening. Later I did a picture at Goldwyn, and the publicity head wanted me to stay on. He went back to New York, and then for no reason he said he was sorry but he couldn't have me. I could only assume Louella had got word that I was there.

"Finally, I got a call from a New York publicity man who represented Rodgers and Hammerstein among others. I was up for the job of unit man on *Oklahoma!* I met Rodgers and Hammerstein. They liked me. They wanted me to do it. The producer of the picture was Arthur Hornblow. Hornblow had come over from MGM. He called me in his office two or three days after I had come in there and said, 'How are your relations with Louella Parsons?' I said I didn't know, all right, I guessed. 'Well, she doesn't seem to think so. She tells me she couldn't use your copy. It's no good. It's not accurate.' He said I'd better straighten out my relationship with her.

"I didn't know what the hell to do on that—so I didn't do anything. This had been going on since 1939. Then a couple of days later Hornblow said, 'Hey, it's okay.' And I found out Mike Todd had heard about it and Todd was a great friend of Joe Schenck. He apparently spoke to Schenck, and Schenck said, 'Well, for Christ sake, does Louella know that if we fire him, he could sue her for a million dollars for running her private blacklist?' And that ended that. Anyway Rodgers, Hammerstein and Todd were New York people, and they didn't care what she thought."

Early in 1939, even before the *Post* article, sensing that there was growing resentment toward her on the part of a number of Hearst editors, Louella realized she had to dramatize her value and impact to the syndicate. She decided to demonstrate her popularity by undertaking a vaudeville tour. The talent would by supplied by Hollywood's brightest starlets, whom the studios would lend her. With the help of friends, she began surveying the best young contract players and finally chose June Preisser, Arlene Whelan, Joy Hodges, Susan Hayward, Jane Wyman and Ronald Reagan. In addition, she took along a close friend of hers and Docky's, Mecca Graham, who was under long-term contract at Warner's. He was to play her secretary onstage and to act as her escort at social functions. She broke in the production in Santa Barbara on November 13, went from there to the Golden Gate Theater in San Francisco, then on to Philadelphia in a big TWA plane emblazoned with LOUELLA PARSONS AND HER FLYING STARS.* From Philadelphia she proceeded to Pittsburgh, where thousands jammed the railroad station at 7 A.M. to greet the troupe when they stepped off the train. At the next stop, Baltimore, someone broke Louella's dressing-room window, but instead of being irritated, she said she was flattered since it made her feel like a glamor girl. New York, Washington, D.C., and Chicago followed. When she arrived in her former hometown, she was presented with the key to the city.

Throughout the tour, the troupe presented three, four or five forty-minute shows each day, depending on the demand. They played to standing room only. In Philadelphia such hordes turned out that an extra detail of police had to be called to restore order outside the Earle Theater.

The format that engendered all this excitement cast Louella as a columnist and the actors as would-be stars who hoped to entertain her and earn a plug in her column —which some critics saw as Louella's sly way of sending herself up. In fact, the opening number, sung to the tune of "Oh, Susannah" went:

> Oh, Louella, won't you mention me?
> For a movie star in Hollywood,
> That's what I want to be! . . .

Then Louella pretended to write her column, while the starlets sang, acted and danced. Later Louella answered questions from members of the audience about their screen favorites.

This may not sound very diverting, but it was generally well received. As a Washington, D.C., critic put it, "the worst that can be said [for Louella] is that the Capitol stage seems a silly place to write a gossip column." Louella thoroughly enjoyed herself and confided to Hearst

* At a stopover in Albuquerque, New Mexico, the Pueblo Indians made her an honorary tribe member and named her Ba-Ku-Lu or Starmaker. She was also presented with a sword and made the only female colonel on the New Mexico governor's staff.

columnist Dorothy Kilgallen on December 15: "I feel like a real professional now. We've done 120 performances and I'm so accustomed to the stage I even ad-lib."

June Preisser, who in terms of the era was personality plus, was the audience favorite, although a great deal of interest centered on the offstage romance between Jane Wyman and Ronald Reagan—an interest that proved a box-office factor with little old ladies.

Despite the fact that Louella was fifty-nine years old, she, like Hedda, was blessed with enormous vitality and actually seemed to thrive on the early-morning rehearsals, the four-a-day schedule and the general excitement. One reporter described Louella's face as "smooth and pink -as a baby." * Most commented upon her unexpectedly slim figure. The female reporters were impressed with her luxurious mink and the style of her simple black frock. Perhaps her greatest asset was her trick of putting herself down before anyone else could, thereby disarming would-be critics. A disgruntled former co-worker in Chicago, columnist Herb Graffis, did get in his own dig: "I hope Lolly makes her income tax payment out of the act. She has made America her debtor by convincingly demonstrating that columnists should stay out of stage shows and in their own business."

Meanwhile, back in Hollywood, Louella's friend Bill Wilkerson, publisher of the *Hollywood Reporter*, praised her for defending Hollywood before women's clubs and needled Hearst executives by announcing that their columnist was considering "two better offers."

Louella's ploy worked magnificently. On January 17, 1940, *Variety* announced that backstage at the Chicago Theater she had signed a three-year contract with Hearst's International News Service. *Variety* didn't quote her salary, but other sources set it at $850 a week.

Nonetheless, Louella was not about to give up the $3,000 plus a week (after paying all expenses except income tax) that the tour brought her. In fact, in early October, 1940, she set out with a second edition, which

* What portion of the baby's anatomy he had in mind was left unspecified.

included Ilona Massey,† Sabu, Binnie Barnes, Mike Frankovich, William Orr, Robert Stack and Brenda Joyce. This time under the tutelage of choreographer Nick Castle, Louella, characteristically admitting that she would never be an Eleanor Powell, even attempted to dance. She obviously enjoyed herself. "Maybe it's the ham that makes me so excited to get back to the footlights as though I were an honest-to-goodness actress instead of just a hard-working reporter," she said.

With the money from this tour, her weekly salary as a columnist and her earnings as a radio performer, Louella had come a long way from the days when she worried about "buying baby shoes." And so had "baby," for on September 28, at Marsons Farm, Harriet wed King Kennedy, an actor-playwright-radio writer, who was a member of a family that moved in Los Angeles society. Louella was certain that there were even better things to come for her child.

---

† Miss Massey was called to Hollywood to fulfill a film assignment, and June Preisser, hit of the first edition, and Virginia O'Brien joined for the remainder of the tour.

X

Being a Hollywood reporter as well as an actress I'm more or less on both sides of the fence.

—HEDDA HOPPER

HEDDA said that writing a column was the only job ever handed to her on a silver platter. "I'd worked so hard finding picture parts that many times I pushed my luck away from me. The need was so great I couldn't relax," she wrote in *From Under My Hat*. "This, I've learned, is the worst method—being overanxious. But I didn't discover it until I was pushing 60."

She never really discovered it. As Hedda's column began to create a stir, instead of relaxing, she increased the pace as if frightened that her newfound success would suddenly evaporate. In addition to turning out columns, she continued to broadcast regularly and make occasional films. All this activity seemed to stimulate rather than tire her.

"She'd come sailing into the office in the morning, calling out, 'Hi, slaves! How's everybody?' And then she'd start: 'Get me Walt Disney and that son of a bitch at Columbia!' We'd ask which one and she'd say, 'The bald-headed one,' " said Patsy Gaile, an actress whose practical-minded aunt had insisted she study shorthand and typing. During a lean period, Patsy went to work for Hedda for two weeks and stayed for the remainder of the columnist's life. "We'd say, 'Who are we fighting today? What's the battle?' And there would be a crusade. About anything—all kinds of things—that's what made it so fascinating. Trivial things, but behind all this folderol there was a solid set of values.

"Hedda dictated the column. She said she couldn't spell, but she really didn't have the patience to write. She liked action. I happen to be a very fast typist and she liked to hear the clatter of the keys. Suzie [Traynor] used to say Hedda would have enjoyed it more if the typewriter had colored lights and bells. She dramatized things.

"She'd get to pacing up and down, acting it out. That was why her column was different from anyone else's. Hedda never sat down to write. She never opened a thesaurus to find an obscure word. She spoke . . . spoke directly to you. And that's why fifty million readers around the world responded to what she had to say. Behind the fireworks, there was this solid sense of values.

"I don't mean—look, she was completely human. She had—you'd get irritated as hell at her at times. Something would happen, and she'd throw open the door and say, 'Well!' You made a mistake!' and sometimes we weren't the ones. But later she'd come out and say, 'Well, I guess I was a little hard on you girls this morning.' And that is something you don't get from everyone."

Hedda adapted to situations easily, but now as a columnist she aspired to omniscience and omnipotence. "Never let anyone know there's anything wrong with you physically," she often cautioned friends, "or they'll assume you're not up to par mentally."

Her new status indisputably involved her in the great world beyond Hollywood. Politically, social and cultural activities interested her almost as much as acting. With the outbreak of the war in Europe, Hedda preached isolationism and urged American women to take a firm stand against foreign wars. She said she was keeping her ear tuned for an American voice in the wilderness but failed to detect one.* Editors' cries that she was hired to write an

---

* Ironically, in the light of what followed a few years later, Hedda recommended Dalton Trumbo's *Johnny Get Your Gun*

entertainment, not a political, column, were ignored.

Hers was a limited vision, but she shared it with millions of Americans. Personally, she told her readers, she was prepared to fight and to give her life to defend her country, but she was unwilling to solve European quarrels—however much she might disapprove of Hitler. Hedda's lack of empathy for the Jews in Germany was at least partially responsible for her reputation as an anti-Semite, despite her earlier attacks on prejudice.*

Hedda's greatest concern was that Bill might be called into the armed forces, although the two of them were no closer than they had ever been and increasingly irritated each other. As Hedda admitted to writer Dwight Whitney, "I love my son, but he is so much better when I'm not around." Thus, on January 24, 1940, when she announced his marriage before "someone" scooped her, she could hardly conceal her surprise.

Bill's actress bride, Jane Gilbert, was the sister of Margaret Lindsay, and the couple had eloped to Mexico. Hedda claimed she couldn't be happier. "She's a darling, and as for Bill, he always was lucky." Hedda added that she had intended to give the couple a big wedding.

The last statement indicates that Hedda was *not* happy over the marriage. Certainly a worldly woman such as she realized that readers would infer from it that the bride's parents were not in a financial position to underwrite the wedding. Thus, Hedda fired the first public shot in the war that developed between her and her daughter-in-law.

The fact is that she undoubtedly would have resented any girl Bill chose as a wife. Jane Hopper quickly concluded that her husband's problems—and her own marital ones—were created by his mother's complex attitude to-

---

as a book everyone who wanted to keep the United States out of war should read. It was a moment in history when the aims of the right and the left temporarily coincided.

* Her inability to resist a wisecrack also contributed to it. When it was suggested that she visit Israel, she wanted to know why she needed to when she lived in Beverly Hills. Yet such close friends as Louis Lurie, Charles Pomerantz and Frank Liberman, all Jewish, maintain that if any prejudice existed, it was unconscious.

ward him. Hedda relentlessly pushed him, pressed him to become an achiever, and when he resisted, she openly deplored his laziness, his love of swimming and sunning and his lackadaisical attitude toward the very things in life that she considered important. Although he was twenty-five years old, she still attempted to instill in him her drive to succeed and acquire powerful friends.

She went out of her way to arrange contacts—or seemed to. Sometimes her methods left something to be desired. On one occasion publicist Herb Stern was sitting in her office and overheard her ask Bill to escort her to a black tie function. There was a pause; then Hedda exploded: "What! You have no dinner jacket!" There was another pause, then: "Oh, well, just wear a dark suit. It doesn't matter. No one will look at you when you're with me anyway."

Whenever Hedda and Bill were together, she nagged at him, and he went to great lengths to avoid outright conflict. Sometimes he found it impossible and protected himself with the benumbing effects of alcohol.

After succeeding as a columnist, Hedda, like Louella, began to use her power to "help" her offspring at the studios. Much to his embarrassment, she occasionally succeeded in pressuring some producer or director into testing him for a role for which he was physically or temperamentally unsuited. In other instances, finding he had tested for a part, she would badger the producer for a favorable decision. In her anxiety to help, she only humiliated Bill. But it was not until she began to promote him in her column that he heatedly told her to stop. Hedda considered his attitude unfathomable.

Although, according to her lights, she had always behaved impeccably, subconsciously she appears to have suffered a deeply felt guilt that somehow as a mother she had let him down. She had been a devoted daughter and, when Joan was born, would become a devoted grandmother. In fact, after Joan's birth Hedda temporarily abandoned Bill and lavished her repressed mother instinct upon this one small child. Jane Hopper saw what was taking place and tried to modify the relationship—with the result that the resentment between grandmother and mother developed into open conflict.

But family life had never been, and never became, of paramount interest to Hedda. Nor was she willing to commit herself to any romantic relationship or even to consider casual dalliance. Instead, she worked even harder at making a success of her column and her thrice-weekly radio shows.

On the air, she engaged in a game of wits with the continuity acceptance department. Disgusted when the censor prohibted describing *navel* oranges, she took to slipping double entendres into her scripts. She also inserted items that were specifically designed to irritate the censors so that she could remove the "offensive" material and retain some bit of eyebrow-raising gossip. In later days, Hedda facetiously credited herself for turning Ernest Martin, CBS's continuity acceptance representative, into a millionaire Broadway producer, claiming she had raised so much hell that radio became unbearable for him.

The column thrived, although any spectacular growth was impossible with the small Esquire Syndicate. In mid-February, 1940, Hedda mentioned that Gene Herrick, head of *Look's* West Coast office, had introduced her to Gardner and John Cowles, two publishers whose low-key, relaxed approach to life impressed her. No reference was made to any business discussions, but since the Cowles controlled the Register-Tribune Syndicate, what was left unsaid was clear to knowledgeable readers. And on June 1, 1940, Hedda's column was taken over by the Cowles group.

With each advance, Hedda assumed additional mannerisms of the stereotype news hen. Her vocabulary grew rougher, and she developed a "hardboiled" exterior. Where Louella concentrated on romantic items, Hedda sniped at racketeer union organizer Willie Bioff for the illegal practices to which film extras were forced to submit. She baited "Reds" and hailed the visit of Congressman Martin Dies, explaining that once the guilty were publicly identified, the innocent who walked in the shadow of suspicion would be cleared too. To a woman as inconsistent as Hedda, what difference could it make that Shirley Temple had been named by this man's committee as a Red sympathizer?

Curiously, Hedda, like Louella, seemed to prefer the journeymen stars to the truly gifted. A good word about Katharine Hepburn, Vivien Leigh, Laurence Olivier and even Garbo was given somewhat grudgingly.* She violently attacked Marlon Brando, although she hardly knew him.

In the interest of controversy, Hedda assumed the outlook of a small-minded, small-horizoned Hollywood provincial. She foolishly complained that studios were being too generous in publicizing Florida and cited as evidence *Palm Beach Story, Nothing but the Truth, Happy Go Lucky, Flight Command* and *My Life with Caroline.* During 1942, she took the chairman of the War Manpower Commission, Paul McNutt, to task for omitting motion pictures as one of the United States' thirty most essential industries and babbled on about closing the theaters and refusing to sell films to the armed forces. "I wonder," she mused, "how our fighting men would like that." Perhaps she reached the heights of inanity upon learning that New York film critics had chosen Katharine Hepburn "best actress" of the year. Hedda perversely claimed that the award would do Miss Hepburn more harm than good, " 'cause we've always resented their telling us who's best!"

"Hedda Hopper's Hollywood," as the column was called, burgeoned under the Cowles clever promotional methods so that even without her six one-reel shorts distributed by Paramount in 1940, Hedda's 1941 income exceeded the $110,000 gross of the previous year. She bought a home located on Tropical Drive in Beverly Hills from Ernest Torrence's widow, and the July 14 issue of *Life* carried a picture feature, "Life Goes to a House Moving," purporting to show how Hedda's celebrity friends had turned out to help her move. Hedda's helpers included Cary Grant, Rosalind Russell, Cobina Wright,

---

* *Even* Garbo, because Hedda once volunteered to work free in order to appear with the Swedish star, and after a sitting by Garbo in MGM's still photo studio, Hedda would appear to select favorite Garbo poses—like a true fan.

Jr., Eddie Albert, Anna May Wong, Robert Stack and Bill Hopper. Miss Wong exploded Chinese firecrackers to drive away any evil spirits that might be lurking about, and Roz Russell brought a gag gift—a garbage pail. Bill Hopper was photographed carrying his mother across the threshold.

To decorate her new residence, Hedda hired her old escort Harold Grieve (by this time married to silent star Jetta Goudal), who turned the place into a "little candy-box of a house." Hedda couldn't have been happier. It was, she decided, where she wanted to live for the remainder of her life.

When, shortly after moving in, Hedda was signed to appear as Paulette Goddard's Aunt Harriet in Cecil B. DeMille's *Reap the Wild Wind*, her joy was complete. "Give an actress a whiff of greasepaint, give her a chance to get her little toe on stage and she's off her trolley! Up at six, shower, breakfast, studio at seven, make-up room and they start putting mud on my nice clean face. Anyway, it looked like mud," she exulted.

With her success consolidated, Hedda, who had always yearned to make life easy for her mother, was able to do just that. The last year that Hedda lived on Fairfax Avenue, her eighty-three-year-old mother had flown to Hollywood and when questioned about her flight had airily replied: "Oh, it's the only way to travel!"

During Mrs. Furry's visit, Hedda and Ken Murray took the old lady to a premiere at the Carthay Circle Theater, where she whispered in amazement to Murray, "They all seem to know my little girl."

When Hedda introduced her to Hedy Lamarr, Mrs. Furry told the star that she was so beautiful she ought to be in pictures. "But mother," Hedda said, "this is Hedy Lamarr!" "Well, couldn't she change her name? You did!" was the retort.

Assuming that her mother would enjoy meeting the current ranking film beauties, Hedda invited them to a tea in Margaret Furry's honor. Mrs. Furry, who was deaf, sat entranced and after the tea was over said, "It was lovely, Elda. They all had such lovely, sweet faces." "Oh, Mother, what a pity you couldn't hear them!" Hedda said.

When Mrs. Furry again visited Hollywood in 1941, Hedda saw to it that she had a hearing aid. Once more, Hedda gave a tea with most of the same beauties in attendance. After the festivities, Hedda asked, "Wasn't it wonderful, Mother! Didn't you enjoy it much more now that you could hear everything?"

Mrs. Furry responded by reaching up and gently removing the hearing aid, which she placed in its box and handed to Hedda. "Dear," she said, "I want you to take this back. They had such sweet, smiling faces at the first party, but this time I could hear all the ugly things they said about other people. And you, Elda, took the Lord's name in vain!" *

That was Margaret Furry's last visit. She died in Altoona at the age of eighty-four on December 27, 1941.

When Hedda reported it, she observed: "She is gone—into life eternal. And I'm alone.

"Son?

"Yes.

"Friends?

"Yes.

"But you can't realize that utter aloneness until you've lost your mother. . . ."

"Comebacks, as Hollywood knows them, are for the most part anticlimatic, often bordering on the pathetic. Hedda Hopper's re-emergence in the film limelight since 1940, however, may be cited as one of the few spectacular exceptions," *Current Biography* commented.

At fifty-seven, still a trim 130 pounds, Hedda had emerged as a real power, collecting kudos from friends and grudging fear from others. The fear was justified—even in friends. On March 4, Hedda ran an item about

---

* Occasionally Hedda would become aware of her use of profanity and resolve to reform. The year that she was national chairman of the Easter Seal Fund for Crippled Children, she bought a six-inch bell bank and placed it on her desk. "Now every time I swear I'm going to make a contribution to the crippled children," she announced. "And every time anyone else swears, they are too." There were no exceptions. In fact, some press agents and actors, hoping to win her favor, contributed for past offenses.

all Hollywood turning out to meet the "One World" candidate Wendell Willkie, who was being backed by the Cowles brothers. That initial item was innocent enough, but the following day, her readers were treated to a story that was both politically naïve and domestically embarrassing to Willkie. According to Hedda, Norma Shearer had proved that she was still the First Lady of Hollywood when the politician drove from the Biltmore Hotel in downtown Los Angeles to Santa Monica to pick her up and escort her to Gene Herrick's party in Beverly Hills. "And at midnight when Norma was tired, he took her home, which broke up the party," Hedda added. The furor that ensued can easily be imagined, but Hedda was moving forward.

Wthen she had signed a three-year contract with the Register-Tribune Syndicate, she had been promised a wire service which the Cowles had been unable to deliver. So when the Chicago Tribune-New York Daily News Syndicate approached her, the Cowles released her even though her contract with them still had some time to go.

THE QUEEN IS DEAD, LONG LIVE THE QUEEN! *Variety* cried.

Time noted that the old Queen Louella with her 17,500,000 circulation was not exactly moribund, but that when, on June 1, Hedda's gossip replaced John Chapman's production notes in the New York *Daily News,* she would be acquiring an additional 5,750,000 daily and 7,500,000 Sunday circulation.

To turn out the columns and radio shows, Hedda worked an incredible 130 hours each week and enlisted the services of two legmen, a rewrite woman, two secretaries, two girls to take care of fan mail and the ever-energetic Dema Harshbarger. Just as Louella had, Hedda also developed her army of stool pigeons: dentists, beauticians, nurses, furniture salesmen, servants, laboratory technicians and morticians, to say nothing of close friends of stars, who loved to dish out secret information—simply to prove that they were in the know.

Of the string of legmen, Hy Gardner stayed only briefly before leaving to concentrate on his own column. Fred Banker was drafted for military service in 1943 and was succeeded by Spec McClure, a young Phi Beta Kappa who had been working as a publicity man. McClure was with her sporadically for many years. When he, in his turn, was drafted, he was replaced by King Kennedy, Louella's son-in-law. (Kennedy and Harriet were divorced in 1946.) In addition, there were, among others, Jaik Rosenstein, Joe Ledlie and Rod Voit.

In thinking back over why Hedda had succeeded where so many others failed, McClure did not discount the assistance the industry provided in building a rival for Louella, but he was inclined to place heavier emphasis on Hedda's flamboyance. "When she went to the Newspaper Publishers Convention every year in New York, Hopper had a radiant vitality," McClure said. "She bowled over those editors. A lot of the job of doing a damn column is selling it. That's why Florabel Muir never made it, and Florabel was a twenty times better reporter than either Parsons or Hopper, but Florabel couldn't shovel it the way they could. The ability to write wasn't it. Neither Parsons nor Hopper could write worth a damn.

"I never was on an interview with Hopper that the stars she was interviewing weren't fascinated by her gossip. The people she was interviewing would ask *her* things. You see, as long as you're not exposing them, everybody is fascinated with gossip.

"Even her enemies miss her today. She kept things lively. They loved to get up and see what she'd said about somebody else. This is the whole damn secret about who supports the columns. Practically everybody who can read. Now old Spencer Tracy was a great man for gossip. He liked to hear every dirty detail. But you put his name in a column except in a professional way, he was likely to kick things over.

"Gossip is a silly job for a man, and people don't have the same good humor toward a man. Have a woman write a column, it's kind of like pulling for a ball team with a woman pitcher, trying to guess what she'll do next.

"One time, when she was just getting popular, Hopper got the idea Bing Crosby was holed up in the Waldorf with a young actress. Hopper was always protective toward these young girls, afraid they'd get hurt. So she called

Ted Saucier, the hotel's press agent, and told him she knew all about it and to have Crosby get in touch with her or she'd blow the whole thing wide open. Crosby wrote her a long, handwritten letter swearing he hadn't done any such thing, so Hopper never printed the story. Now Crosby is somebody you'd think wouldn't give a damn."

On another occasion, McClure recalled, Dean Martin's press agent asked Hedda to intervene. Martin and Jerry Lewis were not yet in films, but during a nightclub engagement, Martin became involved with June Allyson. "It got so it looked as if the things was going to break, so the press agent took Hopper into his confidence. 'It doesn't make any difference to me what they do, but not at the airport at three o'clock in the afternoon!' he said. See, Allyson had gone out to see Dean off, and they embraced right there. Well, Hopper got on the phone and warned them. When they didn't listen to her, she printed a couple of hints. That did the trick."

Because of her candor, Hedda sometimes was the recipient of physical violence. When she printed items romantically linking Joseph Cotten and Deanna Durbin, much to the distress of Mrs. Cotten, the actor asked her to stop and told her what he would do if she didn't. Hedda persisted. When the usually debonair Cotten encountered her at a party, he made good his threat. He planted a kick to her posterior that sent her staggering and warned that there would be another if she ever mentioned him again.

Later when Hedda began to harry Cary Grant unfairly, Cotten, according to columnist Leonard Lyons, sent Grant a shoe and the suggestion of how Grant should use it. Eventually, however, the Cotten-Hopper quarrel was patched up—as many of Hedda's quarrels were—and she became one of the actor's greatest boosters.

Why had Hedda succeeded?

"Impact," McClure said. "A fresh approach. She wasn't a worn-out journalist. It was her greatest strength and her greatest weakness at the same time. She'd come up with some offbeat point of view. As long as she lived, this town never ceased to interest her. Every morning she'd come in, arms loaded with books—she was a great reader—and she'd be rarin' to go. Maybe the night before, when she left the office, she seemed about to collapse, but she had the ability to recoup. Every day she was born anew. When you think of it, writing a column's the same thing day after day, but I never heard Hopper say she'd like to be out of the business. It seemed to regenerate her. She'd get on the telephone, be hamming it up, acting. It was like a transfusion.

"She wrote . . . dictated the column. It would be typed up, and she'd read it through and make corrections. One of the worst things, I'd say, was this thing she had about brevity. Hell, she'd type out verbs. When I tried to explain about a dangling participle, she said, 'Let it dangle.'

"We kept one copy in the office. If Dema was there, she'd blue pencil anything libelous. If she wasn't, I'd take it to the lawyer in the building. Hopper'd think the LA *Times* had done it, and she'd get to raising hell about cutting; but she was never in serious libel trouble until she wrote *The Whole Truth and Nothing But*. That was in the 1960's.

"Anyway she forgot quickly. You see, Hopper never spent time rehashing herself or her columns. If a person tended to sit down and read a column after it was in print, he'd see what was left out and worry. Or what could have been better. She'd just glance at it and go on to something else.

"One trouble with both Hopper and Parsons was that they couldn't maintain interest in anything long enough. If Hopper'd written about Mitchum two days in a week and then a legitimate story broke, she'd say, 'Who the hell cares? We've already had him this week.' She didn't evaluate the news content."

Nevertheless, Hedda controlled the column. At one point Pamela Mason was quoted in *Time* as claiming that it was ghosted. McClure voluntarily leaped to Hedda's defense. "I wrote *Time* a letter, and I said I told Miss Hopper if it were me, I'd sue both *Time* and Pamela Mason, and if she did, I'd be the first one to testify."

When McClure wanted to hold extended discussions with his boss, he discovered the best method was to ride with her from the Hollywood office to her home. It was only then that he could hope for her undivided attention. "And the way I used to get her to do a story was by saying something like 'We can't do anything on Greer Garson, can we?' Hedda would bristle and ask why not. If you got Hopper on the defensive immediately, you could be pretty sure she'd say you could do it.

"Frankly, I don't know if Hopper had a friend in the world. I mean a real friend. Now people say they were, but one of the tragedies of her life, I always felt, was that she lacked the capacity for either deeply loving or being loved. Her whole life was more or less work. She had a recognition that the gossip column wasn't the end-all and be-all, but she pushed it way back in her mind. As I said, she wasn't analytical. I was once talking, and she said, 'My God, I wouldn't analyze anything I've ever done in my whole life.' And I don't think she ever did."

After all the years of being taken for granted—which she was careful to hide—she began to sweep into parties completely ignoring people with whom she was angry. When McClure asked how she was able to do it, she barked: "Don't see them. Don't see the bastards at all!"

There were some celebrities, however, who were always in her good graces, among them Tyrone Power, Alan Ladd, Clark Gable—and Howard Hughes. "I don't know, I think she had a strange synthetic attitude toward sex," McClure said. "She wasn't capable of loving much. She was just an innocent Quaker girl—innocent in the sense of not having experience. She didn't have an innocent mind.

"She had this thing for Gable. She loved to tell Sam Goldwyn's story. He was talking about what made a star one night. He said, 'Well, when a person like Robert Montgomery comes on the screen, you know he's got balls. When Clark Gable comes on, you can hear them clacking together. That's the difference.'

"When Hopper was on the phone with Gable, nobody in the office listened in. And one time when she was feuding with Arthur Hornblow, who was the producer of a Gable picture, she and Gable sat in the dressing room talking and held up production. Hornblow walked back and forth fuming, but he didn't dare say anything. That was part of her power."

Beneath the surface there was indisputably much loneliness. Once in speaking to Margaret Sullavan, Hedda momentarily let the mask slip, saying, "Get married. Don't wind up an old lady in a big house like I am." Yet on a day not long after, she observed she wouldn't marry anyone unless her future husband's complete sex life were known to her. When McClure volunteered that he would be glad to recount his, Hedda replied, "I always thought you would, you son of a bitch. That's the reason I never asked you."

"She seemed to shy away from any real love," McClure said. "To keep people at a distance. I think that's why she had a strange attraction to fags. They were good dancers. A lot of them were witty, talented people. They didn't paw her. The only problem she had when she got home was to keep them from coming in and drinking all her liquor."

Hedda's life remained essentially simple. At a time when her earning power became enormous, she continued to do much of her own housework. Even though she employed a cook, she liked to putter around the kitchen. And every Sunday she took her current dog for a walk.

"She should have had everything, but she couldn't," McClure concluded. "The servants tyrannized her. It was the only family she had—in a sense. After Bill married. Once she got sore at old Maude, who was with her for years, at home, and with Dema and me for getting drunk at the office. She sat at her desk and spluttered, 'My God, where do I go? I can't get any peace at home, and I can't get any at the office.' Even then she couldn't resist a gag. She said, 'And I'm too old to become a streetwalker—so where do I go?' "

Sometimes an item was written simple to create a furor —to allow her to brag about how many letters of complaint she had received for saying, say, that John Wayne would be miscast as Edward Rickenbacker. After she ran a facetious item that those notorious satyrs Errol Flynn and Charlie Chaplin were to appear in *Are These Our Children?*, Flynn sent a letter of protest which Hedda privately answered by warning him that if he wanted the real truth told about him, she was the one to tell it. But at the end, she was unable to resist wisecracking: "And when your body is on the floor, I'd like to be there with it."

She sarcastically referred to Lana Turner as "Metro's big star" and said she had done it again—got married. The groom, Steve Crane, Hedda assured readers, was not from a Chicago millionaire plumbing family, but instead had once operated a plumbing store in a tiny Indiana town. She reported that the romantically inclined Rita Hayworth and Victor Mature were referred to in Hollywood as "The Beauty and the Beast." And when Greer Garson was upset at Hedda's report that the actress was marrying Richard Ney, Hedda retorted that she supposed Miss Garson got carried away at the Norma Shearer wedding but on "sober consideration" decided the relationship might not work out. "After all, when Richard Ney was playing her son in *Mrs. Miniver,* he gave his age as 23," she said bitchily—although she did restrain herself from giving Miss Garson's age. Then, eventually, Hedda was proved right when the couple married.

After feuding bitterly with Marlene Dietrich for several years, Hedda agreed to make up with her. When they met, Hedda hugged Miss Dietrich and inquired what they had quarreled over. "If you don't know, I'm not going to tell you," the star replied. Later she observed: "If I'd told her, she might have started it all over again."

Merle Oberon was in and out of favor for no apparent reason. When Miss Oberon was out, Hedda sarcastically referred to her as Lady Korda. (She was then married to Sir Alexander Korda.) After one sustained attack, Jerry Hoffman, who had become a publicist, arranged for the two women to meet at the Brown Derby. Miss Oberon was already there when Hedda arrived and greeted her effusively. After a perfunctory exchange, Miss Oberon suddenly asked: "Hedda, will you tell me what possibly inspired all the vicious things you have been writing about me?" Whereupon Hedda leaned over, patted the star's arm and said, "Bitchery, dear, Sheer bitchery."

The enmity between Hedda and Louella was often genuine. Nothing was too petty to quarrel over. Since

Hedda's hats were her trademark, Louella commissioned John Frederick to create a Gay Illiterate bonnet for her— to publicize her book and irritate Hedda.

After Twentieth Century-Fox bought the book for a reported $75,000, Hedda announced that she had told Darryl Zanuck of Twentieth that she wanted $50,000 to appear in the film and $75,000 to stay out of it. Upon reading Twentieth's announcement that the central figure in Louella's life would be played by Elsa Maxwell or Claudette Colbert, Hedda raised Louella's hackles by inquiring, "What, not The Gay Illiterate herself? Or isn't she the type?"

Fully cognizant of Louella's pride in being the first to know, Hedda wickedly and publicly congratulated Florabel Muir for scooping the town on the Herbert Marshall divorce. When Hedda had a C-47 ambulance plane named in her honor during World War II, Louella wanted one named for her, too.

Then, as a change of pace, Hedda proposed that they make a truce, suggesting that they reserve adjoining tables at a popular restaurant. At a given signal, they would begin a public exchange of carefully rehearsed insults until they had the attention of everyone in the room; then they would confound onlookers by rising, linking arms and exiting with a line from *Sunday:* "That's all there is—there isn't any more."

Louella at first favored the idea. But the publicists who played one against the other were concerned lest their double-dealing might be discovered. A few well-placed hints that Hedda had no intention of sticking to the script scuttled the plan. Louella's excuse: Her husband forbade it for health reasons.

Privately, Hedda bemoaned the lost opportunity. "Why won't she play ball?" she asked. "It would do us both a lot of good. Well, if she wants it, she'll get it."

When Louella heard this, she replied that she didn't need such stunts. Speaking of Hedda to a magazine interviewer, she observed bitterly: "She's trying to do in two years what it took me 30 years to do. And I resent some of the things she says about me."

But whether Louella liked it or not, her pretense that

Hedda's only outlet was the Los Angeles *Times* no longer fooled anyone. Hedda, with 85 metropolitan papers, 3,000 small-town dailies and 2,000 weeklies, was a formidable adversary whose power was still growing.

XI

Louella had attained absolute perfection in deceiving herself—as well as almost everybody else.

—DALE EUNSON

WHILE others, including Hedda, were inclined to ridicule Orson Welles' pretensions and his beard from the moment he arrived in Hollywood, Louella welcomed him. Welles arrived on the scene at a time when the $10 billion international industry faced the crisis of having 40 percent of its foreign market disappear as the European war spread. Louella remained optimistic that despite economic cuts, "quality" could be maintained as long as such talented newcomers as Vivien Leigh, Bill Hopper,* Harriet Parsons and Orson Welles continued to develop.

Beginning in 1938, Louella chronicled Welles' successes in the theater and on radio—being particularly fascinated with his notorious *The War of the Worlds* broadcast, the pseudodocumentary that sent panic-stricken citizens rushing into the streets to escape the mythical invaders from Mars. According to her, Samuel Goldwyn, Warner's and RKO all were proffering contracts to this supershowman.

---

* Louella always praised him, and Hedda was invariably complimentary to Harriet. Reflecting on this, one observer came up with the explanation that each felt that "with a mother like that, I'm not going to add to that child's troubles."

She announced that Welles was going to—and then not going to—play Napoleon. He was eager to—and then reluctant to—appear in Sinclair Lewis' *It Can't Happen Here.*

Finally, Welles signed with RKO, scheduled to make his debut as the bewhiskered Captain in Joseph Conrad's *Heart of Darkness* unless he did Cecil Day Lewis' *Smiler with a Knife* or the film version of *The Man Who Came to Dinner.* Louella was confident that he could more than fill the wheelchair of such idolized predecessors as Monty Wooley, Clifton Webb and Alexander Woollcott in the role.

On a couple of occasions, she gently needled the studio for allowing the "boy wonder" to squander money and Welles for talking too much before actually accomplishing anything in the film medium; but on the whole her attitude toward him was friendly, and he seemingly reciprocated.*

On July 31, 1940, Louella's column announced that she could hardly wait for the next day to visit the set where they were shooting a scene from Welles' new film—something called *Citizen Kane*—so that she could assess his screen acting and directing techniques. Instead, she chose to attend a preview of *Boom Town,* thereby losing an opportunity to learn something about the Welles film.

What followed can only be viewed as a cruel put on by Welles. He entertained Louella at a five-course luncheon in his dressing room. During the luncheon she asked him about *Citizen Kane's* subject matter, and Welles replied evasively—as quoted in a long, laudatory Sunday interview: "It deals first with a dead man. You know when a man dies there is a great difference of opinion about his character. I have everyone voice his side and no two descriptions are alike." This only bewildered Louella, who thought it seemed a complicated idea. Later she claimed

---

* Hedda was more forthright in criticizing him. On January 22, 1940, she confronted him like a ruffled mother hen, demanding, "Why are you wearing a beard in the first place? Are you going to make a picture? How long do you think you can keep going without producing anything?" Writer Dwight Whitney said Hedda resented beards because "It was something she couldn't do."

she had asked Welles point blank whether the film dealt with Hearst and he denied it.

Even though Hearst editors warned Louella that there were rumors that the picture was about the Chief, she was unable to believe Welles would lie to her, responding to him as she did to anyone she admired—especially a male who flattered her. Welles appeared to be friendly, sending chatty notes and wiring her good wishes when she opened her second vaudeville tour. In Chicago, he visited Louella backstage at the Chicago Theater when he was passing through town. It is easy to believe he wooed her, led her on, used her and finally intentionally humiliated her.

As for Louella, she mentioned him favorably on August 7 and 11, and on August 19 she told her readers that in spite of a broken ankle which confined him to a wheel-chair,* Welles was thirteen days ahead of schedule on *Citizen Kane*. Even as late as September 16—when the picture was more than three-fourths finished—Louella prattled on that "the boy genius photographs like a million dollars" . . . and claimed that RKO had sent a "special ambassador" East to show president George Schaefer that they had a "tall, dark, handsome leading man on their hands." She predicted that additional scenes would be shot to "give the girls a chance to sigh over young Welles."

On October 23, after eighty-two days before the cameras, the $686,000 production, based on a script by Welles and Herman Mankiewicz, finished shooting. Those involved in the production claim that Welles took great precautions to maintain secrecy. Producer-director Robert Wise, then a cutter at RKO, later said that the picture was sneaked into production, and five or six sequences (Welles claimed they were tests) had been completed before the front office, discovering that a film had begun, agreed to grant Welles complete autonomy. When Sid Rogell and other executive types appeared on the set, Welles called off shooting and played baseball until the unwelcome interlopers left.

One way or another Hedda managed to attend the first

* Accident-prone he was, accident-prone he remained.

screening. Peter Noble quotes attorney Arnold Weiss-berger in *Fabulous Orson Welles* as saying that the screening had been set up for *Life*, but that Hedda found out about it and insisted on attending. A former manager of Welles' said that it was specifically scheduled for Hedda by Welles, who not only anticipated but also set out to provoke the attack he knew would come from Louella and the Hearst press. In later years Hedda claimed that by making frequent visits to the set, she discovered, or at least suspected, that the character was based on Hearst and that when she told Welles so, he offered to let her judge for herself at the first showing of the film. He assumed Hedda would respond to the film's artistry because of her long experience before the cameras. In this, he misjudged her, for Hedda was "appalled." To her *Citizen Kane* seemed "lacking in originality," "a dubious box-office prospect" and so "chopped up" that it was impossible to judge Welles as a picture performer. Following the screening she informed him that he wouldn't get away with it, but he insisted he would. "Cockiness I can take," Hedda later wrote, "arrogance, I abhor." According to her, she passed the information through channels to Hearst.

Louella maintained that Hedda not only cooperated with Welles in double-crossing her but also bypassed channels by rushing from the screening room to call the Chief to say that she couldn't imagine why Louella hadn't alerted him concerning the content of the picture. Although Louella claimed that Hearst never blamed her for failing to discover the subject matter of the film, the enraged tycoon ordered her to see *Citizen Kane* at once.* Those close to the situation say that he was even on the verge of paying off her contract and giving her the sack.

Louella called George Schaefer and demanded that a screening be set up for her and two Hearst lawyers, Oscar Lawler and A. Laurence Mitchell. Also in attendance was her butler-chauffeur Louis Collins. Sound man James

---

* Whether true or not, Hearst always maintained that he was one of the few people involved who never viewed the film. Schaefer said Hearst requested and saw a print.

Stewart, who was head of the RKO dubbing department in 1940, stated that while Louella swept out of the screening room before the film ended, ignoring Welles (to whom she never again spoke), Collins remained to the end. According to Weissberger, the butler-chauffeur paused on the way out to comment: "That was a right fine picture, Mr. Welles."

Louella, in tears, implored the lawyers to call Hearst to tell him of the libelous content of what they had witnessed. They refused. Finally, she wired Hearst the unpleasant news. Hearst at once demanded that RKO defer the release under threat of legal action. Schaefer's reply was to announce that the studio would give the film unprecedented prerelease advertising.

In turn, Hedda suddenly planned to devote six segments of her radio show to a profile of Awesome Orson. Louella, as Hedda told it, immediately called every powerful film executive in Hollywood, urging them to apply pressure to persuade her to drop the project. Hedda refused.

Mention of Welles, *Citizen Kane* or anything else connected with RKO in either editorial or advertising columns was forbidden in the Hearst press for two weeks in January—which only increased curiosity about the picture. Dissension developed among RKO executives, who were becoming fearful lest Louella should decide to reveal certain industry secrets to which she was privy. She is also reputed to have asked Nelson Rockefeller how he would enjoy having a story on John D. Rockefeller in Hearst's *American Weekly* Sunday supplement—if the film opened at the Radio City Music Hall in Rockefeller Center.

Hedda said that rumors were everywhere that "the refugee situation" in relation to the industry would be looked into by Hearst reporters, that "private lives" would not be ignored and that soon "there will be a lot of heads that formerly were accustomed to satin pillows reposing in baskets." She doubted the film would ever be released.

The situation became so ominous that Robert Wise was sent to New York with a print. One midnight it was shown at Radio City Music Hall to such major RKO stockholders as David Sarnoff of RCA and Floyd Odlum of the Atlas Corporation. The object was to decide what course to pursue.

One faction proposed that the major studios contribute to a fund to buy the film, giving hard-pressed RKO a reasonable profit. Then the new owners would destroy the film. Schaefer, according to Hedda, said he'd reject even a $3,000,000 offer for it. Another group suggested that by making judicious changes in some scenes, mostly in dialogue, the work could be salvaged. "Finally," Wise told a reporter, "after six weeks of diddling, the picture was released." That leaders of the industry seriously considered destroying what has come to be regarded as a film classic in order to placate a publisher and his irate gossip columnist indicates the power of both the Hearst press and Louella.

The opening date, February 14, was canceled, but at last, after Welles threatened legal action against RKO, the film opened on April 10—to good notices and excellent business. Strangely, as critic Arthur Knight pointed out almost thirty years later, critics initially regarded "the whole thing as a spectacular, precocious stunt." In 1952 an international poll of motion picture critics found Kane just missing inclusion in the top 10, all-time great films, but in 1962 essentially the same critics called it "the best film of all time." Nevertheless, an unofficial boycott made the going rough at first.

Hedda had already changed her own mind by April, 1941. She said the consensus was, even among people who disapproved of the story, that Welles had proved himself a genius. It was, she assured readers, nonsense to think that the Academy Awards would be canceled to prevent him from winning. Indeed it was. Louella had managed to so inflame some members of the film colony that whenever the picture was mentioned during the Academy Awards ceremonies, there were boos. Privately, many of the same people who booed conceded that it was a superb film, but the popular public stance was to pretend disapproval.

Louella never forgave Welles. No mention of his name was included in her column unless it was attached to some derogatory item. During World War II, when he produced and starred in the *Mercury Wonder Show,* to which servicemen were admitted free and whose profits went to the Assistance League, the Los Angeles *Examiner* ran a feature on the production, mentioning both Rita Hayworth and Joseph Cotten but ignoring producer-director-star Welles completely. His name did appear, however, in a paid advertisement.

Only when "the self-proclaimed genius" could be branded "a civilian love thief" who wooed and won Miss Hayworth away from Coast Guardsman Victor Mature or a homewrecker who had come between Dolores Del Rio and art director Cedric Gibbons or blasted as a tax dodger who had fled the country—only under such circumstances was Welles a newsworthy figure in the eyes of Louella. Her fury even extended to his associates. When New York film critics chose Agnes Moorehead as the best actress of 1942 for her work in Welles' *The Magnificent Ambersons,* Louella sniffed that the decision was unpopular in Hollywood.

Naturally, this gave Hedda an opportunity to get into the act. "When a fellow columnist takes a crack at Agnes Moorehead and says that the news that New York critics chose her as the best actress of the year was received with uplifted eyebrows in Hollywood, she's taking in a lot of territory. On the contrary, most eyebrows, including mine, are in their normal place. Now that's a lowdown crack if I ever heard one, and undeserved by Miss Moorehead, who's a superb actress. Could it be that the unkindness was prompted because Agnes' career was backed by Orson Welles, who, as you remember, did *Citizen Kane?* If it was, that's a poor reason to attack the decision of splendid critics with no ax to grind." *

At the very time Louella was doing her utmost to torpedo Welles' film career, she grew mysteriously enthu-

* Apparently Hedda had forgotten her assertion that a similar kudo from New York critics only a year before had done Katharine Hepburn more harm than good in Hollywood. In regard to Welles, Louella, like an elephant, never forgot. Ten years later she was sniping away. She hoped that the seventeen-year-old Swedish miss Welles had just signed wouldn't have as much trouble getting her salary as Betsy Blair had.

siastic about Herbert J. Yates' Republic Studios, which gave the public not only John Wayne and Gene Autry, but also—eventually—Roy Rogers, to say nothing of Vera Hruba Ralston. Republic, which had specialized in quickies, would no longer be the butt of such jokes as the one about the actor who was called to the telephone and returned to find his picture had been finished, Louella reported in January, 1941. She added that if asked to choose the studio that had made the greatest strides in 1940, Republic would have to be designated. Now she was pleased to announce that Yates had spent $50,000 to obtain rights to *Sis Hopkins* as a starring vehicle for Judy Canova and would invest an additional $750,000 in a first-rate production. What was more, Republic's *Meet the Stars* was the best short of its kind Louella had ever seen. *Showman's Trade Review* and *Film Daily,* she was happy to announce, had also singled it out for praise. Not so incidentally, they had had complimentary things to say about the producer, too—one Harriet Parsons.

In March, Louella undertook a new half-hour radio program, *Hollywood Premieres,** which was in many ways similar to the defunct *Hollywood Hotel.* The first show featured Universal's *The Flame of New Orleans,* with Marlene Dietrich and Bruce Cabot. Later CBS listeners were treated to Republic's *Sis Hopkins,* with Judy Canova, Susan Hayward and Jerry Colonna. Almost simultaneously, Yates gave Harriet a producer-director-writer contract. "Never thought I'd be the mother of a movie producer, to say nothing of a director," wrote Louella, who only a few weeks earlier had been predicting that if King Kennedy (then still wed to Harriet) continued to write plays like *Yesterday's Laughter,* she would soon be known only as his mother-in-law.

With each passing month Republic grew more prominent in the Parsons column. Its upward climb continued

---

* Not coincidentally, the Screen Actors Guild issued an ultimatum that its members were no longer to appear on radio programs for less than their customary fees except for charity. Pressure was put on Louella, who signed an agreement to pay guests their regular fees upon the expiration of her thirteen-week contract—which doomed the show's chances for renewal.

on August 26, when Moe J. Siegel called to give Louella a scoop. The studio had received "the most original story idea" Siegel had read in years. It was about a hayseed Mata Hari and was an ideal role for Judy Canova. The idea was Harriet's brainstorm and was to serve as the basis for her first feature production. While the film was being prepared, Harriet was struck by another inspiration. This one was about a group of fifteen- and sixteen-year-old prodigies, who, finding they were already has-beens in Hollywood, got together to tour the nation as a swing band. Harriet called it *Keep Swingin'*—and Louella proudly said that her daughter was living up to her own title.

Meanwhile, Republic signed Joe E. Brown to co-star with Judy Canova in what was now called *Lazybones*. The Brown-Canova combination, Louella thought, promised to be the best comedy team since Abbott and Costello. However, by the time the film was reviewed in the trade papers under the title of *Joan of the Ozarks,* Louella had dropped all pretense of promoting Republic. She did quote the *Hollywood Reporter*'s assessment that Harriet had made "an exceptionally bright debut in the feature field" and *Variety*'s "Harriet Parsons turned in a well-supervised piece of entertainment." But experienced Parsons readers might have guessed that things were not exactly going well at Republic when Louella issued a stern lecture to Judy Canova upon the dangers of becoming known for her temperamental outbursts and added that she had never known of a temperamental actress who didn't emerge second best. Moreover, on May 11, 1943, Louella reported that it sounded like wishful thinking on someone's part, but Republic claimed that it had interested Tallulah Bankhead in appearing in *For Women Only.*

Three months to the day after that item appeared, the secret was out. Louella confided that her "favorite producer" (guess who?) was "parking her typewriter" (guess where?) "under a long term contract." Yes, Harriet had been signed by RKO, whose activities had received short shrift in Louella's column following the release of *Citizen Kane.* How RKO would fare in the column now and how

Harriet would do at RKO were matters of common discussion in Hollywood.

On December 8, 1941, Louella was in New York attending a performance of *The Land Is Bright* when, between the first and second acts, President Roosevelt broadcast his declaration of war. Afterward the audience spontaneously joined in singing the national anthem, which brought a lump to Louella's throat and a resolution to do everything in her power to ensure victory—just as she had in World War I.

Louella soon was distributing her time among the Red Cross, Bundles for Blue Jackets, the Buy a Bomber Fund and the Marion Davies War Hospital, while Harriet devoted herself to the American Women's Voluntary Service and the Hollywood Canteen.

Less than a week after war was declared, Louella's nephew Gordon Maynard was inducted into the Army, and a little more than a month later her friend Carole Lombard was killed in a plane crash while returning from a tour on which she had sold $2,000,000 worth of defense bonds. Louella sniped away in her column at Mae West for "not doing her part" by failing to appear in a show for the Merchant Marine and ominously warned Greta Garbo that she had better offer an explanation of why she had refused to join the Victory Caravan if she had any intention of continuing her film career.

On May 13, Louella's fifty-three-year-old husband volunteered for service in the U.S. Army, temporarily interrupting more than twelve years of marital happiness. Louella said that once America entered the war, she instinctively knew that Docky would try to get a little action. She attempted to ward off the inevitable by reminding him that they weren't kids anymore, but the day came when he showed her a letter making him a major in the Medical Corps. Outwardly, she claimed, she attempted to accept it bravely, but when she was alone, she often had to dry her tears and remind herself that she'd had twelve happy years with Docky, that she was no young war bride.

Louella was right. On that May 15, 1942, when Major Martin reported for active duty at Ross Letterman Hospital in San Francisco, she was less than three months away from her sixty-first birthday, but since so many of their close friends were young, the Martins seem to have related to an age group at least a quarter of a century their juniors.

Weekends at Marsons Farm were discontinued as Louella traveled to San Francisco to be with her major. There the head of the hospital escorted her on a special tour of the facilities, prompting her to assure families that their loved ones couldn't be in better hands.*

Although civilians were prohibited from entering the waterfront area, when Martin shipped out, Jake Ehrlich, knowing how much Louella longed to see her husband off, arranged for her to distribute farewell gifts. Louella was touchingly grateful and assured him that she would never forget his kindness. "And when she wrote her book," Ehrlich said, "sure enough, the whole incident was there, including my name—which she misspelled!"

Professionally she had become so well known that with a little nudging even her hometown recognized her as extraordinary. In September, 1942, Dixon staged a "Louella Parsons Day"—and Bob Hope, Bebe Daniels, Ann Rutherford, Ben Lyon, Jerry Colonna and a local Dixon boy, Ronald Reagan, accompanied her to make it a gala event. It seemed an appropriate time for self-assessment, reevaluation and a certain amount of self-congratulation.

---

* About this time Louella took the necessary steps to formalize her affiliation with the Catholic Church, whose services she and Docky had been attending for the past dozen years. For her conversion she needed documentary evidence that her former husbands had not been members of the church and her letter to Captain Jack dates from this period.

XII

You can't fool an old bag like me.
—HEDDA HOPPER

WHEN Hedda learned that Louella had contracted to Doubleday Doran for her autobiography and intended to call it *The Gay Illiterate*, she announced that if she ever committed her story to paper, she would entitle it *Malice in Wonderland*.

Hedda, now in her mid-fifties, entered the 1940's in disarray. After she had hungered so long for power, the sudden overwhelming success she was granted came at a particularly difficult time. Hollywood, as Leo Rosten observed in his study of the movie colony and the moviemakers, was then perhaps the last manifestation of a lush and profligate world, and even it seemed to sense the shape of things to come.

Hedda was in command of two powerful bases—a syndicated newspaper column and a radio show—from which to disseminate her feelings. Yet she was hardly qualified by temperament, education or experience to analyze and assess the issues she held forth upon. The result was that she fumed and fussed and sometimes actually gave the impression that she was arguing with herself—almost always at the top of her voice.

Hedda's beliefs were rooted in a less complex era when

it was commonly assumed that hard work, thrift and honesty were invariably rewarded; that right was might and vice versa. She was a product of a Quaker upbringing (despite her pugnacity) in a stable, relatively isolated environment. She believed dignity, freedom and self-government were God-given prerogatives. Her outlook was formed at a time when the American dream was bright and new and attainable to any WASP or WASQ.

Everyone was equal, but as this unselfconscious item from a September, 1943, column illustrates, she, like the majority of middle-class Americans, assumed that some were more equal than others. "Not a pleasant sight, listening to a Negro taxi driver bawling out a Lieutenant in the United States Army when the taxi cut in front of him and the Lieutenant remonstrated. My Irish driver whispered, 'That such a thing could happen in this beautiful country.'" Yet if anyone had accused her of prejudice, she would have been astounded, arguing that she liked Hattie McDaniel, Butterfly McQueen and Stepin Fetchit.

In seeking a vacuum-packed, unchanged America, she embraced isolationism. She was determined that American life would not again be corrupted as it had been by World War I. Since hers was a felt, rather than a reasoned, position, it led to some unlikely associations, strange reversals of opinion and some mystifying verbal gymnastics. At one point, she went so far as to claim that she detected an improvement in Hollywood films now that motion pictures were made with wholesome American tastes in mind rather than the jaded foreign market.

But Hedda was a realist who recognized that to succeed, one needed advocates in strategic positions. Thus, she overcame a twenty-year antipathy toward onetime film magnate Joseph P. Kennedy, who, as ambassador to Great Britain, had urged American neutrality. In 1940, when he was a house guest of Marion Davies, Hedda sought him out to urge him never to stop speaking against American involvement in the European struggle. She even went so far as to suggest a public debate on defense spending with her old friend Bernard M. Baruch—whom she now opposed.

In April, 1941, when she visited Washington, D.C. the

patriotism instilled in her as a child triggered a thrill at the thought of actually stepping inside the White House and meeting the President—even if he happened to be a Democrat. Franklin Delano Roosevelt's charisma swept her up, but in admitting it, she allowed politics to intrude by noting that it was easy to see why "they" called this the "Charm School." Attending his press conference, she wrote that the President "gives himself a wonderful time—and reports little information." She added that "to pin him down as to where that one billion, eighty million* went is like trying to get an eagle to tell you what happened to his tailfeathers."

Naturally, after Pearl Harbor there was a change. Hedda threw her weight behind the war effort and urged Americans to do their utmost. Even though she sold bonds, worked at the Hollywood Canteen and went on jaunts to entertain troops at military bases, she still betrayed unconscious traces of ambivalence. One day she would suggest that each new ship be named in the memory of a sailor, soldier or marine lost in action. Another day she might introduce an inconsequential item about a beauty contest with the incredible lead-in "Wars may come and wars may go, but our beauty parades . . ." or she might praise actress Fay Holden for her patriotism in uprooting her prize-winning chrysanthemums to plant a victory garden.

But as the impact of the war struck home, Hedda adopted an all-out pro-Allied attitude. In the light of what was to come, she unbelievably enough endorsed sending Paul Draper and Larry Adler on a tour of Russia. Adler and Draper were described as geniuses, and Hedda predicted that through Adler's harmonica playing and Draper's dancing the two would build up more goodwill than all the politicians together. (Yet before the decade was out, she approved hotelman Glen McCarthy's cancellation of Adler, observing: "Glen employs no one who even looks to the left.") During the war Hedda even had a good word for Stalin, whom she referred to familiarly as Joe. She said he was smart enough to keep the film

---

* In the national budget.

theaters open twenty-four hours a day during the sieges of Stalingrad and Leningrad. "There's a man who recognizes the value of pictures and makes the most of it. . . ."

After a flurry of friendly items about the Russians, Hedda returned to worrying about American Communists. She took on the Writers Guild for criticizing the Motion Picture Alliance for the Preservation of American Ideals. All the MPA was trying to do, she said, was to expose Reds in the name of patriotism. What was "harmful" or "irresponsible" in that? Furthermore, it was beyond her why any $2,000- to $5,000-a-week writer "could be a Commie"—unless he hoped to get in on the ground floor in the event of a take-over.

Since all was not war and Communism or Fascism, she was concurrently enjoying the Welles-Parsons fracas, sniping away at Charlie Chaplin as "The Little White Father," scolding Rosalind Russell for not getting on with the Sister Kenny picture, making snide remarks about Melvyn Douglas, accusing Helen Gahagan Douglas of being vapid and inveighing against the tendency of United States citizens to raise their standard of living with every increase in their earning power.

On a more positive note, she triumphantly announced that her unrelenting campaign to persuade Walt Disney to re-release *Snow White* had caused him to do so—somewhat reluctantly. As a result, the picture would earn an added $12,000,000 gross.

One person Hedda did not go all out on—a person who was, in fact, conspicuously absent from her column—was her son. Readers often asked why there was so little news about Bill in the column—either concerning his war exploits or his picture career. Hedda explained that Bill had asked her to keep his name out of the things she wrote. He wanted to make it on his own.

"You're damned right I did," Bill said. "I never had a damn thing to do with her column. Except once in a while I'd try to do something for somebody. I'd call her and see if I could. Sometimes I could, and sometimes I couldn't.

"There were times when it got to you. Years ago I was tested for a contract at Twentieth. I was all set to sign—and then it died. A year later the agent told me what happened. In those days things like stock contracts went through various channels. This took time. Hedda got to Harry Brand, who was a good friend of hers. Harry got it all set; but he went over the head of the guy in charge of these unimportant deals, and the guy got furious. Dead. There was no meaning of harm on her part. She was just trying to pull the damn plug—you know."

As she became more powerful, anxiety increased. Several times she dropped word that Bill should be interviewed for a picture. Whenever he heard about it, he stopped it, but word was slow in getting around. On one occasion, Bill was sent to a producer to read for a part of which he said, "I was dead wrong for the role. The producer and the director knew it. I knew it. But the producer was worried. He said to my agent, 'I talked to Bill and he's not right for this part, but what the hell is Hedda going to do if I don't give it to him?' The agent told him what I'd told him to say, 'Hedda's not going to do anything to you. She's completely out of it.' But that was the feeling they had."

In 1940 the only mention of Bill in her column was the announcement of his marriage, and in 1941 she limited hreself to reporting that he spent the Christmas holidays in bed with the flu. Nevertheless, she did not desist in pressuring her son to associate with the rich and powerful who were in a position to help him. She bemoaned his marriage. 'Any girl who'd have won her approval would have had to be a master psychologist," said one of her most intimate friends. "Hedda was like my mother. If my brother had married the Queen of England's younger sister, Mother would have said, 'Oh, dear! I never did much care for them.' And I don't think Jane was overly tactful with Hedda."

Bill solved the problem for a time by not speaking to his mother and then by speaking to her only over the telephone. When they met, they clashed. "Hedda would tell friends that she was so disgusted she didn't care if she never saw him again, yet she loved him and sacrificed for him," Frances Marion said. Miss Marion and others who were among the inner circle, recognizing how seldom the two spent time alone together, made it a point to be absent when they knew he was going to visit her.

In 1942 he joined the Coast Guard and the OSS before transferring to the frogmen's underwater demolition Team Number 10, operating in the South Pacific. Its eventual—and, as it turned out, unnecessary—goal was the invasion of Tokyo.

Naturally, Hedda could make little reference to his activities while he was in the service, but at Christmastime in 1946 she reminisced that during the war, Jane, Joan and she had made up a Yule package of small gifts, including a one-jigger bottle of scotch, samples of Jane's powder and perfume and a tiny bag of earth labeled "The latest dirt from Hollywood." Bill deposited the bag on a Pacific beach, envisioning the amazement of some U.S. marine who would come upon it later and wonder how it ever got there.

"I guess my belonging to Team ten was the first thing I ever did that pleased her," he said. The irony was that he had asked for a transfer to escape exactly the type of commanding officer Hedda would have gone out of her way to cultivate. "We had this stupid commanding officer —I won't even mention his name—he was one of those Boston types, and finally one day he found out I had more ancestors than he did among the DeWolfs and the Hoppers. That did it. From then on it was just—well, I got into underwater demolition."

When Bill was manned out of the service in 1945, he solved his career problems by turning his back on acting and hiring out as a used-car salesman. Although he remained in that business for eight years, he was not suited to it. He refused to capitalize on his Hollywood connections—which was one of the reasons he had been hired. And when the situation was particularly shaky, Hedda came roaring to the rescue like the United States cavalry in an old-fashioned melodrama—offering to finance her handsome son if he wanted to purchase a dealership. He turned her down flat and returned to acting.

If Orson Welles was Louella's bête noire, Charlie Chaplin was Hedda's. Hedda attributed Chaplin's dislike for her to the breaking of the Joan Barry paternity suit. Initially her resentment probably stemmed from the fact that he ignored her, but however deeply she might oppose his liberal leanings and disapprove of his alleged predilection for teen-age girls, Hedda acknowledged his genius. Yet even after she had for all intents abandoned acting for writing, he continued to snub her, never complaining when she excluded him from her column (supposedly the worst possible punishment for a star) and never responding to either praise or criticism. It was galling.

As late as October 16, 1941, Hedda still indulged in a kind of doublethink. Commenting on *The Great Dictator,* she allowed that Chaplin was "still without peer in pantomime, satire and comedy," but added, "for unadulterated feeling, I'll take Jimmy Stewart or Judy Garland." Translate "unadulterated feeling" to "patriotic Americanism," and it becomes clear what she means.

One afternoon, while Hedda was dictating to Treva Davidson, one of her secretary-assistants (and the wife of legman Spec McClure), a highly distraught redhead appeared in the office and asked to speak to the columnist. Patsy Gaile volunteered to help, whereupon the redhead began to weep and sobbed out the information that her name was Joan Barry, that she was a protégée of Chaplin's, that he was the father of her unborn child and that he had thrown her out. Miss Gaile interrupted Hedda's dictation.

The story was repeated to the columnist, whereupon Hedda called her own physician and took the girl there for an examination. She was indeed pregnant and *had* been engaged by the comedian to play the leading role in a projected film version of *Shadow and Substance.* According to the actress a romance had ensued. It and the plans for her to play the lead in the film went sour. Around New Year's of 1943, she claimed Chaplin had caused her to be arrested on a vagrancy charge in Beverly Hills. She had been given a ninety-day suspended sentence. "Someone" had provided $100 and a tourist-class ticket to New York. Halfway across the country, she had changed her mind and returned to California.

She sought out Hedda, she said, because on her twenty-second birthday the columnist had written a piece on a tinseled package labeled "Fame" * awaiting any girl who would play the lead in the Chaplin film. The piece had ended with a warning that after a brief fling at the top almost invariably Chaplin's leading ladies had subsided into obscurity.

Hedda was outraged.

On the night that Miss Barry visited Hedda's office, she went to Chaplin's estate, and during the exchange that followed between the girl and the comedian the police were called. Miss Barry was arrested and eventually given a thirty-day jail sentence.

An agent arranged for Judge Holland to represent Miss Barry. Her release was secured, and she was transferred to a Santa Monica hospital.

After considering everything, including pressure to suppress the story, Hedda broke it. She later explained to magazine writer Collie Small that she had done it as "a warning to others involved in dubious relationships." She claimed that the impact had been so tremendous that at a cocktail party she attended, all she had to do was waggle a finger at an erring married producer across the room for him to get her message and break off an affair he knew she had discovered.

At the same time, Hedda also raised other questions in connection with Chaplin. Was, for instance, a genius entitled to special privileges? She repeated the story of his arriving in this country poor and unknown and refusing to become a citizen after America made him rich and famous. She brought up his refusal to contribute to the operation of the Motion Picture Relief Fund Home.

Hedda's disclosure of Miss Barry's sensational charges caused the fifty-four-year-old Chaplin to postpone his marriage to eighteen-year-old Oona O'Neill, which had been scheduled for June 1. When, a couple of weeks later, Chaplin gave the scoop on the wedding to Louella Parsons —even though his best man was Hearst columnist Harry Crocker—he explained the delay had been due to "un-

---

* "Strip away the phony tinsel of Hollywood," Oscar Levant once said, "and you find the real tinsel underneath."

fortunate circumstances." For those who never read the headlines, Louella explained that 'Chaplin meant the paternity suit which Joan Barry brought against him 10 days ago."

Hedda, who thought she knew something about relationships between young girls and aging roués, was further outraged by the marriage. She also interpreted the scoop to Louella as a personal affront. If Chaplin was so eager to have a second front, she'd give him one. In a series of items she slugged away day after day. She claimed that Mary Pickford had known of the wedding four days before anyone else; that Oona O'Neill Chaplin considered herself too big a name to play "second fiddle" to anyone on the screen; that a couple of renowned British actors telegraphed Chaplin a happy Father's Day message after he returned from his fourth honeymoon; that upon his first public appearance after the wedding the groom called newspaper photographers "morons"; that *Shadow and Substance* had been shelved; and that the paternity case would "provide the nation with its first Hollywood circus since the affair Flynn." *

For almost an entire month in the fall of 1943 Hedda seemed to have forgotten about Miss Barry and Chaplin, but on October 6 she crowed that on the very day Miss Barry had had her baby, Chaplin had leased space to another company at the sudio where he had made so many of his films "and, of course, many screen tests of girls he's discovered, which have never seen the light of day."

At the end of November she denied any possibility existed for an out-of-court settlement between Miss Barry and Chaplin. She also reported that he had just signed a new girl, Alice Eyeland.

Two weeks prior to the opening of the trial, Hedda announced that "a Beverly Hills scratch sheet—you scratch me, I'll scratch you—" had written of Chaplin: "There are men and women in the far corners of the world who have never heard of Jesus Christ, yet they know and love

---

* This referred to the statutory rape charges brought against Errol Flynn—who was acquitted.

Chaplin." * The same writer, Hedda said, made the accusation that "the Fascist clique is hounding Chaplin."

"Lord love us, Eddie Hoover, isn't that a new low for you and the FBI?" she added in an aside, implying that the writer had equated the Federal Bureau of Investigation with Fascists.

Louella's announcement of Oona O'Neill's pregnancy and the fact that the blood tests confirmed that Chaplin could not be the father of Miss Barry's child were ignored.

Covering the trial, Hedda gave all kinds of human sidelights, but her readers were left in the dark about the blood tests. She did, however, find room to comment on the histrionics of Chaplin's lawyer; Joan Barry's nervousness; how becoming Chaplin's white hair was; that the jury looked as if it were made up of everyone's next-door neighbors; and that Lord Beaverbrook's correspondent was writing two versions of the proceedings—one for England where Chaplin was idolized and another for Australia. Miss Barry was ultimately awarded child support.

Whether or not Chaplin actually fathered the child was beside the point for Hedda. She felt that Chaplin had used Miss Barry and cast her aside. No monetary settlement would have seemed adequate to the columnist. A publicity man who knew Hedda both professionally and socially claimed: "Hedda was like a big kid. Chaplin had slighted her. She hated his politics, disapproved of his affairs. His treatment of the Barry girl was just too much for her. Anything she could have done would have been justified as far as she was concerned. Let me put it this way. Louella took her column seriously. Hedda took herself seriously."

Hedda brushed aside the case in a 1946 story. "I suppose," she remarked, "Charlie Chaplin will be peeved at me for the rest of my life because I broke the news of his relations with Joan Barry. Joan came to my office and told me the story. I printed it. Then there was hellzapop-

* Consider the impact of publishing this statement by thinking of the uproar that followed when one of the Beatles asserted in this permissive age that they were better known than Christ.

pin. I wish somebody would remember I write stories one day and forget them the next. . . ."

That was what the lady said, but dozens of unfavorable items appeared thereafter.

In April, 1947, she reported that the Chaplins were "camping out at the Waldorf." This proved incorrect, so she retracted. "The Charlie Chaplins ain't camping out at the Waldorf—they couldn't get in. I always get a kick out of Jim Tully's line on Chaplin: 'He praises the poor in the parlors of the rich.' "

In March, 1950, she was speculating on how effective the $500,000 Chaplin was spending on public relations would be in improving his image in America. "This is one mind he won't change," she boasted.

"If Charlie Chaplin—the man who came to dinner and stayed 40 years—had known just what the Immigration Department was up to, he would never have allowed his dancing feet to wander away from our shores" was one of several entries in 1952.

Nor had she shaken the obsession in 1957, when she reported that the comedian's hatred of the United States, which had given him "fame and fortune," had gone out of bounds in *A King in New York*. "He thumbs his nose at the Statue of Liberty," Hedda wrote. "I don't believe even the English will like it, but in Russia, they will eat it up." She lamented that playwright Eugene O'Neill was not alive to write a tragedy about Chaplin's use of his son and O'Neill's grandson to put across a message of venomous hatred against the land that made a multi-millionaire." It was a subject that she thought "would bring tears from stones."

From time to time she reported that Chaplin was bored with Switzerland and was about to settle in Mexico, England or some other country. And in November, 1965, she speculated upon the possibility that *The Countess from Hong Kong* with Sophia Loren was being made as a ploy to "try to soften us up for a return ticket here. . . . I don't know about the rest of you," she wrote, "but personally I feel better when an ocean separates Charlie and the land of the free. Let's keep it that way."

Apparently even the thought that the man she had once

called a genius should have his name on the Hollywood Boulevard walk of stars represented a threat to her, for she was persistent in opposing moves to include him. Two days before entering the hospital for the last time, she told Florabel Muir during a telephone conversation: "I hear that son of a bitch Chaplin is trying to get back in this country. We've all got to work together to stop him!"

XIII

Louella, Louella, Louella
Everyone loves you. . . .

Press agents love your column
Everyone's hustling you. . . .
—HAROLD ADAMSON and
JIMMY MCHUGH

THE years of 1944–1951 were a time of public triumph
and private defeat for Louella, who fostered the illusion
that her life was a succession of glittering successes that
had turned her into a legend in her lifetime. She reinforced
this image with *The Gay Illiterate,* which was stacked high
in Hollywood bookstores weeks before Christmas, 1943.

It was a commercial success, selling approximately
150,000 copies. *Look* reported that one studio gave a copy
to all employees with instructions that they "say something nice about it" the next time they saw Louella.
Twentieth Century-Fox purchased film rights for $75,000
and assigned producer Bill Bacher and writer Eleanor
Griffin to the project—even though three Fox executives
later stated that there was never any intention of doing
the picture. The cash outlay was marked up to public
relations.

Critically, the book was treated as a literary oddity. In
The New York *Times,* Frank Nugent observed that the
book was "most revealing when she least intends it to be."
Characterizing the self-portrait Louella had drawn as "an
elfin creature . . . half child, half catamount," Nugent said
that no one so unworldly and the victim of such extraneous

forces could also be the no-holds-barred gossip writer. *Times* sardonically contended that in exposing a "small-town, intensively feminine mind," *The Gay Illiterate* was as much an American document as *The Education of Henry Adams*. *The New Republic* ponderously flayed Louella for writing a book as "undecisive," "undiscerning," and "cliché-ridden" as her column. *Newsweek*'s dismissal was flip. *Variety* enigmatically reported that the book was providing amusement for insiders who were familiar with Louella's career. The Dallas *Morning News'* reviewer criticized Louella for inaccuracy and in so doing allowed two factual errors to creep into his notice—which only goes to prove how easy this is to do.*

Ashton Stevens, the Chicago drama critic, responded with affectionate amusement. The tone of his review reflects the emotion she seems to have aroused in many co-workers, ranging from the men in the composing room (who printed a testimonial to her when she left the *Morning Telegraph* to join the New York *American*) to Ruth Waterbury, who for a time wrote Louella's radio show. Stevens called *The Gay Illiterate* "the best show in town" and composed a public love letter. "There is self-laughter in this little book that rings silver bells in every corner of my bean," he confided. "When you call yourself a sucker for flattery and declare 'I love it!,' I rock in a chair

---

* A press agent quipped that a plant in Parsons was as good as two—one when she committed the error, another when she corrected it. Sometimes the correction raised eyebrows, too. Once she announced that Judith Anderson and her husband, Luther Green, "had dated the stork." Later she revised the squib to read that it "is Judith Anderson's secretary, who has dated the stork, it appears, and not Judith."

As Louella grew older, she adopted a self-congratulatory attitude toward her errors, claiming she made more because she printed more facts. She also tended to make light of her weakness. "He makes almost as many mistakes as Parsons," she'd say.

When John Farrow pointed out that her godchild's name was Maria, not Marie (and not yet Mia), Louella apologized and said the error was a typo. Then she added an aside to the boys in the composing room, saying that this explanation didn't count. Her relaxed attitude can probably be attributed to the Chief, who, she explained, was not a man to worry about a few mistakes.

that has no rockers." The book then was Louella's *version* of her life.

Harriet, meantime, was experiencing career difficulties. William Dozier, who became executive assistant to studio head Charles Koerner shortly after Harriet was signed at RKO, summed up the credits and debits of being Louella's daughter years later when he said, *"Citizen Kane* was still going on when Harriet came to the studio. I'm sure it helped get her hired—and probably actually brought it about. But Harriet never got enough credit for her ability. She was a damned good producer. Effective. *Enchanted Cottage* was a marvelous picture. Also, *I Remember Mama* was a damned good picture. Also, *Susan Slept Here.* But she never got enough credit for the fact that they were tastefully done. I was there and worked very closely with her, and she really produced those pictures. The trouble was—people figured—oh, if she's Louella's daughter, she can't possibly be there because she has talent. But she had."

Harriet, who gained a reputation for keeping a sharp watch on budgets, was particularly ingenious in developing projects around properties already owned by the studio. Soon after she arrived, she began looking through the inventory and came up with the suggestion that Sir Arthur Wing Pinero's *The Enchanted Cottage*—with its theme of internal versus external beauty—be rewritten to make it applicable to disfigured war veterans. Harriet wrote a short outline explaining her idea, then DeWitt Bodeen developed it into a full treatment and eventually into a screenplay for which he shared credit with Herman J. Mankiewicz. Director John Cromwell was instrumental in hiring Mankiewicz, who had been experiencing problems because of his drinking and after writing the screenplay of *Citizen Kane* for Orson Welles. Since Welles and Mankiewicz had quarreled over the authorship, Louella offered no opposition.

Harriet also discovered that RKO owned a book by Kathryn Forbes called *Mama's Bank Account,* a tender, comic group of sketches about an immigrant Norwegian family's experiences in Pre-World War I San Francisco. What it lacked was a cohesive plot line. Harriet activated the project by interesting Greek actress Katina Paxinou in playing Mama. Miss Paxinou, who had scored a triumph in *For Whom the Bell Tolls,* was considered box-office bait. Bodeen was hired to do the screenplay.

Then suddenly *The Enchanted Cottage* was snatched away from Harriet and given to writer-producer Dudley Nichols, who planned to transform the disfigured, plain heroine into a prostitute to be played by—of all people—Ingrid Bergman. Louella was willing to do battle, but like Bill Hopper, Harriet resisted parental interference. To make matters worse, Mary Rodgers, daughter of the composer Richard Rodgers, happened to read *Mama's Bank Account* and recommended it to her father as a likely Broadway property. Two weeks before the picture was scheduled to go into production, Rodgers and Oscar Hammerstein II persuaded RKO to defer filming until they could present John Van Druten's dramatization of the book on stage. RKO agreed, and the play scored a smashing success with Mady Christians as Mama, Barbara Bel Geddes as the incipient writer and Marlon Brando as the oldest son.

What Louella dared not do, Hedda did. She questioned in her column what was going on at RKO when talented Harriet Parsons was given such shabby treatment. From the tone of her inquiry, it was apparent that if RKO wasn't careful, the studio would have Hedda on its back. Miraculously, *The Enchanted Cottage* was returned to Harriet. Dorothy Maguire was signed for the lead with Herbert Marshall, Robert Young and Mildred Natwick in other prominent roles. Cromwell was still to direct and Jack Gross to act as supervising producer.

Louella, who was in the East undergoing a series of medical tests, had little to say during the filming. But on February 16, 1945, she announced that she was proud of her child and agreed that Harriet deserved the rave reviews her picture was getting in trade papers.

In announcing that RKO was tapping Harriet to produce *I Remember Mama,* as Van Druten had retitled *Mama's Bank Account,* Louella confessed that she had promised Harriet not to discuss her career with RKO executives, but as a newspaperwoman she could still release items such as this because they came under the category of *news*.

The Enchanted Cottage was scheduled for a minimum of five weeks in New York, and it thrilled Louella to be able to report that in the Salt Lake City trial run it had broken every record except the one set by Bob Hope's *The Princess and the Pirate*. When the film opened at the Astor Theater in late April, Louella promptly spread the good word that there were long waiting lines for every performance.

Finally, in June, Louella reviewed the picture.* She admitted that she couldn't claim to be 100 percent impartial but rationalized that if anyone else had turned out such a moving film, she would have rushed into print urging one and all to see it. Acknowledging Harriet's warning not to go overboard, Louella said that there was enough glory for director Cromwell, writers Bodeen and Mankiewicz and stars Maguire, Marshall, Young and Natwick, but that she still felt impelled to make a deep bow "to you, Miss Parsons, from me, both as a mother and a critic."

The worry over Harriet's career had disappeared, but both Louella and her husband were in precarious health. During October and November, 1944, she left the column in the hands of her staff. Dorothy Manners, her assistant of ten years, received the by-line and was assisted by legman Neil Rau and secretaries Dorothy May and Dorothy Trelor.

Somehow word got out that Louella was undergoing a series of medical examinations, and rumors spread that she was terminally ill. But on November 29 Louella was back at her desk, pooh-poohing the report that she had one foot poised on the edge of the grave. As if to reinforce her claim, she embarked on a fifteen-minute Sunday night gossip broadcast on the Blue Network, immediately following Walter Winchell, then at the peak of his popularity.

* Hedda reviewed it in December, 1944. "Harriet Parsons' *Enchanted Cottage* is just that. It's an enchanting love story done beautifully by Dorothy Maguire and Bob Young."

Winchell had chosen Louella, having vetoed Hedda for the spot.

In the first flush of enthusiasm, Winchell facetiously suggested renaming the town Lollywood. Such flattery made Louella a fierce partisan, and she was soon reporting that when Winchell said Errol Flynn might sue a magazine for misquoting him, "a certain other radio commentator" had telephoned Flynn to ask permission to deny the statement. Flynn refused, Louella chortled, telling the certain other radio commentator that it was time she got her own stories instead of denying other people's.

Her ardor was somewhat dampened when she heard that Winchell had begun complaining about being followed by someone so inept, and she responded by saying that she wasn't crazy about his delivery either. But the two had no serious break until he broadcast one of her exclusives on his show. She had customarily held these items for the later edition of her papers, thereby protecting their exclusivity. What she had failed to take into consideration was that the three-hour time lapse between New York and California gave Winchell an opportunity to raid her column. He did, and after that, her hatchet was unsheathed. The two were locked together for six years, however, since their joint sponsor, the Jergens-Woodbury Company, was perfectly satisfied.

It is a part of the fascination of Louella that at sixty-four and in poor health, she did this weekly Jergens-Woodbury radio broadcast, turned out her column, covered hard news stories, reviewed films for *Cosmopolitan* magazine and wrote or touched up columns and stories bearing her name in *Photoplay* and *Modern Screen*. As if that weren't enough, she undertook what later became known as a "cameo" role in *Without Reservations*.

When the picture was released in May, 1946, she unselfconsciously gave it a glowing notice and awarded Mervyn LeRoy *Cosmopolitan*'s citation for the best direction of the month. At the end of the review, she added a PS that a radio columnist was played by "one Louella Parsons." This was followed by a PPS, admitting that Louella Parsons would never win a citation from *Cosmo-*

politan—or even a booby prize. It was an old game—but it suddenly seemed flatter than usual.

The reason became clear on May 16, when a news story revealed that she was "rapidly recovering" from major surgery. The operation, performed by Dr. John Jones, had taken place at the Good Samaritan Hospital. Dr. Jones, Dr. John Flick of Philadelphia and Louella's personal physician, Dr. Verne Mason, had concurred that her condition was excellent. Special prayers were being said, the story added, at the Beverly Hills Church of the Good Shepherd, of which she was a member.

Although official records are unavailable, Louella suffered from a diaphragmatic hernia. "It caused a lot of bleeding," Fieldsie Lang said. "She went East to have an operation, and this famous doctor wouldn't touch her. He said the odds against success were too great. So she came back and put up a big front. There were many times when she was not nearly as strong as she pretended to be. But she never complained. In those days, you didn't talk about things. The word 'cancer' was taboo. But you'd catch her off guard, and you knew what she was thinking."

Her fears proved unjustified, and by the time she made her first public appearance at a dinner dance given by Gene Tierney and her then-husband Oleg Cassini, she was well on the way to enjoying eating and drinking once again. The first week in September she took to the airwaves with her new radio show and shortly thereafter resumed full-scale activity. "She felt fine for many years," Fieldsie said. "But she was supposed to go in for checkups all the time. She never went. She just didn't have time. And then she had this old-fashioned way of dressing, getting up in those heavy old corsets and tying them too tight. So eventually she had trouble again."

Even without health problems, the immediate postwar years would have been difficult for Louella. Although she had long ago deserted Roosevelt's politics, she retained a genuine affection for the man, dating back to the days of Peter Brady. His death saddened her, as did the demands of labor. The violent 1945 strike against the studios by the Conference of Studio Unions* moved her even farther away from the prolabor positions she had held in the 1920's.

She had always been short-tempered. Leonard Riblett, who processed her column, claimed that a man had never had a fight with a woman until he'd tangled with Louella. "For openers," he said, "you'd pick up the phone and hear, 'You dirty son of a bitch . . .' and she'd go on from there." Stars, directors and studio heads were not exempt from her tongue-lashings. Press agents who double-planted were banished. Once when Stanley Musgrove had a hard news story that was about to break and was unable to reach her, he gave it to Hedda. The next day Louella called in a cold fury to accuse him of "burning both ends against the middle." His clients were banned until he came up with another story too tempting for her to ignore.

Her assistants, though innocent, were often hapless victims when she was outwitted by some other reporter or double-crossed by a star. Ruth Waterbury was an exception. She had been there only three days working on the new radio show when Louella lost an important news story. Storming out of her inner office, she marched over to Miss Waterbury and proceeded to berate her. In the midst of the tirade, Miss Waterbury stood up, walked to the closet, put on her coat and went home—totally ignoring Louella's response. When Louella called to apologize, Miss Waterbury made it plain that she was not prepared to serve as whipping girl for someone else's mistakes. Louella apologized and never again spoke crossly to her although on several occasions Miss Waterbury saw her flush, open her mouth and then think better of the course she was pursuing.

Almost any criticism of Hollywood brought a counterattack. On occasion, she might applaud Sam Wood for admitting that as a producer-director he was retrenching, but it made her fighting mad when a friend sent her Charlie Chaplin's article from *Reynolds News* in London

---

* A conglomerate union that attempted to represent—among others—set decorators, plumbers, cartoonists, story editors and publicists.

in which the comedian said that unless Hollywood abandoned its assembly-line mentality and began to realize that masterpieces couldn't be mass-produced like tractors, then Hollywood would die.

The old Hollywood was gone. She found it difficult to regard the newcomers as authentic—just as she felt vaguely uneasy about what was happening to her other love, newspapers. Having worked with many of the pre-World War II columnists, she had long been immune from criticism, not only in the Hearst press but also from its rivals. But the end of the war had brought a new breed of columnist, personified by John Crosby. These were young, witty, professional cynics who regarded Louella and her work as quaint. Her "exclusives" amused them as trivia. They found her halting enunciation and pronunciation on radio the epitome of amateurishness.

Louella, of course, was hurt, but not so hurt that she was incapable of putting her detractors down while simultaneously attempting to adjust her perspective. She no longer talked of pickaninnies in her column and even boldly urged that Eric Johnston ban the showing of all films in Memphis, Tennessee, so long as their local censor, Lloyd T. Binford, eliminated scenes that were moral (she favored cutting immorality) simply because they showed Negroes. If Johnston followed her advice, she predicted, Memphis movie fans would make short work of the bigoted Binford.

She also swung with the crowd in taking up the cry against Communist infiltration in Hollywood (although Hedda got there first), bragging that her initial radio editorial on the subject, urging actors to refuse to utter subtly subversive ideas, had brought unprecedented response. This aspect of her writing was totally unpredictable. At various periods she'd become temporarily exercised over Red writers, directors and actors, but clearly her heart was not in politics. After a strong opening statement on the dangers of the "Red Tide," she'd suddenly shift gears and caution that care must be taken that good Americans were not falsely accused.

John Garfield, for instance, was defended on the grounds that Louella felt he had "done so much for the underdog" that he was being wrongly branded left-wing. "I'd stake anything I own that Communist ideologies attributed to John are as repugnant to him as they are to me." When his associations became public, she denounced him. But a few months later she began touting his work in *Body and Soul* as of Oscar quality. Garfield, who had "been on the wrong side politically for some time," had told her he'd given up all politics.

Like many of Chaplin's friends, Louella tended to dismiss his liberal views as muddy thinking, but when she learned that he had involved himself in the Peace Congress, she was astounded that he'd have the nerve to announce plans for a new film. She assured him Americans would never pay to see it. Ten months later she changed her mind. While she was dining with Mr. and Mrs. Samuel Goldwyn at the Pavillon in New York, Chaplin dropped by their table, and Louella found him more like himself than he'd been in years. She was certain he'd got those leftist ideas out of his system.

This is not to imply that Louella was "soft on Communism"—far from it. She never questioned the fact that the Communist Party had not been legally banned, nor did she disapprove of the techniques employed by the House Un-American Activities Committee. In fact, she herself indulged in guilt by association to harry a national magazine's bureau chief whom she blamed for an unfriendly story about her. Why, she demanded, hadn't he long ago fired an employee who turned out to be a liaison agent for the Communists? She was proud, too, that her name was banned in the Soviet press as an agitator. Louella's problem was that she found it inconceivable that people she knew and liked—John Garfield and Larry Parks, for instance—could embrace an ideology the Chief had spent years exposing.

Amid all these unsettling factors there was one area of her life that provided solace—Catholicism. When the world became too much for her, she retreated to a convenient church and lost herself in prayer. And whenever she traveled, it was now always a meeting with Francis Cardinal Spellman or some other Catholic luminary that represented the high point of her trip. Interviewed after a two-month European vacation in 1948, Louella said the best part had been a private audience for her and Dr. Martin with Pope Pius XII, who had spoken highly of William Randolph Hearst and had complimented the publisher on his unrelenting fights against Communism.

Louella herself once said that no book about her would be complete without Hearst, who provided opportunities, seldom questioned her judgments and always forgave her mistakes. Early in their relationship, Hearst had autographed a picture of himself "To Louella, the only Louella, the best Louella, from her admirer. . . ." After years in his employment, she received a photo of him standing in front of the White House. It was inscribed: "The happy smile is always worn after reading your column." Shortly before his death, he probably gave his most spontaneous summation of Louella in response to Bebe Daniels' question of whether he recalled the time Louella had appeared with her riding pants on backward. "Why shouldn't she put her pants on backward?" he asked. "Louella never did anything like anybody else."

Louella repaid his faith with self-serving and genuine adoration as she proved by her behavior after he had picked up the tab for a testimonal dinner honoring her thirty-five years in the newspaper business—twenty-seven of them in his service. Although he was too old and enfeebled to attend, 800 other notable Parsons partisans crowded into the Cocoanut Grove. Among them was his beloved Marion Davies, whose unsteady progress to her table in the center of the room was quickly noted by gossips. It soon became apparent that she was in an obstreperous mood. Louella's arrival to the accompaniment of "Lovely to Look At" seemed to strike Miss Davies as hilarious. But her mood changed when waiters wheeled in a six-foot-high anniversary cake in the shape of a motion-picture camera and guests joined in singing the special lyrics of the Harold Adamson and Jimmy McHugh song:

Louella, Louella, Louella
Everyone loves you. . . .

Press agents live for your column
Everyone's hustling you . . .

During the singing, Miss Davies turned her back on the dais with its luminaries ranging from Governor of California Earl Warren to Louis B. Mayer. Louella found her old friend's conduct alarming. As Dwight Whitney reported in *Time*: "Louella had a hard time trying to smile and watch Marion Davies at the same time. Finally, she dispatched a photographer to confer with Marion. He did and Marion threw Louella a wave and a rowdy greeting."

Printed accounts quoted her as saying, "Hello, you old bag, you!" but a guest recalled it as "Hello, Louella, you old shit!" Her impatience seemed to increase as Louella modestly accepted the tributes of a parade of celebrated admirers. After listening to Bob Hope ("You turn the whole nation into a sewing circle without too much needle"), Darryl Zanuck ("Louella, whether or not you can spell names correctly is unimportant. You have a heart as big as the church itself"), and Dr. Martin's ("I don't think there's any doubt who is the forgotten man of 1948"), Miss Davies was heard to grouse that *she* had been in Hearst's service longer than twenty-seven years, but nobody had offered her any testimonial dinners. Finally, in the midst of Jack Benny's speech, she collapsed and was helped or carried (again sources differ) out.

Early the next morning Louella placed a telephone call to publisher Henry Luce, whose publications *Time* and *Life* were anti-Hearst in tone. When she learned that he was out of the country, she put in a call to Clara Boothe Luce. "I'm not asking Mr. Luce to be kind to me," she is reputed to have said, "only to Marion because Mr. Hearst is old and sick." How Mrs. Luce responded is unknown, but in *Time*'s story Marion Davies got off lightly—which was what Louella wanted for the man who presented her (by way of his son David) with a gold engraved letter, complimenting her upon her "courage, accuracy, fairness and curiosity."

The testimonial dinner had presented a minor tactical problem for public relations people—how to kowtow to Louella without offending Hedda, but it was simple compared to the potentially explosive situation created by their reconciliation. After a decade of infighting, the two women appeared together at Romanoff's for lunch thirteen days after the testimonial dinner. Press agents, who had been playing one off against the other for years, shuddered. The restaurant—and then the movie industry—buzzed. As Hedda had told Louella earlier, "Darling, if you and I ever compare notes, we'll rock this town on its heels." Witnessing the actual reaction, she said to Louella, "Doesn't this prove to you what a lot of shits there are in this town?"

The resumption of friendship had come about in a logical but unexpected way. A few days earlier Louella had attended a preview of *I Remember Mama* and spotted Hedda. "I expect Harriet's picture will be very good, but I know one person who won't give it a good review," Louella bitterly told a friend. When Hedda's notice appeared in the New York *Daily News*, Harriet, who was in that city preparing for *Mama's* opening, read it and called to ask her mother whether she'd seen it. Louella reminded her she never read Hedda. But Harriet insisted, reportedly saying that Hedda had done for her what nobody else would. After reading the review in which Hedda had symbolically thrown all her hats in the air, Louella called to thank her and the luncheon was arranged.

The tenor of the proceedings was distinctly girlish with the two columnists agreeing to share Charles MacArthur's news that Alida Valli had been cast in *Trilby*—even comparing deadlines. Later Louella made a remark that Hedda pretended to take exception to and warned, "One more crack like that, and I'll slug you," to which Louella replied, "That's all right, dear. As long as you let me have an exclusive on the story." Who, Hedda wanted to know, said Louella had no sense of humor?

Their reconciliation was as widely publicized as their feud had been, causing Harriet to wire Hedda (in a faintly familiar style): YOU AND MA WOULD MANAGE TO TOP ME STOP YOUR HISTORIC LUNCH HAS NOW CROWDED I RE-

MEMBER MAMA OFF THE FRONT PAGE STOP YOU GALS
MIGHT HAVE WAITED FOR BABY

For a brief time friendly relations prevailed, but in 1949 two major stories reactivated the old rivalry. In Louella's heyday, the triumph of romantic love over seemingly insurmountable odds was a favorite film theme. It so inspired her, in fact, that she attempted to construct her life according to its conventions. In their separate ways, the seemingly disparate romantic situations in which Rita Hayworth and Ingrid Bergman found themselves enmeshed fit this pattern and consequently stirred Louella to outdo herself. From the beginning, Louella ignored condemnations heaped upon Miss Hayworth and Aly Khan, the older son of the spiritual leader of the Ismaili Moslems, for traveling the world together. In Louella's view, Cinderella had finally met Prince Charming. Louella had first encountered Rita when she was Marguerita Cansino, a Spanish dancer in nightclubs; later Louella had known Rita as the chattel of automobile dealer Ed Judson, still later as the puppet of Orson Welles and most recently as America's "Love Goddess"—so what could be more natural than that she should be the only reporter invited to the wedding? What if Elsa Maxwell had introduced them?

Hedda scoffed at the idea, saying she had it on good authority that Aly Khan wanted no press coverage. To thwart those angling for invitations, he had scheduled the wedding at his chateau, L'Horizon. Furthermore, Helen Morgan, Rita's press agent, had assured her no reporter would be present.

Dorothy Manners, who was substituting for Louella, offered to bet anyone that her boss would be there with Rita's agent, Johnny Hyde. She confessed that she had been eavesdropping on an extension when the invitation had been extended. Hedda said Louella wouldn't get within a mile of the ceremony.

Louella did manage to wangle a luncheon invitation, following a series of telephone calls to Miss Hayworth from Los Angeles, New York and Paris. She bought an antique handkerchief that had once belonged to Marie Antoinette for the bride to carry at her wedding and took it along to lunch, where she made it clear she expected an invitation.

Miss Hayworth nervously picked at her food which Louella attributed to premarital jitters. Others said it was because she was faced with her future husband's ire if she capitulated to the columnist's siege and with Louella's vindictiveness if she didn't. In the end, Louella emerged clutching one of the prized pink disks—identifying invited guests—in her plump pink little hand. Gendarmes, she said, would be on hand to control press people and other would-be gate-crashers.

All her maneuvering suddenly became meaningless when the French Justice Ministry ruled that the wedding must take place in public. Mayor Paul Derigon ordered the ceremony held in his office. Louella's explanation was that the Communist mayor and Communist newspapers were opposed to allowing rich capitalists special privileges.* The truth was that among the scores of angry newspapermen assigned to the story was a canny Frenchman who cited an almost forgotten law forbidding private weddings if any citizen objected. He objected, and Louella's exclusive became public property.

An estimated crowd of 10,000 curious spectators converged in the area surrounding the mayor's office on the day of the wedding. Since Louella had been one of the last to learn of the change, the switch tested her ingenuity.

As she later explained, she gave up her seat with the family and close friends† and sat at the back of the room so that as soon as the ceremony was concluded she could reach the only phone in the building. When the time came, she leaped up, fell, skinned her knees, arose and sprinted to the phone, which she presumably had reserved. When

---

* For an amusing account of Louella's "lyrical, sociological and political dispatches"—sometimes three a day ("prose was evidently running off her typewriter now like sweat off a baseball player"), see A. J. Liebling's "Right Up Louella's Ali," *The New Yorker,* June 11, 1949.

† This was unusual. As queen of the Hollywood press corps, she seldom relinquished royal prerogatives. For instance, when visiting poet Robert Frost was honored at a reception, Louella joined him in the receiving line.

she first approached Derigon about the reservation, she claimed he pretended not to understand either her English or her attempts at French. Undaunted, Louella knew another language. "The more franc notes I pulled out of my purse, the better he understood me," she observed. As a result, her by-lined story was on newsstands in the United States two hours before anyone else's.

In January, 1949, Louella ran a seemingly innocuous item that Ingrid Bergman was going to devote an entire weekend to playing hostess to Roberto Rossellini and that they might make a picture together. At that time Louella could not remotely have imagined that before the end of the year she would be caught in the crossfire of abuse aimed at a screen saint turned sinner. Nor could she have believed that in revealing the facts of the Bergman-Rossellini case, she would—involuntarily—become a pioneer in the new candor.

Soon after Miss Bergman began filming *Stromboli,* on the island of the same name, there were rumors of a romance—denied—and an impending divorce—denied, then confirmed. The general public's response was almost a sense of personal betrayal. Having accepted the virginal image of the actress, a surprising number of otherwise intelligent men and women were outraged. In the industry the shock came not because she had had an affair, but because she had flaunted it. There was speculation that she was pregnant. Such things had happened before, but the principals involved had gone to great lengths to hush up the facts for what was thought to be the good of Hollywood.

Hedda flew to Italy in August to find out what was transpiring. After a pleasant interview in which Miss Bergman seemed willing to discuss her problems candidly, Hedda asked if she was pregnant. The actress laughed. "Oh, my goodness, Hedda. Do I look it?" Hedda accepted this evasion as a denial and filed a story saying that Miss Bergman was not pregnant and would sue Italian papers for spreading this falsehood. Imagine her outrage then, when six months later, over Louella's by-line, Hedda read:

INGRID BERGMAN BABY DUE
IN THREE MONTHS AT ROME

A mysterious message delivered just as Louella was beginning her radio program put her in contact with her informant. When she asked why he hadn't contacted her before the broadcast, he said the story was too important to fritter away on radio. Louella always refused to divulge his identity, describing him only as "a man of great importance, not only in Hollywood, but throughout the United States . . . who had connections in many other parts of the world—including Italy."

Speculation on her source centered upon Howard Hughes, as Louella may have intended. Hedda, however, was convinced that it was public relations man Joseph Henry Steel, who was employed by both Miss Bergman and Hughes. Two newsmen familiar with the background of the story recently suggested that Hearst, who naturally preferred newspapers to radio, gave the news to Louella. They believe that WRH's Rome correspondent, Mike Chinigo, obtained the story, forwarded it to Hearst and that Hearst gave it to his star entertainment reporter.

Whoever provided the information placed Louella in a position that temporarily made her almost as controversial as Miss Bergman. Even though Louella realized that if she was proved wrong she would be liable for damages, she was unshaken. "You see, when she went on a story, she was really a bird dog," Ruth Waterbury said. "I mean she turned into the damnedest beagle. It didn't make any difference. She was on a scent, and she was going to hold on. You know everybody hit her with everything. Other papers denied it. They made fun of her, and she never deviated so much as a hair. She said, 'I know my source on this, and I've got it.' The point is Louella did not back down on a single thing."

Dr. Martin appears to have been less certain. In *Tell It to Louella,* she paints a bemusing domestic scene as she tells of entering her husband's bedroom and finding him devoutly bent over his beads. Hearing her enter, he looked up and explained, "I'm saying my beads and praying your story is right." * Louella admitted that she too prayed that her story was correct—and that Ingrid would find happiness. Not only did it prove true, but Hedda later acknowledged she had been left with egg on her face. After losing ground consistently to Hedda, Louella in 1949 had staged a strong comeback.

The triumph was marred by the fact that the two most important males in Louella's life were ill. Hearst was suffering the complications of advanced age, but Dr. Martin's problems were more specific. "Docky never really had been well after he came back from Australia. He put out he'd contacted some rare tropical disease in the service, but he knew what really was wrong. He didn't tell Louella —I think it was out of kindness. He didn't want to worry her. But when I had a lung operation [1947], he arranged it. After I got home, he secretly told me he had leukemia. He went all over—Johns Hopkins, the Mayos—more as a guinea pig than in hopes of being cured," Fieldsie Lang recalled.

By 1950 it was clear that he was seriously ill, and 1951 marked the end of an era. In January Dr. Martin checked in and out of the Mayo Clinic, and on April 15 he entered Cedars of Lebanon Hospital in Los Angeles. Death came on June 24. Less than two months later, on August 14, William Randolph Hearst also died.

Louella, seventy years old but indestructible, was back at work within two weeks. Although shattered by her double loss, Louella concentrated on the main chance. Following Hearst's death, the submerged hostility between his family and his mistress surfaced. His body was removed from Miss Davies' home without her seeing him. (Having attempted to drown her grief in alcohol, Miss Davies became hysterical and had been put under sedatives by the attending physician shortly before her lover's death.)

Faced with the choice of going to Miss Davies as other

* Louella said that for the only time in her career WRH asked whether she was sure of her source. If he supplied the tip, this may be another example of his elephantine humor—similar to the note he sent to Louella prior to her wedding inquiring why she never got after Marion Davies for remaining single.

friends, including Hedda, did or going directly to San Francisco to attend the funeral, Louella, who was in New York resting when her employer died, never hesitated. She went where she belonged—with the family.

XIV

To make these female gossip columnists happy,
you've got to wear a suit made out of the stars
and stripes; hang a placard around your neck,
saying, "I love Hollywood"; take them out to
dinner; buy them roses; wipe the dust off their
shoes and declare "I love you! I love you all!"
—PETER SELLERS
to Hank Grant in the *Hollywood Reporter*

IN HER sixties, Hedda combined the elegance of a 1929
Rolls-Royce with the sportiness of a Thunderbird. She
maintained that appearance was the first line of attack.
Attack before you're attacked professionally or personally.
When Bill was cast in a film with Walter Brennan, he told
his mother of his good luck. "I was excited," he recalled.
"I'd never met Walter. And all Hedda said was that I was
dead. I wanted to know what she meant, and she said,
'He's a scene stealer.' I told her she was out of her skull.
You work with somebody much better than you, and they
pull you up. There isn't any such thing as a scene stealer
unless he's working with another one. So this first scene
I had with Walter was a fifty-fifty, a two shot. We did it,
and Walter said, 'Bill, don't look at me with both eyes.
Look at me with one or you won't get your kisser in the
camera.' My God. I'd never thought of that and said so.
'Neither did I until somebody told me,' Walter said.

"I told Hedda the story and reminded her of playing in
Midnight with Claudette Colbert and John Barrymore.
Jack and Claudette both knew how to take a scene when
they wanted to. After three weeks she called a truce,
telling Jack, 'I won't if you won't.' He agreed, and that

270

ended it. But Hedda was always saying they're dead or you're dead. Because it was her idea that everybody in a picture was fighting everybody else. You couldn't convince her otherwise."

This attitude was both Hedda's strength and her weakness. It made it possible for her to persevere in the face of seemingly impossible odds, to achieve material success and an amount of power. It also prevented her from obtaining what she longed for—artistic fulfillment.

Preoccupied with externals, Hedda progressed only slightly beyond the lesson she had learned by investing in expensive gowns for *Virtuous Wives*. Even so, King Kennedy said, "Hedda dressed for Hedda. Clothes had no date on her. She gave a beautiful party for Tallulah Bankhead once. Bea Lillie and Ethel Barrymore, among others, were there. Everyone raved about the hostess gown Hedda was wearing. One of those trailing things. Well, the next day she told me Adrian had designed it for her to wear in an MGM picture twenty years before.

"She loved Adrian, and she was crazy about Mainbocher. She had a real clothes sense. She needed no one to style things for her. I've seen her in the office looking like the Prisoner of Zenda. Somebody would be coming in to say hello. She'd go to the washroom, comb her hair, grab one of her hats out of a box and put it on. She'd sit behind the desk, creating a picture that left her visitor enthralled."

Each year Hedda bought approximately 150 hats. Her favorites came from Lily Daché, Sally Victor and Rex, but she also wore novelties created by fans. There was a fake hand with painted red nails, a miniature Eiffel Tower and a lobster shell creation. She'd wear anything—anything except one modeled upon a miniature Japanese bedpan which had been sent her by a not-so-proper Bostonian. So famous did her headgear become that the Internal Revenue Service allowed her an annual $5,000 deduction as a business expense.

The wardrobe was ornamentation, but Hedda was equally concerned with the foundation beneath the façade and waged a well-planned campaign to retain a healthy, youthful vitality, regarding it as part of the equipment of a public personality. Under the guidance of Dr. William Branch, Hedda was a guinea pig in glandular therapy. "That meant taking hormones by mouth," Dr. Branch said. "At the time there was talk that this practice caused breast cancer. But finally the American Medical Association came to the opposite conclusion. But I maintain that much of Hedda's energy came from the therapeutic action of the drug. The keenness of her mind—the timbre of her voice—the quality of her complexion. There's much medical evidence to back it up now, but when she began, there was a lot of speculation on the danger. She helped debunk it. She was a tough-minded gal when you knew her well."

In addition to Dr. Branch, Hedda collected a long list of other doctors. "Maybe sixteen or eighteen names," said Molly Merrick, an ex-columnist who went to work for Twentieth Century-Fox and became one of Hedda's most intimate friends. "Patsy Gaile used to say she thought when Hedda wanted medical attention, she must have stuck a hatpin in the list and said, 'I'll try him this time.' Periodically, she went on the Bieler diet. I think she had as much faith in Dr. Henry Bieler as any of her doctors. He took care of her for a long time. She used to drink some dreadful mineral soup made out of squashes and beans and I don't know what all that he had her fix in a blender. When she had a cold, that would stop it. I hand it to him. It looked horrible, but it did work. I used to tell her: 'I'm only jealous of one thing. Your health.' She just had amazing vitality and endurance.

"But she had no idea of medicine. Once she told me she had this pain in her head. She said it was quite bad. I finally got her to go to some German doctor. He must have been a very wise, poised man, because he looked at her head, felt it and asked how often the pain came. Was it there all the time?

"She had taken off her hat and thrown it on his desk. 'I think it's cancer,' she said. 'I'm all prepared to face it.' He looked at her hat and saw this great pin and the hole where she put it, keeping it in the same place so as not to mark the material. He said, 'Do you always use that hatpin?'

"'Oh, yes, that's what holds my hats on, goes right

through the thick part of my hair.' Well, the hatpin was pressing on a nerve, and it hurt. That was the cancer."

In later years, at the suggestion of Bernard Baruch, Hedda also visited the Niehans clinic in Switzerland, where shots distilled from the embryos of unborn animals revitalized such public figures as Somerset Maugham and Pope Pius.

On a less dramatic plane, at sixty-two Hedda's exercise program included daily bending and lifting activities, including 100 scissors to retain her shapely legs. "Appearance was a part of her profession, but personally she was also utterly feminine in her little vanities," her friend Gypsy Rose Lee said. "In later years, we used to appear on TV game shows and Hedda would always tape two in one evening. They paid five hundred dollars each and her reason for it . . . well, I'll explain that later. I'd be in the makeup department and Hedda would appear, her hair done, her makeup on, her hat, her dress—looking absolutely beautiful, very soignée. And I'd say, 'My God, Hedda, you put on the most wonderful makeup.' And she'd say, 'Well, honey, if you'd been putting it on as many years as I have, you could put on good makeup too!' That was the feminine part. The reason she did two shows in the same evening was that she'd hire this makeup man, who charged her a hundred dollars. He put it on with all those hooks and strings under the hair and hat. But she wouldn't admit it.

"She'd talk to me and say, 'Gypsy, I'd love to get my face lifted. I'm scared to death.' And mean it. She was afraid of the pain. She was afraid of the anesthetic. She was afraid of what it would do to her. She was afraid that maybe she wouldn't like the looks, that she might look pulled. Or that it might interfere with her personality, with her projection. And I tried to reassure her that none of those things would happen, that she could just have a very loose lift, an easy little tuck-up like I'd had several times. That was the time to tell me about the television makeup man, but she wouldn't say it. You know she kept her secrets well, and this was her little female secret."

Exuding vitality to the end of her life, Hedda counseled youngsters to accept every party invitation—even if they stayed only five minutes. Who, she asked, knew what opportunities awaited? One type of opportunity Hedda resolutely rejected was romance. One evening at Ciro's when magazine writer Kyle Crichton pinched her leg, Hedda yelled loud and long. In 1947 when she grew friendly with William O'Dwyer, mayor of New York, Walter Winchell wrote that she was engaged. She denied this and also rumors about her involvement with Bernard Baruch, but in conversation with Olivia De Havilland she counseled: "Well, dear, if you're going to marry, do it quickly. Because the longer you're single, the more self-sufficient you become and the less need there is to marry."

As an actress, Hedda had bathed in the love that flooded across the footlights and, after she entered films, the affection she received during public appearances. Now, as a columnist, she found a substitute in recognition. If there was no deep involvement, she wanted none. For the moment, she was busy enjoying fame.

It was essential to her life plan to be friendly with the rich and powerful, but she also struck up easy camaraderie with sales people, quickly learning their names and their problems for future reference. Once while she was riding an elevator with Molly Merrick, a solid-looking gentleman stepped into the car, spotted Hedda and said he hadn't seen her for ages. "It has been ages, hasn't it?" Hedda agreed. "You look wonderful. How's your wife? Bring her to cocktails someday." In the parking lot, Hedda inquired whether Miss Merrick had recognized the man. Miss Merrick said she had thought he and Hedda were old friends. "I've undoubtedly met him," Hedda said. "But I don't remember it."

"But you mentioned his wife."

"Oh, I'm sure he's married," Hedda said. "He looked so married. And the invitation will brighten their day."

Hedda found it easy to brighten days of superficial acquaintances. A minister's wife from a small Illinois town to whom everyone brought their troubles felt she had no one to whom she could turn. So she sat down and poured out her troubles to Hedda, adding she didn't expect an answer to her letter. Hedda wrote back to say she thought she could understand, adding that she had once sung in a choir. "I'm enclosing something for you and the only provision I make is that you spend it for something you never expected to have and that you spend it on yourself." She enclosed a check for $50.

Occasionally, she would strike up an extended correspondence with a stranger. Once she received a note from a former organist in a silent movie theater who'd become a reporter on a small California newspaper. Perhaps it reminded Hedda how fortunate she had been, for she wrote the woman regularly and at Christmas always sent a $100 check.

As the recipient of lavish Christmas gifts, Hedda was alert to studio workers who seemed unlikely to receive any gifts and sent some of her presents to them—including champagne and caviar to the oldest script girl in the business. These "weaknesses" were fiercely concealed.

In 1950, for instance, she sponsored a young Japanese who came to the United States to study business administration at Santa Monica City College. When talent agent Abner Greshler was in Tokyo during the early 1960's the student, now advertising director of Sanyo Electric, Inc., said, "I am Tanemichi Sohma. I delivered a package to your house on Barrington Avenue in Los Angeles for Hedda Hopper."

"When I spoke to her about it, she was uncomfortable. She hated talking about her kindnesses," Greshler said.

Finally, in 1964, after Sohma had become manager of the New York office of Sanyo Electric, Hedda, who was visiting Manhattan, wrote half a column, recalling that everyone except her eighty-year-old, highly prejudiced cook, Maude Hadley, had liked Sohma. Miss Hadley refused to accept the truce with Japan and carried her prejudice so far that Sohma had to complain that he wasn't getting enough to eat. Eventually, though, he won Miss Hadley over by pointing out, when she was rushing out the door to catch a bus, that she had forgotten to don a skirt.*

* Miss Hadley was also terrified of blacks. When baseball hero Jackie Robinson was in Hollywood in connection with the film based on his life, Hedda arranged to interview him at her home.

"You'll find lots of friends of Lolly's," Frances Marion said. "Not so many of Hedda's. Most people hate to hear the truth and Hedda told it." Patsy Gaile put it another way. "I know damn well you'll get plenty of bitchiness," she said. "People remember that. And I can tell you some, too, but there was a softer side." This hidden side earned her the complete loyalty of her staff and a small band of staunch defenders. "Suzie and I used to say that she was like the little girl with the curl," Patsy said. "When she was good, she was very, very good and when she was bad—well!"

Hedda's interests were catholic. A friend of Louella's, who was not fond of Hedda, put it this way. One evening Louella and this woman dined at LaRue. The maître d' and the waiters outdid themselves catering to the columnist's whims. When Louella's companion ordered Strawberries Romanoff for dessert, Louella gasped. After the waiter left, Louella whispered that it was LaRue, not Romanoff's. "Well, that was the difference," Louella's friend said. "Hedda moved in the great world. She'd have known Strawberries Romanoff were a delicacy of the royal family—not Mike Romanoff's house specialty."

Hedda retained a genuine love of theater and kept up with its development. She was highly enthusiastic about George Kelly, one of America's most underrated playwrights and the uncle of Grace Kelly. She preferred Philip Barry, Noel Coward and Somerset Maugham to Eugene O'Neill, Elmer Rice and Robert Sherwood. She responded to Tennessee Williams of *The Glass Menagerie* but deplored his powerful *A Streetcar Named Desire*. She objected to Arthur Miller's plays on political grounds.

On the way, Spec McClure, aware of her use of weighted colloquialisms, warned her to be careful with Robinson. Hedda gave McClure to understand that she knew how to behave. She must, however, have had her doubts about Miss Hadley, because when she entered the house, she stuck her head into the kitchen and called, "Maude, if you see a nigger around the house, don't be scared. It's only Jackie Robinson." A moment later she entered the library and found herself face to face with the great athlete, who had arrived early.

Aware of her limited education, she read omnivorously —newspapers, magazines, fiction and nonfiction. Once, Spec McClure lent her Thomas Wolfe's *Look Homeward, Angel*. She took it home and the following morning arrived at the office late and bleary-eyed. Slamming the gigantic novel down on McClure's desk, she growled, "Listen, you S.O.B., don't ever do that to me again. I was up all night. I couldn't put the damned thing down!"

Her greatest enthusiasm was reserved for opera. She was thrilled by its music, pageantry, color and the attendant social activities. For years, she dropped everything to fly to San Francisco for the opening of the season— which she publicized generously—and to mingle with old San Francisco society. When she became securely established, she traveled to New York to attend the opening of the Metropolitan—and reprimanded Southern Californians for their failure to provide a suitable house for the San Francisco Opera Company's annual engagement.

Whatever she became to others, to actors Hedda was one of them. Louella, on the other hand, for all her long association with films, remained a "civilian." Gypsy Rose Lee, for example, remained a stripteaser to Louella. Hedda emphathized with Miss Lee, the writer and ex-ecdysiast.

"We became friends in 1946," Gypsy said. "When my son, Eric, was born, the first telegram and the first telephone call I received in the hospital were from Hedda. She was the very first to wish me well. She sensed—sensed, hell, she knew that anyone who had been out of show business for as many months as you have to be to have a baby needed a word of reassurance. She also knew what a kind word in a popular column meant to a performer. And each time when it seemed I needed a professional boost, she was there.

"She was the kind of friend who didn't call to ask whether she could drop in—she just appeared to see what I was up to," Gypsy said. "She lived near Lucy Ball, and on Sunday mornings she'd go right up to Lucy's bedroom whether Desi was there or not. She loved my jelly-making bouts. She loved it when my birds were hatching baby birds. And she loved to have slips of plants taken from

my garden for her garden. Little cuttings. I think it reminded her of Pennsylvania.

"I had two little paintings that Fanny Brice had done.
I'd had them framed, and she commented on them several
times. One Christmas I gave them to her. I'd also made
her some jelly. Eric had made her a silver key ring, and
I'd dried some rose petals for her linen closet. Well, she
thanked me profusely for the jelly and the rose petals and
the key ring—and didn't mention Fanny's pictures. Because the thing she really loved the most was the thought
that I would dry rose petals from my garden and em-
broider them into this little bag for her. That she appreciated and liked more than something of value.

"Her home was very comfortable," Gypsy reminisced.
"It was such a good house for entertaining, and the parties
were wonderful. Gee, they were fun. Because they were
all such a part of her. She put you at the right table. When
she'd have people out in the garden for instance, she would
make certain that pretty young girls were with the men
who appreciated young pretty girls. And the witty women
were with men who were interested in that sort of thing.
And yet she managed to introduce you to everyone at her
parties. And she wasn't the kind of hostess who was absent
all the time. When you needed her for an opinion or a
question, she was there. I miss her parties. Not for the
sake of it being a party, but just because it was a wonderful way of observing Hedda.

"She could be a wonderful friend and a bitter enemy,"
Gypsy said. "I know of some people who had trouble
with her and she was a relentless, unforgiving enemy."

The truth is that Hedda enjoyed a good fight. Over the
years, in addition to Louella and Chaplin, she ran countless unflattering items on Mary Pickford, Deanna Durbin,
Joan Bennett, Joan Crawford, Joan Fontaine, Rex Harri-
san and, as time passed, James and Pamela Mason, Marlon
Brando, Elvis Presley, Elsa Maxwell and Edith Head, to
name a few.

The problem with Miss Pickford grew out of a misin-
terpretation of an item regarding the star's niece Gwynn.
There were several harsh exchanges. When Hedda en-

countered "America's Sweetheart" at a party, Hedda greeted the star: "Good afternoon, Miss Snot." Miss Pickford didn't reply, but the following Christmas she sent Hedda a Pickfair card. Inside was her ambiguously worded greeting:: "Merry Christmas, Miss Snot."

Hedda's problems with Deanna Durbin began in 1948, when both the actress and Universal Pictures were infuriated by an item: "Oh, Deanna! In regard to Deanna Durbin in *Lady on a Train*. Was this trip necessary?" Hedda could have explained that it was legman King Kennedy's line, but she chose to fight instead.

Annoyed with costume designer Edith Head, she referred to her as "Travis Banton's sketch artist"—after Miss Head had won an Academy Award.

Initially, Hedda admired Joan, the youngest of the battling Bennett family. When Hedda and Joan appeared in *Vogues of 1938,* Hedda played Miss Bennett's mother. Feeling unwell one day, she asked to be allowed to do her close-up early so that she could go home. The request was refused. After finishing the scene, Hedda fainted in her dressing room and left the studio weak and shaken. She seethed and sniped away over the years. Finally, when Miss Bennett played Elizabeth Taylor's mother in *Father of the Bride,* Hedda gloated in print that perhaps now the mighty Miss B might discover how it felt to have to wait until the end of the day to do a close-up.

Miss Bennett took revenge in 1950 by sending Hedda a $435 valentine. The $35 went for a skunk which carried a note: "Won't you be my valentine? Nobody else will. I stink, but then so do you." The $400 went for advertisements in *Variety* and the *Hollywood Reporter,* reprinting Hedda's item from the January 5, 1950, column: "Far cry. Joan Fontaine's press agent is working overtime again. Says she's wanted for the Queen Victoria role in *The Mudlark.* She thought she was a dancing queen at Katie and Harry Goetz's when she put on a solo dance atop the thickest carpet I've ever trod on. Exhibitionism, I calls it."

Beside that observation, Miss Bennett ran Hearst columnist Harry Crocker's reply: "Crockery. Hollywood is smiling tolerantly at the inane attack in print by a certain female upon a younger star for her gay New Year's Eve dance. Hollywood realizes that this and similar ridiculous outbreaks are the result of years of frustration as an actress. Small wonder she is seen in fewer and fewer homes. Too frequent are her breaches of manners against fellow guests who are unable to reply in kind. Ah, well, it just means more rides alone on her broomstick for the woman with the conical hat to fit her conical head."

Miss Bennett added: "This couldn't be you, could it, Hedda?"

On February 16, Hedda replied: "Everyone is asking if I received a SKUNK as a valentine present from Joan Bennett. Yes, I did. And it's the cutest thing! It had been prepared for domestication, rather than for the wild fury that prompted the gift. It was a good publicity skunk, and beautifully behaved. I christened it Joan. I was flooded with telephone calls asking for the pet. But the James Masons got their bid in first. They had been looking for one for six months as a companion to their nine cats. Seems there is a great affinity between cats and skunks."

When *Time* magazine asked Joan Bennett why she had sent the animal, the actress said she'd had enough of Hedda's lip. Hedda pretended she was delighted with the gift, but gave Miss B an additional dig when she added that she hadn't thought the Wangers (Walter Wanger was Miss B's current husband) could afford the ads.

The feud with Joan Fontaine arose in the wake of a close friendship. The friendship had begun when Miss Fontaine was contemplating marriage to the aging actor Conrad Nagel and Hedda warned: "Take a good look at me. . . . I married a man five years older than my father. We had a wonderful son and I've worked every day since —without a husband." For whatever reason, Miss Fontaine decided not to marry Nagel, married a divorced actor Brian Aherne, married and divorced producer William Dozier—all the time remaining on a friendly basis with Hedda. Then in August, 1949, the two women met on a Constellation headed for Europe. Miss Fontaine was going to Rome to make *September*. Hedda was headed for Paris. Impulsively, Miss Fontaine invited her to Rome, and

Hedda accepted. Meanwhile, the younger woman met photographer "Slim" Aarons, and a hectic romance developed. Hedda was ignored—and she neither forgot nor forgave.

Rex Harrison outraged both Hedda and Louella when he and wife Lilli Palmer attacked Hollywood after the columnists felt Harrison had been protected against a scandal following the suicide of Carole Landis. Hedda lambasted him on that point and thereafter sarcastically referred to him as "Sexy Rexy"—even when she had nothing more than a bit of casting news about him.

Outrage at the sexual deportment of Rita Hayworth and Aly Khan, Frank Sinatra and Ava Gardner, Elvis Presley and others started her harassing them.

Elsa Maxwell was added to the list when after a party she neglected to pay a tradesman $200 for rented lighting equipment. Hedda and Lady Mendl split the cost. The tradesman sent the receipted bill to Miss Maxwell with a note naming her benefactors. Lady Mendl received Elsa's check within two weeks, Hedda within twenty-four hours —but as Hedda said—Lady Mendl had no column.

The feud with Pamela Mason was, according to Hedda, a "cat fight," which began when Pamela attacked her on television. Pamela, for her part, claimed that she, her husband, her ex-husband, her children and her friends were subjected to unrelenting attack and vicious innuendo.

"One reason Suzie [Traynor] and I stayed and worked for Hedda so long," said Patsy Gaile, "was that behind the fooferaw and folderol, there was real kindness. Real values. And there was always a crusade. She had an all-out battle against pointed-toe shoes. Unimportant things. But she also crusaded against license and misuse of freedom in the motion-picture industry. She felt films could be our greatest ambassador of goodwill. And she came out in her column and fought Communism tooth and nail when it was not popular to do it. That was one thing— she had the courage of her convictions."

Beginning in 1945, Hedda's orientation became increasingly political and violently conservative. She had from the beginning attempted to slip political commentary into her columns, even though the editors and publishers frequently reminded her that she was hired to do entertainment, not politics.*

In 1945, Hubbell Robinson assigned Hedda to the CBS network's team covering the founding of the United Nations in San Francisco. Initially she seemed optimistic about its prospects, noting that assembling the forty-eight participants cost the same as two hours of warfare, but she was quickly disillusioned. Russia's Molotov struck her as a prima donna. She complained about seating arrangements, and, in summing up, told a *Time* correspondent that the session promised to turn into the greatest clambake in history.

For some time her column had been dotted with non-entertainment business names. In addition to such socialites as Mrs. Nion Tucker and Mrs. George Cameron, Mrs. Marjorie Merriweather Post, Jerome Zerbe and Henry Sell, there were such public figures as Bernard Baruch (she proudly displayed his photo "To Hedda, the gallant") and Alben Barkley (they became friends when chosen Grandmother and Grandfather of the year). Publishers Colonel Robert McCormick, Captain Joseph Patterson, Gardner Cowles and Henry Luce were frequently mentioned.

If Louella tended to choose her friends from devout Catholics, Hedda seemed to prefer political conservatives. Senators Robert Taft, Everett Dirksen, Joseph McCarthy and later Senator Barry Goldwater, General and Mrs. Douglas MacArthur and the FBI's J. Edgar Hoover were more than nodding acquaintances. As a Taft partisan prior to the Republican National Convention in 1952, Hedda worked to team him with MacArthur. MacArthur, she said, was willing to run, unlike "another general" who wanted the nomination on a silver platter, which some bankers and internationalists wanted to hand him. She was speaking of Dwight Eisenhower, but after he was chosen, she labored enthusiastically for him. Following his election, Hedda didn't stand on formality. She called the First

---

* Ex-FBI man John Temple said that Hedda would wait until the publishers of the Los Angeles *Times* were out of town to insert some political item she feared they would delete.

Lady to ask if she might drop in at the White House for tea. "She never lost that neighborly spirit from Altoona," Patsy Gaile chuckled, in telling of the incident.

In a small way, Hedda considered Richard M. Nixon as something of a protégé. As a cohort of the "Young Republicans," she joined in urging him to oppose Helen Gahagan Douglas and drive the Congresswoman out of the Senate. When the Nixons attended a party at Hedda's for the first time, Hedda didn't think Mrs. Nixon's hat flattering. So she took her guest aside and gave her a more becoming one. Through the years, Hedda worked hard for the Senator, stumping the Mid-west during his 1952 Vice Presidential campaign, hailing him as "a great man and a great American."

Personal disenchantment set in a few years later when he campaigned in Southern California against John F. Kennedy. Hedda, assuming she had earned special privileges, managed to elude bellboys and hotel security officers to turn up at the presidential candidate's door. Nixon, unaware she could overhear, told an aide to say he was asleep. Hedda decided he was an ingrate and gave him the deep freeze. Mutual friends urged her to put the incident down to campaign fatigue, but she regarded it as a personal slight. "Eventually," Suzie Traynor said, "the thought was gentled, but Miss Hopper was deeply hurt at the time." Cordial relations were resumed, but Hedda never quite regained her initial enthusiasm.

By Hedda's standards, Ronald Reagan had been foolishly liberal in his youth, but when he finally saw the light, he joined her list of patriots.* Prior to his election as governor of California, Hedda wrote a piece praising him; but her death occurred before his victory, and the article was not published.

A favorite quotation of Hedda's came from her grandmother, who counseled: "Child, there are two sides to

---

* Thomas E. Dewey was not admired by Hedda or vice versa. At a reception an aide spied Hedda and rushed off, over her protests, to inform candidate Dewey that Hedda was there. His response, according to her, was, "Let her wait at the back of the line like everyone else."

every question, but only one of them is right." To Hedda that came to mean *far* right.

In 1947 she resolved to spend her vacation with Spec and Treva Davidson McClure motoring across the United States. She hoped to meet "a cross-section of America," to find out what they were feeling and to awaken them to the dangers of thinking pink. Speaking to 6,000 members of the American Legion Auxiliary of Women, she urged that they boycott pictures with actors who had Communist connections. Still, she was willing to grant that some had been dupes, and she conceded that some right-thinking people, notably Jack Warner and Darryl Zanuck, were doing their best to keep "Commie" propaganda off the screen by scheduling pictures exposing "the fifth column activities of the devotees of another dangerous ideology."

Earlier in the year when she reported that Armand Deutsch was studying production methods with Dore Schary, the studio chieftain she distrusted most, she went so far as to say Deutsch couldn't have found a better teacher. But as her identification with the Motion Picture Alliance for the Preservation of American Ideals increased, her tolerance decreased. Among the organization's members were John Wayne, Adolph Menjou, Charles Coburn, Ward Bond, producer James K. McGuinness, producer-director Leo McCarey and Lela Rogers, Ginger's mother —some of whom were not exactly celebrated for their analytical abilities. McCarey, for instance, claimed that he had to keep close watch over pinko writers to prevent them from inserting propaganda into his films. Asked for an example, he said that lefties always portrayed bankers as heartless, thereby undermining faith in the capitalist system. What McCarey failed to mention was that in *Going My Way,* which he produced and directed, a villainous banker was trying to foreclose a Catholic church's mortgage.

Lela Rogers, asked to substantiate her charges that leftists inserted subversive dialogue in her daughter's pictures, came up with the line: "Share and share alike— that's democracy."

Adolphe Menjou, who feared that a Communist take-over was imminent, confided that in the event it happened: "I would move to the state of Texas . . . because I think that Texans would kill them on sight."

Compared to McCarey, Mrs. Rogers and Menjou, Hedda was a model of rationality and a mistress of logic. Yet because her ideas reached millions, she proved far more dangerous. Egged on by other members of the alliance, she pointed a finger at *Mr. Smith Goes to Washington,* a comedy which she felt destroyed faith in the U.S. Senate by implying there were only two honest men in that body. She cited *Meet John Doe.* It portrayed an American industrialist unsympathetically. She frowned upon *The Farmer's Daughter.* It might be a bright comedy, but it ridiculed free elections in her opinion. *So Well Remembered* riled her, not because it was a melodramatic mishmash but because she regarded it as so filled with anti-American sentiments that she predicted it could qualify for a command performance in Moscow. No picture made "under the banners of freedom" could be ferreted out that would so please the Communists, she said.

"There are two schools of thought on such pictures," Hedda admitted. "The lefties argue that by inspiring social reforms through such mediums we may prevent the Communists from taking over the country. I do not recommend the picture as entertainment as it is badly done from a technical standpoint. But I urge you to see it. Then decide for yourself whether or not Hollywood is capable of inserting leftie propaganda in films."

While a major portion of the industry resented the scheduled September, 1947, investigation of Hollywood by representatives of the House Un-American Activities Committee, Hedda welcomed it. Her brand of Americanism was based on fear of change and made no allowances for shadings and differences of opinion. She was outraged when such liberals as Humphrey Bogart, Lauren Bacall, Gene Kelly, Danny Kaye, John Huston, June Havoc and some fifteen others chartered a plane to Washington, D.C., to oppose the investigation and the invasion of a citizen's right of privacy about his beliefs.

When those subpoenaed refused to testify whether (1)

they belonged to the Screen Actors, Writers or Directors guilds and (2) they were or ever had been members of the Communist Party, Hedda was outraged. She printed a letter from a Milwaukee reader urging a boycott of their films. Hedda agreed and urged a thorough housecleaning.

Prior to the confrontation in Washington, Eric Johnston, president of the Motion Picture Producers Association, Dore Schary and other executives resisted pressure. Then at the Waldorf-Astoria in New York, the MPPA and the Society of Independent Motion Picture Producers met at the behest of Spyros Skouras, Harry Warner, Nicholas Schenck, Peter Rathvon and Barney Balaban.

Despite prior assurances that there would be no blacklist, there was to be one after all. Eric Johnston reversed himself for the third time after the meeting, as Hedda quickly pointed out. He had begun the year by saying he'd never go so far as to deny work to a Communist. Twenty-four days later he said that if the Communists had set out to capture Hollywood, they'd suffered a defeat, and then ten months later he called the Communists fools and fakers and said that those who failed to answer questions put to them by the committee presided over by Congressman J. Parnell Thomas* had done the industry a disservice. Johnston, Schary and their ilk, Hedda said, had been set straight by the moneymen in the East on where the industry's real power lay.

Determined to destroy Communism, Hedda was willing to ignore the Bill of Rights. Inflamed by her associates, she increasingly equated difference of opinion with disloyalty. She was highly suggestible. "When you began talking, she might think one way. By the end of the conversation, she was completely on the other side," Bill Hopper said. "But as far as she was concerned, what she thought now was the opinion she'd held all her life."

Temperamentally, she was unsuited to politics. A casual date between Susan Hayward and Hal Hayes led Hedda to speculate on whether Hayes had shown the actress his

---

* Thomas was himself jailed for payroll padding before the "Hollywood Ten" began serving sentences for contempt of Congress.

private bomb shelter and offered refuge in case of atomic attack. He'd promised so many Hedda feared it would be overcrowded—reaching a new high in frivolousness. But in situation after situation she seemed insensitive to the seriousness of the charges she leveled or the issues involved. To give her the benefit of the doubt, she was at times frivolous and callous—if not sadistic. When, for instance, Darryl Zanuck alarmed Charles Brackett by urging that Hedda not be seated on the aisle at the Academy Award ceremonies because she intended to stand up, unfurl an American flag and stomp out if José Ferrer won an Oscar, Hedda lamented that she hadn't thought of doing so, since it would have been a good gag.

Because of this lack of sensitivity, she took potshots at such a varied spectrum as Eleanor Roosevelt, Eric Johnston, Ring Lardner, Jr., Dore Schary, John Garfield, Karen Morley, Harry Truman, Howard Da Silva, Shelley Winters, Larry Parks, Betty Garrett, Humphrey Bogart, Lauren Bacall, Sterling Hayden, Helen Gahagan Douglas, Clifford Odets, Lillian Hellman, Carl Foreman, Adlai Stevenson, Dalton Trumbo, Arthur Miller, Melvyn Douglas, Florence Eldridge, Frederic March, Alvah Bessie, Anne Revere and on and on and on. Hedda felt that wittingly or unwittingly these people had lent their names to groups dedicated to causes inimical to the best interests of the United States. If they were good Americans, let them admit their mistakes.

It was in this area that Spec McClure found Hedda and many of her adversaries equally puzzling. "It was fascinating," he said. "So much of it was surface. Take Bogart. There was the political thing, but Bogie wasn't really political. Bogie without Bacall was a pretty goddamn good Joe. Bogie was a drunk who was liable to take offense and say any goddamn thing. On her radio program, Hopper had a feature 'My Hat's Off,' and for some goddamn reason it was off to Bogie. They'd had these political differences. Bogie was drunk and called up and said, 'I don't want her taking her hat off to me.' I told Hopper, and the next day she called him. I was listening on the other phone, and he said, 'Oh, dear, oh, dear'—he was very contrite about it. He was a belligerent drunk, but he couldn't retain anger very long. You see you're dealing in a world of shallow emotions. There are fireworks. And by the time you or I get interested in the whole damn thing it's over. So unless you catch this feature, you can't explain these people. Because they're not normal people at all."

McClure felt that in a sense Hedda never realized how deeply the knife she wielded cut and was bewildered by the results. She simply enjoyed the sensation of power. "I think with people—even if Chaplin had sat down with her, he could have straightened himself out. I think he thought why should I straighten myself out with her. Let her straighten herself out with me."

Those who attempted to placate Hedda found themselves in a consistently inconsistent world. A case in point was Dore Schary. Neither had liked the other when Schary was a writer at MGM, but when he became head of RKO, it became mutually advantageous to call a truce. They met and talked. Hedda went so far as to praise him in her column as a talented moviemaker who turned out good pictures. But when Schary took his stand against the Un-American Activities Committee's investigation, she once again began criticizing his work.

When he was appointed head of Metro-Goldwyn-Mayer, she griped that he had testified on the opposite side from George Murphy, Robert Taylor, James K. McGuinness and Louis B. Mayer. "It will be ironically amusing to watch some of the scenes behind the scenes now that Dore Schary is the big noise at Metro-Goldwyn-Moscow," she wrote on July 19, 1948. She said that she disliked him for his "pinko" sympathies and for having reversed himself under pressure. Yet when MGM's public relations experts set about wooing Hedda, she again wrote cordially about Schary, calling him "our fastest working executive. You can get him on the phone and receive a definite yes or no within 24 hours. I got an answer for a friend in 20 minutes. That's what I call an executive," she enthused. That was in March, 1949, but by September she was again miffed. Using a technique that increased her reputation for bitchery, she noted: "Dore Schary's in the pink after five weeks at Arrowhead. Said it would take him a week to clean off his desk. A week! Anyone else would be at it a month." If taken to task for using the word "pink," Hedda would have denied malice. Yet nine times out of ten in her column "pink" had political connotations.

When Spec McClure heard that MGM was making *The Red Badge of Courage,* he suggested casting war hero Audie Murphy in the lead to director John Huston. Huston said Metro wanted to use one of its stars. "To show you how these things worked," McClure said, "I went to Hopper, who had never read the book. She called Huston. Then she called Schary about Audie. She kept at it about how perfect Audie was for this part and he finally got it. She—in a way—was responsible for casting a part in a book she never read." *

But at best the Hopper-Schary relationship was a rocky one. Written exchanges were so frequent that Schary kept a file on Hedda's beefs, and she was one of the few people that he ever barred from the studio. Yet when an intermediary suggested that he appear on her radio show, both he and Hedda agreed. The script was prepared. Schary, who had the right to check his statements for accuracy, objected and made changes. On the day of the broadcast, Hedda called McClure and informed him the script was too weak to broadcast. McClure and his wife went to her home and found her in bed.

McClure took the script downstairs. "I didn't change a damn one of Schary's statements or additions. Not one word. But I changed Hopper's questions around so she was throwing knives right and left," he recalled. "She read it and got out of bed and took me to the station with her. Schary came in flanked by a couple of publicity men and we all sat around a table. Hopper said, 'Dore, I changed the script a bit.' He said, 'Did you change my answers?' 'Not a word,' she said. So we started to read. The first thing Schary objected to, I said I think he is

---

* On February 15, 1951, Hedda assured readers that *The Red Badge of Courage* was the title Stephen Crane had given his classic half a century before and had "absolutely no Commie implications." She said that anyone who attempted to change it should "hang his head in shame."

right. So we changed it. The next time, I said, 'I agree with Miss Hopper.' It went on that way. I never thought he'd go on with her, but he did. But I don't think he ever forgave it."

In July, 1951, when Schary replaced Louis B. Mayer as head of MGM, Hedda gave both men the shiv, saying Mayer should be happy since he had once told her Schary was the only man who could save the company. A year later Hedda quoted Schary as having admitted that he now was convinced that Communists were dedicated to overthrowing the government by violence. In a Sunday story, she allowed him to amplify his position by making a distinction between social criticism of the 1930's for improvement of internal conditions and social criticism in the 1950's which would be given worldwide circulation and perhaps used as propaganda by enemies of the country. Hedda was not of a temperament to indulge in analyzing such points. To her it simply meant Schary had retreated. Whether it was a valid position or one dictated by opportunism, Hedda thought Schary could be summed up by her favorite contemptuous dismissal—"a pissant."

Hedda never tired of quoting Arthur Caesar's remark that most people were liberal until twenty-five, but if they hadn't become conservative by thirty-five, something was wrong with them. Perhaps this explains her switch in attitude toward Sterling Hayden. When the actor appeared before the committee in 1947, Hedda observed that after that performance he might not have to degrade himself by starring in any more films, as he had often complained of doing. Yet in 1952 she explained that she could understand his feelings when he was released from military service and was concerned about the state of the country. The only ones who seemed to share his concern were the Communists, he told her. "When I confessed my Commie connections, I did so thinking my film career would be ruined, but now I work as much as before," Hedda approvingly quoted him as saying.

Although Carl Foreman was a couple of years over thirty-five when he sought rapprochement with Hedda, her about-face in regard to him probably caused more discussion than any of her political feuds—with one exception. In October, 1951, she expressed amazement that Gary Cooper would associate himself with Carl Foreman Productions, since Foreman had refused to answer "the $64 question" about whether he still was or ever had been a Communist when he appeared before the Un-American Activities Committee. The writer-producer at once reminded her that he had signed an oath that he was not a member of the Communist Party on September 11, 1950, as a member of the executive board of the Screen Writers Guild. "Okay, Mr. Foreman, that is $32 worth of the $64 question," Hedda replied, "and I believe, knowing Mr. Cooper's Americanism and his contemplated association with you, he would be interested as I am in the remainder of the answer." Apparently Foreman was able to give it. For he won Hedda over completely.

Several of her associates were puzzled at her switch. "Carl Foreman?" Patsy Gaile said. "Suzie and I used to discuss that. He must have a hell of an understanding of human nature and psychology. Her heart was operating in that particular area, because if a person really appealed to her feelings, she would become their champion."

"You didn't have to come crawling to Hopper," Spec McClure said. "That wasn't the angle at all. But if you would just sit down and explain, that was all there was to it. It makes you shiver to think what would have happened if she'd ever met Joe Stalin.

"Hopper's enemies used to say she was more vicious than Parsons," McClure went on. "I don't agree. I don't think she ever wrote a damn thing that hurt anyone permanently with the exception of Larry Parks, and that was a political thing. Hopper was motivated by a different set of beliefs. She believed it was the patriotic thing to do. But I'm sure Larry Parks could have straightened himself out if he'd got to her."

From 1945 to 1948 Hedda ran occasional items praising Parks, yet he and his wife, Betty Garrett, appeared more frequently in Louella's column. Louella reported on his gratitude to the United States as the land of opportunity, his touching devotion to his mother during her terminal illness and other admiring items. Hedda, bolstered by the imprisonment of the Hollywood Ten and Parks' belated admissions, trumpeted that charges of witch-hunting had been disproved. Parks' excuse for not testifying earlier, that the industry was already a "wounded animal," brought Hedda's tart reply that Washington had given Hollywood three years to clean house, which should have been ample time for him to come forward.

Then at a meeting of the Motion Picture Alliance at the American Legion Hall, Hedda made a dramatic attack, disagreeing with fellow member John Wayne, who advocated forgiving Parks his previous errors. "I feel impelled to say some things that I believe speak the minds of the mothers of 55,000 casualties in Korea," she said. "I have read the papers. I have listened to the radio. And then I was shocked as I read the statement of our president John Wayne, which would imply that he voiced the opinion of our Alliance. If it did—we should so express ourselves. It is not my opinion. I wish to be personal from now on.

"I too have sympathy for anyone who sees the light, but Mr. and Mrs. Larry Parks were visited by a member of the FBI four years ago—who pleaded with them to give up their membership in the Communist Party. If they had listened, Larry Parks' appearance in Washington yesterday would not have been necessary. . . .

"Larry Parks read the best script of his career yesterday —but he gave no news. All data was already in the Committee's possession. One, two or ten careers in Hollywood aren't worth a dime unless we are willing to lose them for our country.

"Why so much emphasis placed on one career? Do we know what the careers of those 55,000 would have been if they had not been caught short by refusal of information in our country? And I, for one, believe that the life of one soldier fighting for our freedom is worth more than all the careers in Hollywood.

"How can anyone expect to hold his position in public life who withholds valuable information until put under pressure?

"I suggest before we let the traditional theatrical charity govern our reason that we consider whether the mud of an uninformer is worse than the mud of Korea mixed with the blood of 55,000 boys whose luck ran out before they came to fame in Hollywood or anywhere else.

"Larry Parks says he felt he'd done nothing wrong. I feel sorry for him.

"And I'm wondering if the mothers and families of those who've died and the wounded who are still living will be happy to know their money at the box office has supported and may continue to support those who have been so late in the defense of their country?"

Depending on the point of view, Hedda was Joan of Arc or Medea. Well aware of the controversy her speech had created, she told a representative of the *Hollywood Citizen News* that she was prepared to be vilified to defeat Communism in Hollywood. Had she let it go at that, there might have been no repercussions, but she added that in "some respects" it seemed that HUAC was guilty of white-washing certain industry figures. She claimed knowledge of wrongdoers who had been allowed to deny guilt under oath.

Her attack on Parks and the committee aroused both left and right. Her appearance in New York as one of four mistresses of ceremonies at an American National Theater and Academy benefit turned into a debacle. When a couple of jokes fell flat and Hedda said perhaps she should hence-forth delete her humor, the audience applauded, and some of the orchestra gave her musical razzberries. She finally retreated amid catcalls, boos and foot stampings. Critic Richard Watts of the New York *Post* admitted enjoying seeing her put in her place. *Variety* commented that the antagonism was clearly evoked by her right-wing activities.

In Hollywood rumors circulated that she was sub-poenaed by the committee. But in September Chairman John Stephen Wood of the House Un-American Activities Committee announced he had met privately with Hedda and warned that unless she was prepared to document her whitewashing charges, she had better shut up.

Subsequently the committee's September meetings in Hollywood were ignored by Hedda. On the day Wood re-leased his statement, she concerned herself with guests' re-actions to Harold Grieve's redecoration of her home. Grieve had turned her piano into a bar with a petticoat—

and Hedda claimed everyone would be copying it. But if Wood or anyone else thought Hedda had been permanently silenced, that person didn't understand Hedda.

XV

I can't help it if it seems that doggone moon above
Makes me need someone to love. . . .
    —"Don't Blame Me"
      by DOROTHY FIELDS and JIMMY McHUGH

THE somber period following Docky's and WRH's deaths
was intensified by the cataclysm that television caused in
films, publishing and broadcasting. In the 1950's, events
were telecast into homes almost as they happened. Louella's prized front-page scoops became increasingly trivial.
The Parsons autonomy also diminished after the Chief's
demise. Her disarmingly daffy, higgledy-piggledy syntax
was now transformed into serviceable, plastic prose. Occasionally Louella would call the *Examiner* to cuss out
someone for tampering with her copy, but most changes
went unnoticed or unchallenged. Even with editing there
was still an occasional candidate for the *New Yorker*'s
"Most Fascinating News Story of the Week"—*e.g.,* "When
I was talking to George Cukor on the phone I heard him
let out a yell. A mouse ran over his foot."

Radio—and to a lesser extent other media—found advertisers and stars defecting to television. Louella, who
had returned to the airwaves after a brief retirement,
suddenly found her show canceled in 1951. (Using fan
mail—in her column she claimed 1,000 letters a week
protesting her absence—she managed to return to broadcasting briefly in 1952.)

Motion pictures were harried not only by television, but also by unrepealed wartime taxes, by government-decreed separation of production companies and theater chains, by Red hunts, by the growing popularity of art theaters and by runaway production. "Help! Help!" Louella cried. "There'll be nobody in Hollywood for us poor columnists to write about if the present (and past) exodus keeps up!"

Such television favorites as "Uncle Miltie" Berle, Burns and Allen and Dagmar were of greater interest to her readers than Olivia De Havilland, Terry Moore or Keefe Brasselle. After World War II studios began dropping lesser contract players, and by 1954 Greer Garson and Clark Gable (he had been a top-ten box-office champion for fifteen years) were bidding MGM good-bye.

For Louella, it became increasingly difficult to recognize the new stars. Mary Pickford, Clara Bow, Loretta Young and Marilyn Monroe were unique, but how did a reporter keep ersatz Marilyns—the Diana Dors and Barbara Nichols—straight? And what kind of name was Gina Lollobrigida?

Independent press agents, relatively unimportant in Louella's heyday, couldn't or wouldn't whip stars into line as Perry Lieber, Harry Brand and Howard Strickling had. The Tyrone Powers and Joan Crawfords had been taught to value a break in Parsons, Hopper or Sidney Skolsky, but Marilyn Monroe and Farley Granger ran off to New York to study acting and were indifferent to columnists. Marlon Brando demanded total privacy, causing Louella to suggest he take up another profession. If he persisted in being uncooperative, what did it matter to her that he was potentially the most gifted actor in America? "We Americans," she said, "don't even permit our Presidents the luxury of a private life."

Under the circumstances, it seemed inescapable that Louella would opt for a well-earned retirement. She had long ago accomplished everything possible in her field. She was an Institution—an Institution whose hand and footprints had been immortalized in the cement of the forecourt of Grauman's Chinese Theater. Still, institutions don't last forever, and even Louella admitted that she was "no longer a little girl."

In August, 1952, *Time,* a magazine that had frequently treated her harshly, paid bemused tribute to her, forgiving her weaknesses: ". . . she never avoids phrases like 'the reason is because' unless it is impossible not to do so, and she likes her infinitives split. Louella is aware of these oddities and will talk about them frankly, explaining that she types so badly that it is difficult to read what she has written, and when she dictates she does so at a terrific pace. The result is a chatty, intimate, informal, verbose and, on the whole, knowledgeable hodgepodge." The story emphasized her unwavering loyalty to Hollywood and designated her "Mother Superior" of the motion-picture industry.*

During the next few years, one kudo followed another. The Masquers paid her tribute with George Burns setting the tone. "She's a wonderful woman and you can only say nice things about her. And I'm not saying this because she's syndicated in 1,500 papers. I'd say the same thing if she was only in 1,400 papers . . . I'll never forget one time Hedda Hopper—if you'll excuse the expression—caught me in a picture and in her review, she said, 'George Burns is the lousiest actor I've ever seen.' Louella got very sore. She called me up and said, 'George, we've been dear friends for years. If you've got an item like that, why didn't you give it to me?' "

She was the first woman to receive the Mount Sinai Men's Club's "Heart of Gold." The California Women's Press Club gave her its Golden Flame Award. She appeared on Edward R. Murrow's *Person to Person.* She was awarded an honorary Doctor of Letters degree from Quincy (Illinois) College. The Los Angeles Urban League Guild's Humanitarian Award was bestowed upon her. And William Randolph Hearst, Jr., gave her a luncheon, a scroll, a charm bracelet and a gold typewriter.

Yet in spite of all the honors, there was a sadness about

---

* Louella earned it as she demonstrated after reading Lillian Ross' brilliant account of the tribulations involved in producing *The Red Badge of Courage.* Louella observed that perhaps this would teach executives not to allow outsiders, such as "the Ross woman" to gain access to the industry's secrets.

her. Determination, longevity and courage had turned her into a curiously poignant figure. On mellow days, even Hedda saw her as Hollywood's "Dutch Aunt." Perhaps it was because she doggedly plugged away, asking no quarter and taking immense pride in beating out rivals on such stories as the Tyrone Power-Linda Christian separation or the Howard Hughes-Jean Peters marriage. (Even if Hughes did insist that she run the news in her column instead of on page one where she would have rated a by-line and extra money, too.) But poignant or not, she was as competitive as ever. At a press party, she and Hedda engaged in a tug of war over the hapless Marilyn Monroe. The problem? Which was to be photographed alone with Marilyn—*first*.

Observing Hedda's success in cultivating political power, Louella plunged in and performed as adeptly as usual in areas alien to entertainment. Gazing into her clouded crystal ball, she assured her readers that Ronald Reagan harbored no political ambitions. Castigating blacklisted writers, she naturally managed to confuse two men and name the innocent one. But nowhere is there better argument for keeping apolitical commentators out of political matters than in her self-contradictory response to Robert Rich's script. In 1956, she reported: "The spiritual and religious quality of *The Brave One* has delighted both the Mexican Consul and President Adolfo Ruiz-Cortines of Mexico. Said the President: 'Irving Rapper directed the picture as if he were really a Mexican himself.'" Yet in 1960, after she had discovered that Robert Rich was none other than the notorious Dalton Trumbo, she lectured Frank King of the King Brothers, who had contended that Trumbo should be given the Oscar his writing had earned. "I don't feel he's entitled to any recognition from the film industry," Louella said. Louella was accurate. Like Hedda, she *felt*. She seldom analyzed, reasoned or thought.

Nepotism was as strong as ever. Whether Harriet was producing *Susan Slept Here* or the television pilot *How to Marry a Millionaire,* Louella was in there plugging. She went to the TV pilot reluctantly because she had a bad cold but happily trumpeted that she had found the little program so diverting that she had stayed for two showings.

In the same vein, when her godchild Barbara Bebe Lyon married, Louella flew 6,000 miles to be present. Yet it says something that she had earlier passed up attending Grace Kelly's marriage to Prince Rainier. Avoiding any specific mention of health, Louella simply said she couldn't go.

Loyalty to family and friends was of increasing importance to her. A case in point was designer Orry-Kelly.* When her old pal found himself bankrupt, Louella organized a show of his paintings. At the opening of the exhibition, Louella divided her time between seeing that Kelly didn't get drunk and insulting and pitching his paintings. She sold socialite Gladys Knapp three; Mrs. L. B. Mayer two; Mrs. Jack Warner, Joseph Schenck, Mrs. Nate Spingold, Mrs. Al Hart and Gracie Allen one each. She also pressured Carnation Milk, sponsors of Burns and Allen's television show, into purchasing a still life of red carnations for their stars. Even such relative newcomers as Gordon MacRae didn't escape. Consequently, the show sold out, and Kelly was rescued from financial ruin. Ironically, not long after, the temperamental designer

---

* Louella, who greatly enjoyed Kelly's company, once invited him along when she was appearing before students at the University of Southern California. Kelly and Docky stayed outside in the automobile drinking. When Louella finished her talk, they began driving up Sunset Boulevard on their way to dinner. Suddenly Louella announced that they must locate a ladies' room at once. Since none was available, Docky pulled to the curb, and Louella scurried behind a billboard. Kelly, who was feeling no pain, stepped out of the car and began his spiel, "Now ladies and gentlemen, if you'll look closely, you'll see the pee of Miss Louella Parsons, the Hearst columnist, one of the unusual sights of Hollywood. . . ." Suddenly, Louella's exasperated voice came from behind the billboard: "Orry-Kelly! Stop that!" "Yes, ladies and gentlemen, this is—" "Orry-Kelly! You stop that or I'll never speak to you again!"

But later when one evening Kelly staggered out of a Beverly Hills party, made it to the center of the street and hailed a police car, which he mistook for a taxi, it was Louella who sent Docky to the police station to bail him out while she got busy on the phone to keep it out of the newspapers.

took offense at an item in Louella's column and defected to Hedda.

Louella ignored that. Yet when aroused, her needle could still prick. Shelley Winters learned that after Louella read some anti-Hollywood remarks attributed to the actress in *Newsweek*. Miss Winters heard Louella was displeased and claimed she had been misquoted. Louella replied that she certainly hoped so. "Because you were 'Miss Nothingburger' before Garson Kanin's and Ruth Gordon's *A Double Life*."

As recipient of a David Selznick memo accusing her of allowing others to vent libelous spleen against *A Farewell to Arms* in her column, Louella publicly dressed him down: "David dear, you and I have been doing business since you were a little boy and you know better than to accuse me of letting anyone 'use' my column. I must repeat that a picture that was snowbound, changed directors in midstream and lost three top technicians has had its troubles."

Beginning in 1952 and running through the 1950's, Louella experienced an Indian summer. In 1956 a sixty-minute television drama devoted to the more positive aspects of Louella's career appeared on CBS-TV's *Climax*. Asked who would be suitable to portray her, Louella vaguely indicated that anyone would do. Submission of a list of twenty candidates proved none were acceptable. Louella finally chose Teresa Wright—stipulating that the actress not "make me too sweet." Apparently, Miss Wright, who spent some time studying the columnist in her Maple Drive home, took Louella at her word. At least the New York *Times'* Jack Gould found the portrayal "fairly dripped with lilac-scented acid." The New York *Post's* Jay Nelson Tuck suggested that for the week, the program should have been retitled "Aunti-Climax." But Louella enjoyed it. It was one of the most star-studded hours ever seen on television, she noted in self-congratulation.

Also contributing to Louella's happiness was Jimmy McHugh. While no one could ever take Docky's place in Louella's life, she admitted that Jimmy's humor, attentiveness and understanding did much to revitalize her. Jimmy had been one of Docky's pals, as well as a member of the elite Catholic circle in which the Martins became increasingly prominent as Louella became more deeply involved in her adopted religion. Initially, Louella accepted Jimmy's attentions as those of a sympathetic, but casual, family friend. Certainly in 1952, she exhibited no possessiveness. *Rendezvous Time,* she said, based on the life of "one of my favorite people and one of the world's greatest songwriters," was being considered by Warner Brothers. The plot was to be built around Jimmy's being inspired by beautiful women to write "On the Sunny Side of the Street," "I'm in the Mood for Love" and other standards.

Nor was there any hint of jealousy when she reported his dinner date was "Miss Hawaii" shortly after the *Rendezvous Time* item. But the situation could not prevail. Jimmy was the perfect candidate to fulfill Louella's need for a dominating masculine presence in her life. He was a jovial party man—and Louella loved a party. He was a man of distinction (with some twenty scores for musical shows) to his credit—and Louella respected achievement. His songs were deeply sentimental and figuratively Louella wore her heart on her sleeve. Furthermore, he was engagingly frank, describing himself as "a born hustler—just a little smarter than the average kid. A little more hip, a lot more ambitious."

Louella understood that Jimmy was an operator. She was also enough of a realist, despite her romanticism, to accept the give-and-take underlying all relationships. If Jimmy was a man who was always doing something nice for someone, he naturally expected reciprocation. But most important to Louella was the fact that Jimmy enjoyed a good time almost as much as she did.

Many of Louella's friends, aware of Jimmy's attraction to young beauties,* felt he was simply exploiting her. In a sense there was some truth in this. Like many creative

---

* When Mike Todd's *As the Girls Go,* for which Jimmy wrote the music, was trying out in Boston, members of the company were amused and astonished as this preswinger swinger would drive his beautiful outgoing guest to the airport, see her off and pick up her equally beautiful successor, who had just arrived— or was about to arrive—on an incoming plane.

people who recognize that their ambition exceeds their talent, Jimmy invariably took advantage of others. So did Louella. They were a matched pair. But to focus solely on this aspect of the relationship is to overlook what Louella represented to the Boston-born Irishman who had had to fight his way to the top. Louella was powerful and kowtowed to. She was demanding of the most celebrated people and yet sweet and somewhat deferential to him. He enjoyed her company. To say that he might not have sought her out had she been Louella Jones or Smith is beside the point. She was LOUELLA PARSONS.

"Louella," Jimmy said after her retirement, "was a wonderful lady. She *was* Hollywood. They called Mary Pickford Hollywood's queen, but Louella was the uncrowned queen. No one made a move unless she knew about it. You heard about Bob Hope. When he was going on one of his very wonderful, very generous trips to entertain our service boys, they wanted to know who should be notified in case of accident. He said, 'Louella Parsons. She'd never forgive me if she wasn't the first to know.'"

As the Parsons-McHugh friendship developed, Jimmy retained his admiration for her but also assumed that certain prerogatives had accrued to him. If Louella began taking him for granted or failed to mention him in her column frequently, his phone calls diminished. His enemies interpreted this as proof of exploitation. (Yet after she retired, he faithfully visited her at least once a week.)

"Louella was willing to be a dear friend to anyone who gave her a chance. Big or small," he said. "She would fall in love with people if they offered a friendly feeling or a kind word. She was a clearinghouse for Hollywood. And I would also say that I'm sure I was fortunate in that there was very little that this lady didn't discuss with me at some time or other. Take her books. I don't know how well I liked them. She didn't think too much of her writing, but she was well educated. She knew commas, periods and question marks."

In charting the course of their friendship, it is significant that in 1951 there were two or three casual mentions of Jimmy in the column. In 1952, there were twenty. In January, 1953, Hedda commented that since Louella had taken over Jimmy McHugh's "life, career and entertainment," a film scenario of his life was in preparation. "But that romance," Hedda predicted, "may hit rock bottom before the script hits the soundstage." *

Hedda to the contrary, the McHugh plugs continued, and the relationship deepened. What Hedda, at the time, called a romance, Louella described as friendship, and Jimmy viewed himself as being part of the family. Probably each was partially correct. "They were the goddamnedest cutest people," public relations man Bill Doll said. "She made Jimmy nicer, and she was nicer on account of him. See, this relationship had residuals for both of them."

Probably Louella's feelings toward Jimmy began to deepen when she suffered a seizure that prevented her from writing the column in the late summer of 1952. Upon her return to work on September 3, she acknowledged the thoughtfulness shown her during her illness. Although she did not name him, Jimmy had been especially attentive. And after her "rest" in Laguna Beach, there were numerous clues that she was falling in love. She sported a new svelte figure—118 pounds. She limited her calorie intake to an incredible 800 a day. She made arrangements for an entire new wardrobe and began wearing her hair differently. As her escort for her first night on the town, she chose Jimmy.

Three days later he gave her what turned out to be the start of a series of parties that they arranged for one another. This particular one was a "get well" party to which Jimmy invited not only the elite of the entertainment industry, but also—and more important from Louella's

* Jimmy had briefly squired Hedda to several parties in the early 1940's. Always alert for self-promotion, when he was assigned to write music for Frank Sinatra's first film, *Higher and Higher*, in 1943, Jimmy took the young singer to Hedda's house, unannounced, late one evening. He asked her to come and meet a talented young man. Hedda refused, and the Hopper-McHugh friendship foundered. Hedda felt she was being used. In telling of the incident twenty-five years later, Jimmy still expressed rancor.

viewpoint—Monsignor Patrick J. Concannon, Father Thomas English and Father John O'Donnell.

Thereafter each year on her birthday, Jimmy would celebrate the event with a gathering that was always duly reported by Hearst's society editor, Princess Conchita Sepulveda Pignatelli. One year, kilt-clad Scotsmen played bagpipes as the guests arrived and then gave way to a calypso band that provided music until dawn. The guests were a mixed bag, too, including Fred MacMurray, Tommy Sands, Irene Dunne, Zsa Zsa Gabor, Lizabeth Scott, Ann Miller, Clark Gable, Fabian, and Barbara Stanwyck, plus newspaper, recording, nightclub, film and church figures.

In 1959 he held a dinner for Louella at L'Escoffier. She said she had never had a birthday party to equal it and that the decorations were so beautiful and the food so excellent that if she never had another birthday celebration, the memory of this one would suffice.

Conversely, Louella gave Jimmy natal fetes, including other friends whose birthdates were close to his. Columnist Mike Connolly; hotelier Hernando Courtwright; John Haskell (Dorothy Manners' husband); and, in later years, super-public relations executive Patricia Newcomb were honored. Each received a small cake. Jimmy's was always an extravagant concoction: a piano with a Louella doll atop it; a miniature of the Hollywood Bowl; a stack of gold records—always some symbol of an important event in his life.

In addition to the birthday parties, there were countless others. While the motion-picture industry was suffering one of its recurrent slumps, Louella, who was attending three or four parties each night, told her readers that the atmosphere around town was more festive than at any time she could recall. On New Year's Eve, for instance, she and Jimmy dropped in at Harriet's, went from there to the Tex Feldman's, then on to Arthur Cameron's (where Louella confessed dancing so hard that her feet ached for two days) and then to Jack Gibbs'. Dawn found her enjoying scrambled eggs at a late spot on the Strip. If, occasionally, at parties, she catnapped before dashing off to another or to a nightclub, it was understandable. She was past seventy.

For those who recalled Louella's commitment to the labor movement during the Brady days and her fascination with medical developments during Docky's lifetime, her suddenly developed enthusiasm for popular music was a significant clue to where her heart lay.*

Her column suddenly became a veritable cornucopia of tidbits about Jimmy's new nightclub act which included, "a beautiful bevy of singing protégées." Among them were Darla Hood (formerly of *Our Gang* comedies), Dorothy Coulter, Eve Marley, Beverly Richards and Judy Clark. After *Variety* hailed the act as "the best show ever to play Reno and good enough to go, as is, anyplace . . . ," Jimmy and the girls were booked into Ciro's. Immediately Louella set to work promoting the event as if it were the comeback of D. W. Griffith. When the engagement proved successful, Louella went East to attend the Eisenhower inauguration and not so incidentally to nail down Jimmy's booking at the Copacabana.

Through her intervention, producer Joe Pasternak tested Jimmy and his protégées for an upcoming MGM extravaganza. And when Warners failed to hand over hard cash for *Rendezvous Time,* Louella announced that it looked as if Ross Hunter might snatch the project from competitors. The campaigns she had staged for others who were close to her were mini-powered affairs compared to the one she was engineering for Jimmy.†

Initially, one might not see much connection between Goddard Lieberson, Mamie Van Doren, Cole Porter, The Mills Publishing Company, Jake Ehrlich, Senator John Kennedy, Lauritz Melchior, and Audrey Baer. What did they share in common? Jimmy McHugh! Lieberson assured Louella Jimmy's romantic songs would be sung as long as the world responded to music. Louella would never

---

* It took her almost no time at all to discover that it was rhythm and blues and not "rhythm and blue," as she first assumed.

† She still found space to herald Harriet's *Clash by Night,* and Harriet reciprocated by casting Louella's voice in her new undertaking *Susan Slept Here.*

have believed any performer could have improved so enormously as Mamie Van Doren had under Jimmy's tutelage. Cole Porter was visibly touched when Jimmy introduced him at the Coconut Grove as the greatest composer in the world. The Mills Publishing Company sent word to Louella that the three top standards for mid-July, 1953, were written by Jimmy. Jake Ehrlich gave a party in San Francisco for Freddie Karger, Jane Wyman, Jimmy and guess who? Jimmy introduced Louella to Senator John Kennedy and his pretty bride outside the Mocambo. Lauritz Melchior and Jimmy headlined at rival hotels in Dallas. Audrey Baer, columnist Mike Connolly's attractive date, won the prize for the prettiest costume at Jimmy McHugh's Gold Nugget Ball, staged to raise funds for his Polio Foundation in Palm Springs.

One thing Louella did not record in 1953 was that on Jimmy's birthday, she presented him with an expensive watch, inscribed "To Jimmy, with Love, Louella." In 1954 Jimmy was elevated to columnar stardom. After serving as a featured player for well over a year, Jimmy, Louella apparently decided, was well enough established with her readers to stand on his own. Even a visit from his Boston relatives was taken note of for the edification of readers in Hong Kong and Beirut. A confidant of Louella's said: "By that time, she had this fantasy going. There always *had* to be a man in her life. She chose Jimmy, and it turned out to be a terrible frustration for her. Because, you see, it was"—long pause—"*nothing*. Oh, he liked her. He enjoyed her company, but she wanted real romance. Well, it just wasn't possible."

Bill Doll, to whom Louella had always gone out of her way to be kind, realized how serious she had become about Jimmy when suddenly Doll's office couldn't get any items in the column. "I couldn't figure it out. What happened, Jimmy was in New York and brought this Copa girl to lunch. Now he just happened to have a stack of her glossies he wanted planted in the papers. ———— was going to the Coast to try to get in the movies. After she went to Hollywood, Louella got jealous. She raised hell with Jimmy, and he told her he'd met the girl through me." Monte Proser, formerly of the Copacabana, confirmed

Doll's story and added that Louella had virtually run her young rival out of town by effectively closing all studio doors to her.

Louella continued to give Doll the freeze until 1957, when she attended the post-premiere party of Mike Todd's *Around the World in 80 Days* at Madison Square Garden. That night she made up with Doll, scolding him for being "naughty and introducing Jimmy to that terrible girl." Having forgiven Doll, Louella not only mentioned his clients but began to include his name in her column frequently.

A contrast between Hedda and Louella can be seen in the Hopper-Sinatra-McHugh and the Parsons-Eddie Fisher-McHugh stories. "Eddie was hot. I hustled him to sing some of my songs and got to like him," Jimmy explained. "One night he came back from Korea—as a matter of fact, I was one of the people who told him to go there in his uniform and sing for the soldiers, which he did. And when he came back it was practically the same story as with Frank Sinatra and Hedda Hopper. I said, 'Louella, a kid singer just came back from Korea. I'd love to have you meet him.' It was eleven at night, but we drove up to the Beverly Hills Hotel and I called him up in his room. I said, 'I'm down here with a very important young lady, Louella Parsons.' He said he'd come right down. He came down and spoke to her for about half an hour or so. About three or four days later, Louella in her usual manner wrote everything beautiful about Eddie Fisher. As a matter of fact, it must have been three or four paragraphs. Then everyone knew about Eddie Fisher because she had a very large reading public."

It is indicative of Jimmy's regard for Louella that he should feel Fisher, who had had several gold records to his credit before entering the Army, had only become a recognizable personality after Louella had written about him. Expanding on the point, Jimmy said, "Louella played a large part in Eddie Fisher's life because she gave him more space than almost any of the Hollywood actors of the time."

* * *

If the 1950's had begun on a troubled note for the industry, changes accelerated enormously by the middle of the decade. Within a short period both Dore Schary and Nicholas Schenck left MGM. Darryl Zanuck decided to step down as head of Twentieth Century-Fox to become an independent producer. Louis B. Mayer and Harry Warner died. Joseph Schenck, confined to his Beverly Hilton Hotel suite, was allowed no visitors. During 1958 and 1959 Harry Cohn and Cecil B. DeMille and such relatively younthful men as Tyrone Power and Errol Flynn died. Gracie Allen retired. Y. Frank Freeman ended his long association with Paramount. Joan Crawford, a widow, first told Louella that she was dead broke—then denied the story. Studios suspended work or closed permanently. Then on December 4, 1959, Louella's friend and agent of twenty years Wynn Roccamora committed suicide.

Yet it is a measure of Louella's resilience that the column continued to roll on. And, in a sense, the world of popular music into which her association with Jimmy McHugh had taken her provided figures with which younger readers could identify. Fisher's romance with Debbie Reynolds moved Louella as deeply as Jack Gilbert's courtship of Greta Garbo or Gable's wooing of Carole Lombard. "Louella loved Eddie and always believed in him," Jimmy said. "And I may say as long as he sang my songs, he was always in her home. There were times . . . you know . . . 'What's the matter, Jimmy?' And I would tell her. Because we were all that close. But if I ever had any trouble—if Eddie wasn't singing something—or somebody else wasn't—I'd just happen to mention it. Maybe I shouldn't have, but many times on the impulse of the moment, you do something. You can't help it. Could be the parish priest, and I would still say it."

The result was that the offender would be given a subtle warning that Louella was displeased. "But there was never anything wrong other than what we call a plug couldn't cure," Jimmy said. "Nothing the singer of a song—especially a Jimmy McHugh song—couldn't cure."

The McHugh-Todd-Parsons relationship neatly illustrates the wheeling-dealing world in which Louella operated. In 1948, Jimmy and lyricist Harold Adamson had written the songs for Mike Todd's Broadway musical *As the Girls Go*. The show opened to tepid notices in Boston, and as was often the case, Todd found himself pressed for funds. He tried to borrow $5,000 each from the songwriters. Adamson refused. Jimmy wrote out a check.

Meantime, Todd's press agent, Bill Doll, persuaded Walter Winchell to use an item implying that the show was a combination of low comedy and sizzling sex. The result was a big advance sale which helped build a Broadway run of 420 performances.*

Union contracts assured the songwriters their royalties, but Todd failed to repay the loan. Later, when he turned up in Hollywood to raise funds for his film *Around the World in 80 Days,* Louella's close friend Joseph Schenck was about to invest several millions in it. Jimmy complained about the $5,000 to Louella, who immediately contacted Schenck's lawyer, Gregson Bautzer. "Greg called Mike to be in his office at noon next day," Jimmy recalled. "I was there. Mike came in and saw me. 'Jimmy! Good to see ya. I love ya. What're we doing here?' And Greg said all we wanted was my five thousand in cash by that afternoon—or no six million dollars. Mike turned to me. 'Tell him. I love ya. Was anybody nicer to ya?' And I said, 'Yeah, yeah. We had a big romance, Mike, but you owe me five thousand dollars, and I need it, Mike. Uncle Sam is looking for me.' So at five o'clock, he had the five thousand. But when Mike hired Adamson for the *Around the World* theme, he got another music writer [Victor Young]. I got my five thousand, but Adamson got a hit."

Nevertheless, such are the vagaries of show business relationships that when Todd moved to Hollywood and married Elizabeth Taylor, he joined the Parsons-McHugh circle since he was a good friend of Eddie Fisher's, and Eddie Fisher was a good friend of Jimmy McHugh's.

Periodically, Jimmy and Louella would descend upon Las Vegas where they would attend two or sometimes three shows each night during their stay. Louella

* In recognition of Doll's wizardry, Todd had previously inscribed a photo to him: "You made me what I am today."

thoroughly enjoyed gambling*—craps, 21, and the dollar slot machines. But Las Vegas, like the music business, was also a source of news when Hollywood was undergoing one of its increasingly frequent lulls. Wherever Louella went in the desert gambling resort, she was pursued by telephone calls from press agents offering items and begging her to dine and see the show at the hotel each represented. "Ringside table naturally for Miss Parsons," Jimmy recalled. "Every place we would go, the singers— whether it was Johnny Mathis or Patti Page, Sinatra or Dean Martin, whomever might have been there. They, many of them, would sing my songs and would dedicate them to Miss Parsons." Press agents and personal managers insisted upon this, having deduced that a medley of Jimmy's songs ensured an enthusiastic mention in Louella's column. In some cases, singers were persuaded to insert a McHugh number for a single performance that Louella was attending.†

"And then she used to delight in going to five o'clock mass there," Jimmy said. "That was five o'clock in the afternoon. Louella would never miss mass." Knowing her devotion, Jimmy was inspired to present her with a gift that provided immense comfort, an electrically wired, ten-foot statue of the Virgin Mary for the back lawn. "She used to worship out there on her lawn," Jimmy said. "She was a great favorite of the Blessed Virgin's. She used to go out there and pray. And it was a great source of peace

---

* When Louella went to the races, she would bet $2 on each horse. She enjoyed bragging she had picked the winner.
† In the 1950's, the final lines of "Louella, Louella, Louella" were revised to read:

> Someday you'll pick out a sweetheart
> Maybe my dreams will come true
> Louella, Louella, Louella,
> Can I be the fella for you?

Pat Boone recorded it in 1957. Later RCA-Victor released Urbi Green's instrumental of the song, and a German singer, Lys Assia, recorded it. "I have seldom had as big a thrill," Louella admitted. "It's beautiful."

and contentment for her. The mere fact that the Blessed Virgin was there."

Louella needed this reassurance. In public, she maintained a swinging, indestructible image, but the years following Docky's death were punctuated with warnings of her mortality. She suffered from nervous exhaustion, temporary loss of voice, surgery to remove a lobster claw from her throat, a bout with pneumonia and an accident in which a bus rammed into her automobile. The accident produced nervous shock that aggravated her heart condition. During a trip to the Middle East and Europe, she was felled by a massive heart attack, from which she privately admitted she had not expected to recover.

So at dusk, it was a comfort to her when the Blessed Virgin lighted up. Evenings, after returning home from a late party or when she was restless or ill, Louella could rejoice in the glowing presence. Someone was watching over her.

XVI

I love to laugh and make other people laugh.
What I am is a ham.

—HEDDA HOPPER

HEDDA began working on her autobiography in 1950,
and by July, 1952, the first of two installments of *From
Under My Hat* appeared in the *Woman's Home Companion,* followed by the hard-cover edition in September.
The New York *Times* called it "a conversation piece pure
and simple," and the New York *Herald Tribune* dismissed
it as "the longest of all possible gossip columns." Producer-
director Cecil B. DeMille, reviewing it in the Los Angeles
Times, found courage, generosity, tolerance and good
humor where the other reviewers had detected egotism
and malice—and since the book contained all these qualities, it is fair to assume the reviews more accurately reflected the reviewers than the contents of the book.

Within seven days after publication, *From Under My
Hat* was a best seller. Its success set Hedda darting like
a hummingbird from Massachusetts to Iowa to Indiana to
Colorado and back to California for autograph parties
and lecture dates (the latter at $1,500 an appearance).
She was also guest of honor at the San Francisco Press
Club where the only other female honorees had been
Lillian Russell, Madame Chiang Kai-shek, Eleanor Roose-
velt and Gertrude Lawrence.

To Hedda it proved that the general public remained fascinated by Hollywood. Of course, being Hedda, she spiced gossip about Brando and Bogart with attacks on Chaplin, Adlai Stevenson, José Ferrer and Judy Holliday and by doing missionary work for Senator Joseph McCarthy.

Six months of hectic activity were halted in March, 1953, when she entered Good Samaritan Hospital for surgery, assuring everyone that it was nothing serious. But a combined hysterectomy and hemorrhoid operation proved too much even for Hedda, causing her to miss the Publishers' Convention in April for the first time since she had begun her column. Temporarily, too, it cooled her feuds. A chance meeting with Dore Schary found the two of them embracing and planning lunch so he could convince her of Brando's brilliance in *Julius Caesar*. "You have to be hospitalized once in a while to realize how nice everyone is," she announced, in a revealing remark that exposed the depth of her loneliness.

Two months after the operation, however, she had recovered sufficiently to travel to London for the coronation (which she felt "out DeMilled DeMille") and to promote her book. At a literary luncheon honoring her at the Dorchester were 800 opinion makers, including Donald Zec, who had skewered her with: "Take one black widow spider, cross it with a scorpion; wean their poisonous offspring on a mixture of prussic acid and treacle and you'll get the honeyed sting of Hedda Hopper." Eventually, Zec was to be sought out as a friend. It was a part of her pattern.

Several years earlier, Hedda had wanted to hire one of the Los Angeles *Times'* crime reporters as a legman. Instead of calling city editor Casey Shawhan, she arranged the transfer through the publisher's wife. Several months later at the Publicists' Dinner, Hedda spotted Shawhan, who had been drinking, and shouted, "Where are you going, you big son of a bitch?" Shawhan feigned surprise that she was speaking to him, and Hedda demanded to know why she wouldn't. He then proceeded to dress her down for going over his head and ruining a good crime reporter. Having made it clear what he thought of such tactics, he stalked out. A couple of days later Hedda called to chuckle over the exchange. "You didn't notice, but there were a dozen press agents standing around, and every one of them was thinking, 'I wish I could talk to that old bitch like that.'" Then she invited him to lunch.

Ten years after the publication of *From Under My Hat,* the pattern remained intact. Jean Meegan, then talent coordinator for an afternoon Merv Griffin television show, booked Hedda on what she thought was an exclusive basis. To Miss Meegan's surprise, the evening before Hedda's stint, the columnist turned up on *The Tonight Show.* "I was wild-eyed with anger when I arrived for my appointment with her at the Waldorf next morning," Miss Meegan said. "Apparently the maid had just left, because Hedda suddenly opened the door, thrust a wet broom in my hand and said, 'Here. This must be yours.' 'I don't think so,' I replied. 'Didn't you just get in?' Well, Hedda screamed with laughter. Now Hedda could take it. I was anything but cordial or charming, but it got her attention. She did the show, and she did it brilliantly. And whenever she came to New York, she called Merv or me—whether we were on the air or not. She was loyal. You know, if a show is canceled, every magazine subscription stops immediately. There are no invitations. You never hear from anybody. But we always heard from Hedda."

"The only way to woo Hedda was to talk up to her," public relations man Frank Liberman said. "And if she barked, bark back. I found that out a little late. I figured at one point I was in such bad shape with her—she wouldn't come on the phone—I figured what could I lose?" As with Miss Meegan and Shawhan, Hedda responded by offering friendship.

Naturally then, she sought out Zec.

After completing her book promotion and her coverage of the coronation, Hedda and Jerome Zerbe (who, she often pointedly said, was the son of a contemporary of hers) set out on what she called "a fling through fantastic Europe," visiting Germany, Austria, Italy, France and Spain. The visit to Spain was prompted by the opening of the Castellana Hilton. While there, Hedda attended two bullfights and became wildly enthusiastic about the sport.

Once, carried away with emotion, she tossed her ostrich-feathered Jacques Fath hat into the ring. "I threw away a hundred-dollar hat, but I got more than a thousand dollars' worth of thrills," she said.*

After a brief return to Hollywood, she flew to New York in mid-August for an appearance on the *Philco Playhouse* and to help Bernard Baruch celebrate his eighty-third birthday. (Part of Baruch's celebration was making a swan dive off the high board at his Oyster Bay estate.) If the trip accomplished nothing else, it proved to her that live television was too demanding for her to consider it on a regular basis. (Three years later, when she was offered the role of a female detective in an Erle Stanley Gardner filmed series, she rejected it with no regrets. She valued her freedom to travel too much.)

Although temporarily quieted by the chairman of the Un-American Activities Committee in 1951, by 1953 Hedda had become so militant once more that the editor of the New York *Daily News* publicly reprimanded her for "trying to settle international affairs." He called her suggestions for boycotting the likes of Judy Holliday and José Ferrer "ridiculous." Even George E. Sokolsky criticized her "bloodbath attitude," saying such extremism gave anti-Communism a bad name. Publicly Hedda refused comment, but privately she felt betrayed. A few years later, she claimed that Sokolsky had told her he was "misquoted."

Nevertheless, accumulated criticism obviously affected her so seriously that with certain liberal friends she avoided the subject. "Politics was something else with Hedda," Gypsy Rose Lee said, "I never talked politics with her. Not that I'm particularly a political being. But I'm certainly not as far to the right as Hedda was. As a matter of fact, she was rather ridiculously conservative. I think she had reached the point where she was no longer

---

* She was outdone only by Mary Martin, who was persuaded by TV producer Tex McCrary to enter the bullring in high heels and a summer dress for his wife, Jinx Falkenberg's TV show. When he suggested Hedda join Miss Martin, Hedda refused, saying she'd thrown so much bull in Hollywood she didn't want to tarnish her record in Spain.

making proper evaluations. In her eagerness to prove certain political points, she didn't see any grays at all."

Public relations man Charles Pomerantz, who became an intimate friend in the mid-1950's, said, "Of course, Hedda's politics were something a lot of people who really liked her got worried about. But Hedda never equivocated. She liked strong people. You notice the people she went for. That was the basis of our relationship. She knew I'd tell her. One of the last things she said to me, I was talking to her on the phone and she said, 'What do you think of Ronald Reagan?' And she had a pretty good idea what I might say, and she said, 'No, no, no. Don't tell me. I don't want to lose you as a friend. I'm not going to argue politics. I have so few friends. I don't want to take a chance of losing anybody.' "

Pomerantz had become a friend when the *I Love Lucy* writers devised a segment concerning Ricky's coming to Hollywood to hire a press agent who would make him as popular as Marilyn Monroe. "The writers came to me and said they were using my name,* and since it would entail working closely with some columnist, would I recommend someone? I recommended Hedda for several reasons. Number one, I knew she had acting experience and she made a good appearance. For what they wanted, whoever it was also had to be social. So Hedda was ideal. Of course, she loved the idea. From that time she became very, very close to Lucy, and she and I got together. I'd dealt with her before, but on a remote basis."

Later Pomerantz arranged for Hedda to serve as national chairman of the Easter Seal Drive. She committed herself fully, visiting several cities to spark the opening of their campaigns. In San Francisco, Pomerantz happened to mention that he would like an excuse to visit the city often. Hedda immediately telephoned both tycoon Louis Lurie and the chairman of the Chamber of Commerce. "This man is great," she said of Pomerantz. "I want him to have some business up here."

"If she liked you, all you had to do was mention something and she pitched in," Pomerantz said. "She called

---

* Hy Averback impersonated Pomerantz.

producers for stars. Or for writers and directors. She made calls for everyone. I was always amazed by her fantastic energy and how far she'd go for a friend."

On one occasion Pomerantz introduced Hedda to a client, Susan Oliver, whom he described as "the world's greatest unknown actress"—and that was the way Hedda described Miss Oliver in a subsequent column. "Then my daughter got married. Susan, who was a personal friend as well as a client, came. Well, Hedda was shocked to see Susan without a hat," Pomerantz said. "I tried to tell her it was a matter of personal style, but Hedda wouldn't have it. She was off Susan. When I'd point out that Susan looked well in something, Hedda would insist someone had dressed her. It took a long time for her to accept Susan again.

"This was a Jewish wedding, and at the reception everything broke down into ethnic dances. One of the highlights was this enormous *hora* with maybe a hundred people on the floor. Well, Hedda, who had to be in her late seventies, couldn't sit still. She'd never danced it and at first didn't know how to put one foot in front of the other. But she outdanced everyone on the floor."

Pomerantz was also impressed by Hedda's practicality. She was always reluctant for her friends to spend money on entertainment and tried to wangle free tabs. "If she couldn't, she wanted her money's worth," he said. Three-quarters of the way through dinner at the Brown Derby with him and a client, she asked the star whether he was finished with his steak. He said he guessed he was. She turned to Pomerantz and said he must be finished, too. Then, she hailed the waiter and told him to slice the meat and put it in a doggy bag with the rolls that were on the table. The waiter inquired whether she wanted the butter put on dry ice, since her dog was going to have a banquet. "Dog hell!" Hedda exploded. "That's my lunch tomorrow. That's expensive meat."

The concern did not extend to film studios, as publicist Herb Stern, who was Columbia Pictures' contact with Hedda for many years, learned. Stern says his feelings toward Hedda were ambivalent: He liked but never quite trusted her. The final break came in 1960, when he invited her to luncheon at the Brown Derby. She accepted and brought along her staff. "The bill was so big that it was broken in half. I got two vouchers for my expense account through a special arrangement I had with the Derby," Stern said. "During the luncheon, Hedda said, 'People must think Harry Cohn is keeping me. I'll prove he's not.'" Stern interpreted the remark as one of Hedda's humorous jabs, but a couple of days later an item appeared to the effect that when Harry Cohn had built his home, the material had been filched from supplies meant for GI's. "Five minutes after I read it, Hedda was on the phone. She began the conversation with, 'Well, I suppose you're hiding under your desk.' The strange thing is she liked me, but there was this bitchy streak. The other thing is that she began each day anew. She expected everyone to forget and forgive. We decided at Columbia to forget her—she was too much trouble.

"Before that, even though I was Hedda's boy for years, she scared the hell out of me. Yet I liked her. I took her to D. W. Griffith's funeral. Hedda and I sat in the back. When the honorary pallbearers—L.B., Selznick and so forth—went by, she said, 'Look at those sons of bitches. Look how white they are. They know they're going next.' She was bitter about the way they had treated Griffith. She knew how it was to be shut out. After the funeral, I took her back to the office. The only time I ever saw her soften up was then. She put her arms around me, kissed me on the cheek and said, 'Thank you for asking me. Do you know there is not another person in town who would have thought that I would have to go to the funeral alone?' A very lonely woman."

Since she allowed herself to trust few people, she had few intimate friends, and the intimacies of family life were still largely absent. Her relations with Bill and his wife had continued to deteriorate, and her fond, yet demanding attitude toward her granddaughter, Joan, did nothing to calm Jane Hopper. Hedda was devoted to Joan, but even with the child she seemed fearful of being exploited. The little girl obviously sensed this. Once when Joan was about to leave a playmate's home, she said she was visiting her grandmother. Her little friend's mother saw her smudged face and disheveled hair and offered to tidy her up a bit. "Oh, no," Joan replied, "it's not *that* grandmother."

Nevertheless, when Joan's drawing of an angel was chosen to decorate the Buckley School's Christmas card, Hedda called the drawing more beautiful than any Picasso or Matisse. And when she went to the coronation or took other trips, she showered Joan with cards and gifts. Then when the little girl came to expect them, Hedda felt she was being taken advantage of.

Adding to loneliness was her puritanical outlook. For instance, when *Confidential* magazine was raising havoc by exposing the sexual peccadilloes of celebrities, the publisher hired detectives to mine Hedda's background. After six months of effort, they had failed to unearth a single tidbit. "They couldn't find anything on me," Hedda told Pat Newcomb. "There's nothing to find. When I go home at night, I wrap my hair in toilet paper, cream my face and curl up with a good book."

Under the circumstances, it is understandable that she was repelled by the *Kinsey Report* and horrified that the word "love" was never mentioned. She felt that no decent woman would have agreed to answer the questionnaire. She was alarmed, too, when the United States Supreme Court struck a blow at censorship, predicting that this would serve as an invitation for foreigners to flood the country with obscene films, which would increase the difficulties of major studios. Those companies that hadn't already folded were teetering on the brink. In addition, none of them seemed familiar anymore. Accustomed to encountering Gable, Tracy and Jimmy Stewart at Metro, she couldn't relate to stars who would have been character actors in her heyday. At Warner's, Bette Davis, Jimmy Cagney and Joan Blondell were long gone, and she was dismayed to see two young actors slouched down, their feet on chairs, when she had lunch in the commissary. She ventured a guess that they were from Elia Kazan's New York group. She was correct. One was Richard Davalos, the other James Dean.

Hedda's initial reaction to Dean was hardly more positive than her attitude toward Marlon Brando, whom she disliked after a single disastrous encounter, in which he grunted answers to her questions. When she asked if he cared to continue the interview, he said he didn't believe so. Then she saw *On the Waterfront* and admitted that she had not been so moved by a film since *The Big Parade*. She now understood the magic of Brando. Had he been willing, it seems clear that she would have made up. Brando did not respond. Even so, Hedda chose him as the best male performer of the year.

Dean was more responsive to her overtures. Soon Hedda was championing him as the best of the new-style leading men. His cocky, yet vulnerable personality brought out Hedda's frustrated motherliness. After seeing him in only one film, *East of Eden,* she went on record that he was not only better-looking but more versatile than Brando. When Dean confided his desire to play *Hamlet,* Hedda urged some New York producer to grant him the opportunity. It was nonsense to think him too young. Knowing him as she did, she was certain that his would be the most original, most moving interpretation since John Barrymore's.

Following the release of *Rebel Without a Cause* (in which Bill Hopper had a part), Hedda trumpeted that Dean had confirmed her estimate that he was the most gifted star to appear in many years. She became so committed to him that she attacked other reporters who wrote of trouble between the young actor and director George Stevens during the filming of *Giant.* Dean had held up shooting only once, she said. Why give him this bad publicity? Privately she admonished him against tarnishing his future by gaining a reputation for being difficult. Whatever Dean thought of her advice, he politely thanked her, and Hedda's enthusiasm grew.

Then on October 15, 1955, Dean's sudden death at the wheel of his racing car produced an emotional outburst such as Hedda seldom permitted herself. Revealing more than she intended, she saw in him another isolated human being longing for love and understanding but being thwarted everywhere. "It will be a long, long time before we see his like again," she predicted. "I loved that boy and I always will."

Hedda campaigned to perpetuate his memory. She

scolded the Academy of Motion Picture Arts and Sciences board for failing to create a special posthumous Oscar for him. The following year she suggested that they award one which Warner's could have mounted on a granite shaft over Dean's grave in Fairmount, Indiana. The award was denied, but as long as Hedda wrote her column, she reported on his continuing popularity.

Two particular favorites of Hedda's followed Dean in her affections. On May 29, 1956, Hedda announced that a young Irishman, Stephen Boyd, had stolen the show in Twentieth Century-Fox's *The Man Who Never Was*. And when she was in Rome during the filming of *Ben Hur*, in which Charlton Heston and Boyd were acting, Hedda showed up on the set. Director William Wyler introduced her to Boyd, who still claims that he was unaware of her profession. "All I knew was that there was very good conversation," Boyd said. "She seemed to have a marvelous sense of humor, and I was happy to meet her. She was a lively woman. She wasn't a person who went along with the normal idea of age making you more placid, more dignified. Hedda seemed to have the idea that she wanted to live life every second. She had a will to live, not just to make a living—to live. Hedda played roles—as everyone does. People who don't are dull. When you seem to take delight in every single second, you're playing a role. I find that approach interesting. It made her a tremendous personality, but I still didn't realize how important Hollywood considered her."

Ben Hur was finished, and when Boyd returned to Hollywood, he found a copy of the story she had written about their visit waiting for him. "I called to thank her and said I hadn't realized she was doing a story and hoped I'd treated her with the respect due her. She said no, I hadn't —and she liked it. I told her since we'd started on a natural relationship, I hoped we'd continue it. She said we would, but if I ever lied to her, she'd screw me. 'You know damn well I'm going to lie to you, because I don't want you to screw me,' I said. It was that kind of relationship." Hedda readily agreed to keep his secrets, provided he never revealed them to rival columnists—and she kept her word.

Like so many of her younger friends, Boyd's political outlook did not coincide with Hedda's. "I became an American citizen for the very simple reason, if you're living here, you want to protect your home or whatever. And you must be able to vote to do that. Immediately after I became a citizen, I thought I must look at the two parties. Now—this is a very personal thing. I found absolutely no difference between them. To me in America, there is no such thing as a political party. I think there are movements—and they go in exactly the same direction. Naturally I heard all her views and what Democrats and Republicans were—and it was all nonsense, absolute nonsense. Because really if you sit down and think about it, there is no difference. It was a tremendous argument we had, but at the end of that, she said, 'Well, of course, I have a memory of the two-party system. And that could influence how I feel. I am adamant in my feelings. You are a stranger in this country. You cannot see in what you call movements what they are, what they mean and where the backbone is. I can see where the difficulty lies for you in making up your mind what you're going to support.' And she wanted to discuss it more.

"She gave lots of advice. I wish to hell I'd have taken some of it sooner. I was under contract to Twentieth Century-Fox and she said, 'Buy yourself out. What the hell are you under contract to one studio for? You need your freedom.' And she was right.

"There were possibly many points in Hedda that were humanly bad," Boyd said, "but I would hate like hell for anyone to miss the thing that really made her tick. She'd done *The Oscar* with me, her last picture. Now about two days before we were due to leave on this tour to promote it, she called to say she wasn't feeling well, but that by the time we got to Philadelphia she was going to try to make it there. If she couldn't, she'd definitely make it to Washington. Well, she couldn't. But she didn't just call Paramount. She called Edith Head, and she called me. When we arrived in Washington, we got the news Hedda had died. Those calls were such a gallant thing to do. She was ill. But she knew we were expecting her, and she made that effort. Well, there has to be a great deal of human response in anyone to do that in her last days."

Probably the actor who touched Hedda most deeply after Dean was Steve McQueen. When she spotted him on television in *Wanted—Dead or Alive,* Hedda told Patsy Gaile, "I like that feisty little bastard. I like the looks of his back. Get him in here for an interview." Following the interview, she began taking a personal interest not only in McQueen's career, but also in his private life. McQueen, who had been a victim of a broken home, responded to Hedda's motherliness. After he replaced Sammy Davis, Jr., in Frank Sinatra's *Never So Few,* McQueen scored a personal hit. Sinatra took him along to New York for the opening of the film. Attempting to keep up with the belters who made up "the Rat Pack," McQueen got drunk and began throwing Mexican firecrackers and cherry bombs out his hotel room window onto Central Park South. His shenanigans brought the police, a narrow escape from arrest—and a stern message from Hedda. In response, he sent her a monkey. Upon his return from New York, Hedda called the actor to her offices and talked seriously to him about making a choice between becoming an important star or a member of Sinatra's entourage. McQueen thought it over and after twenty-four hours promised to apply himself. From then on Hedda was in his corner.

As his career skyrocketed, a camaraderie developed between them. On one occasion when *Look* magazine was doing a feature on McQueen, he suggested including Hedda in the pictures. When the star, the photographer and the writer arrived at Hedda's home, she offered drinks. McQueen countered that he'd rather have something to eat. Hedda exploded. What did he think this was—a short-order house? In reply, McQueen slapped her on the fanny and said, "You know I don't want anything to eat. What I really want to do is ball you!" Spluttering, Hedda disappeared, returning shortly after with chocolate cake and milk for him. Afterward McQueen said that he always treated her like a chorus girl and she loved it.

When Hedda died, McQueen was in the Orient filming Robert Wise's *The Sand Pebbles.* News of her death left him visibly shaken. Shortly after, there appeared on the back pages of both *Variety* and the *Hollywood Reporter* an unsigned tribute to a great lady—Hedda Hopper. Hedda's staff, after some detective work, discovered the anonymous donor of the ads had been McQueen.

Had Hedda been an unenthusiastic tourist, travel would still have been a business necessity. But she loved her jaunts, whether deluxe or austere. Under the latter category came the annual Yuletide trips she made with Bob Hope and his Hollywood stars to entertain servicemen stationed abroad. The first one was made to Thule Air Force Base in Greenland and Goose Bay, Labrador, where within a forty-eight-hour span, Hope and his entourage staged three three-hour shows. The following year, she spent in Anchorage, Alaska; the next, island hopping in the Pacific, ending in Japan; and the final year, Korea.

Reveling that she was doing something for her country, Hedda took deep pride in being able to match her ancestors in enduring pioneer hardships. With the enlisted men, she displayed unfailing good humor. She played grandma to youngsters who were homesick, came on as a world-weary sophisticate for those who responded to wit and style and indulged in low comedy—throwing herself against sexpot Anita Ekberg's dressing-room door "to protect Anita's virginity"—for the men who needed a laugh.

If she was invariably pleasant with the enlisted men, she behaved unpredictably with the brass. In Anchorage, an aggressive major annoyed her one evening. The next morning, when she appeared for breakfast, the major was on hand to greet her and ask the seemingly innocuous question "How are you?" Hedda eyed him coldly and snapped, "My asshole's frozen," as she majestically sailed on by.

Nor were wives exempt. During the South Pacific jaunt, an officer's spouse found herself face to face with Hedda. Perhaps unnerved by the columnist's formidable presence, she nervously inquired whether Hedda had had her shots before leaving the United States. "I certainly did," Hedda boomed. "I didn't want any Army medic sticking a rusty needle in my ass."

Yet she enjoyed the trips and was furious when the State Department became fearful of the effect ten correspondents might have on negotiations for retaining five SAC bases in Morocco. In recognition of their contributions, Hedda, disc jockey Johnny Grant and actress Piper Laurie were honored by the USO's Volunteer Services Committee at the Third Annual Medallion Award luncheon. In response, Hedda maintained that she ought to be honoring them, and close friends realized that behind the gracious response lay a kernel of truth. The holiday treks provided her with a sense of belonging during what was essentially a family season.

In the years prior to and after the trips, sensing her loneliness, such friends as King Kennedy, glamor photographer Wally Seawell and comedian Robert Q. Lewis, among others, made it a point to spend considerable amounts of time with Hedda during the holidays. Jerome Zerbe either invited her to his Connecticut place or flew to California to visit her. The final two Christmases, she spent with society friends in Burlingame, California.

But whatever the occasion, Hedda always had her bag packed. Hilton Hotel openings were special favorites of hers. It made little difference whether the setting was Istanbul or Dallas. Even Fidel Castro's revolution couldn't keep her away from the opening of the Havana Hilton. She explained, "My motto is—Live it up! You're a long time dead!"

Her presence on these junkets proved her Achilles' heel during a 1959 feud with columnist Ed Sullivan. The fight was triggered when *Hedda Hopper's Hollywood,* an NBC television special, was scheduled opposite Sullivan's Sunday night variety hour. Sullivan, who was riding high ratings, had faced a formidable lineup of stars paid minimum union fees on special programs twice before that season without objecting: the first, a tribute to Eleanor Roosevelt, raised funds to fight cancer; the second, a telecast of the Grammy Awards to outstanding recording artists.

Now on an evening when he was featuring opera star Birgit Nilsson, comedians Wayne and Schuster, popular singers Peter Palmer and Frankie Avalon, the Earl Grant

Trio and the Festival Company of Norway, Hedda was promoting Bob Hope, Steve McQueen, Lucille Ball, Judy Garland, Liza Minnelli, Gloria Swanson, Tuesday Weld, Debbie Reynolds, Joan Crawford, Bette Davis, Stephen Boyd, Hope Lange, Don Murray, Mickey Rooney, John Cassavetes, Nelson Eddy, Gary Cooper, Marion Davies, Janet Gaynor, Ramon Novarro, Francis X. Bushman, Ricardo Cortez, and Charlton Heston. Sullivan contended that he was spending $42,000 on talent while Hedda was getting hers for $4,000. His deadpan countenance contorted with rage, he complained to Ronald Reagan, president of the Screen Actors Guild, and Kenneth Groot of the American Federation of Television and Radio Actors that Hedda was obtaining $100,000 worth of talent for the equivalent of a shoeshine man's salary. "This," he contended, "is the most grievous form of payola."

What added spice for the public to the developing feud was that both columnists were distributed by the Chicago Tribune Syndicate, and their columns often appeared side by side in various newspapers. From Sullivan's viewpoint, a request to grant Nelson Eddy (with whom he had a contract) permission to appear with Hedda was unreasonable, but what infuriated him most was that Heston, whom he had paid $10,000 for a dramatic reading, was appearing with Bushman, Novarro and Boyd in a *Ben Hur* bit for $210.

Sullivan accused Hedda of violating ethical standards by approaching performers directly instead of going through their agents. Hedda pretended not to understand his outrage, since he had invited her to be introduced from the audience of his telecast at least six times and she'd always replied she appeared only for money. "He's afraid I'm going to have a hell of a good show," she said to the New York *Post*'s TV critic Bob Williams, "and I'm going to." As for what she was paying her guests, she said it was none of his business. "I don't ask what he's paying and I don't give a damn." Sullivan, denying any invitations to her, claimed they had spoken only once when, meeting her at a Tribune Syndicate party, he couldn't avoid her.

In the brouhaha that followed, Heston withdrew with the lame explanation that he'd thought Hedda had a local program. Joan Crawford found it impossible to leave New York. Bette Davis developed a "roaring cold." Steve McQueen was detained by work in Alaska. The Hopper office denied Tuesday Weld had been asked. And Mickey Rooney, a weekend racetrack regular, sent word he always spent Saturdays *and* Sundays in church.

The Hearst press played the story on page one. Other papers gave the feuding columnists fulsome coverage. So much so that Sidney Skolsky observed: "I can't understand why Ed Sullivan objected to Hedda Hopper's TV show (she's paying performer's scale). Ed acted as if he were the press agent giving Hopper a million dollars' worth of free publicity for free and certainly helping her get a rating."

Following the January 9, 1960, telecast, critic John Crosby wrote: "Miss Hopper, wearing a face that I suspect Loretta Young had loaned her for the afternoon, was discovered on top of the mountain, looking down majestically on the earth people like God. 'This is my town,' she intoned, and I expected a little bush to burst into flame. 'There's no town like it. It's business is make-believe.' "

Despite defections, Hedda presented a star-studded lineup, and Marion Davies, who, along with Hedda, had enjoyed the ministrations of cosmetician Gene Hibbs, was so transformed by clips and rubber bands that she went out on the town for the first time in months. Although reviewers found the entertainment content unimpressive, several thought Hedda should be rewarded for providing Hollywood with an upbeat image, and ratings were high.

Two days after the telecast, *Time* likened watching the feud to seeing "a cigarstore Indian chasing a tufted titmouse with a crabnet." To Sullivan's claim that she had used her column to recruit performers, *Time* quoted Hedda: "He's scared to death I'm going to knock him off the air. . . ." She added that he was a liar.

"This woman just used to hang around the fringes of show business," Sullivan said. "She's no actress. She's certainly no newspaper woman. She's downright illiterate. She can't even spell. She serves no higher function than playing housemother on Conrad Hilton's junkets. And yet she's established a reign of terror out there in Hollywood."

Hedda, who considered herself a close friend of *Time* executives, felt that the story was weighted in Sullivan's favor. "What hurt her," said Charles Pomerantz, who had been hired to handle the publicity on the special, "was that she couldn't believe that they would run the story without at least letting her know. The takeout wasn't flattering to Hedda, but mainly because there was the implication that Hedda was a sort of procurer for Conrad Hilton because she had always gone on the junkets to open the hotels and there were pretty girls around. And that she didn't care what Ed said about her writing ability or anything else. But she was just shattered about the junkets. They had this mutual editor at the New York *Daily News*. I was in a position to hear what they said. 'Listen to this,' she said. They were hedging. They wouldn't say anything to Ed. They wouldn't do anything to his column. And the Chicago *Tribune* let her down dreadfully. And her friends at *Time* when she called them. It was afternoon—about five o'clock in the waning hours of the day. And Hedda was sitting by the window. She said absolutely nothing. She prided herself on not showing emotion, but I had never, never seen her so crestfallen. Finally, when she looked up, she tried to say something, and I could see she couldn't talk. She was crying, and she cried very softly, and she said something about the opportunities to be unchaste, but she never had. She wanted Bill to be able to go anywhere with his head up. But the Hilton crack really hurt. She cried, and after a while, she said, 'Why don't you go home and have dinner with your family? Go on. Don't waste time here.' And she got up and left."

"I went home, and that night I couldn't eat. I started to get a knot in my stomach. Figuratively, all of a sudden I saw Hedda with no real friends she could count on. Not much family life—and now this world shattering around her. And I said to my wife, 'Look, I've got to run over there. I just can't stand the thought of her being alone. So I picked up the phone—we had a mutual telephone service—and asked for her. They said she wasn't in, but they could get her. They connected us. Well! Hedda came on the phone, and I heard loud music and all kinds of noise. And I said, 'Hedda? Hedda, where are you? And what are you doing?' And she said, 'I'm at the biggest goddamn party in Hollywood.' I said, 'You're what!' She said, 'I was feeling low, so I went home, took a hot bath, put on my fanciest gown and went to the fanciest party I could find. What the hell are you doing?'

"I said, 'I can't eat my dinner.' She said, 'Forget it. You can't dwell on the past. Pull down the curtain. You can't worry about things like that. He's just a pissant. Don't worry about pissants.'

"The guts that took. But she said, 'Well, the bigger the names they call me, the more challenge it is.' Hedda was one of the giants. And they are gone now."

XVII

If I knew for sure I could get back in time to telephone the scoop to my city editor, I'd willingly be
the first Lady Astronaut to volunteer to go to the
Moon.

—LOUELLA PARSONS
in *Tell It to Louella*

WITH the arrival of the 1960's, more honors rolled in
for Louella. Each succeeding decade seemed to emphasize
the length of her service, and the industry obviously was
eager to acknowledge its indebtedness. On one occasion,
Hearst columnist Bob Considine complimented her for
preserving what Lincoln Steffens called "a stupid ignorance." Considine explained that this allowed a reporter
to react freshly in print to events that might evoke boredom in another writer. "Herbert Bayard Swope," Considine said, "called columning 'the curse of every-day-ness.'
Louella wouldn't."

Louella didn't. Although the figure she had once fiercely
resented having described as "plump" was now sylphlike
and her ravaged face bore only vague resemblance to the
retouched photograph atop her column, she persevered.
True, she moved more slowly, but she persisted in making
the rounds. Even so, there was no mistaking that more
publicity handouts found their way into her column.
Everywhere she went, press agents would slip written-out
items into her hand, and she would stuff these submissions
into an enormous handbag. It made note taking less of a
chore and diminished chances of error.

On one occasion an autograph hunter crashed a party after a major premiere and succeeded in getting signatures on his program from Rosalind Russell, James Stewart, Henry Fonda and several other major stars before he encountered Louella. Assuming the program he shoved at her contained a hastily scribbled submission, she stuffed it into her purse. Rather than risk ejection, the fan let her keep it. The next morning, when Louella perused the handouts, she studied the various autographs for several moments before handing the paper to one of her secretaries and wailing, "*What* are they trying to tell me?"

Getting the message to Louella became increasingly difficult. Nevertheless, she moved resolutely with the times, determined to survive. How completely her world had changed is apparent in a pre-Christmas 1959 item, reporting Marion Davies in better health than she had been for more than a year. "I haven't seen her for a long time and I'm glad to say she still has that devastating sense of humor that makes it possible to laugh when a less courageous person would be in the dumps." The rift following Hearst's death had never been repaired, but even without it, the ex-star and the columnist who now described teenagers Nancy Sinatra and Tommy Sands as "two of my best friends" could have had little in common.

To Louella keeping *au courant* was a practical matter. Much of her mail came from teen-agers, and she catered to them, making it a point to supplement such familiar musical names as Dinah Shore, Patti Page, Frankie Laine and Frank Sinatra with Frank, Jr., Anna-Maria Alberghetti, Molly Bee, Sal Mineo, Fabian and Elvis Presley.

If, at first, Elvis' pelvic movement shocked Louella, he soon won her approval by demonstrating that he was a modest young man and a dutiful son. Initially, she attacked Tuesday Weld's appearance as relentlessly as she once had Katharine Hepburn's. When, as was her custom, she made resolutions for celebrities in her January 1, 1960, column, she included Miss Weld's: "To keep a dress, comb and a pair of shoes handy in case of being late for a TV date (as with Paul Coates) so as not to appear in a nightgown, tangle-haired and barefoot."

But from the first Fabian Forte, the singing son of a

Philadelphia policeman, was a favorite of Louella's. Because he was too young to serve alcohol, Fabian held a "poptail party." Louella attended and wrote about it as enthusiastically as if it were a Marion Davies gala. "All teen-agers are going to envy me," she announced triumphantly. "Fabian kissed me! So did Dick Clark!" Everything about Fabian appealed to her. She liked the way he dismissed his singing ability (even though his version of "I'm Going to Sit Right Down and Write Myself a Letter" sold 250,000 copies in seven days). He sent her the first Fabian sweater, and by 1960 she considered him important enough to occupy the lead spot in her column. There were frequent mentions of his phone calls, girl-friends and career developments. Obviously they were close—or were they?

In 1970, when artists' representative Robert Raison attempted to arrange for the actor to be interviewed about Louella, Fabian briefly confused her with Hedda and said that they had met only briefly and had talked on the phone once or twice. Nothing so dramatically underlines the decline of columnists' importance to entertainers during the 1960's.* It would have been unthinkable for Jeanne Crain, Lon McAllister or Van Johnson to have confused Louella and Hedda for a single moment.

If approval or disapproval meant little to a Presley, a Fabian or a Brando, there were wheeler-dealers in the 1960's who still set great store by columnists. One was Joseph E. Levine, whom Louella at various times described as "the Boston-born Barnum," "that amazing promotional genius," and "the man who behaves as if it were the good-old days." Beginning in 1959, Louella sponsored Levine in Hollywood, helping to transform him from a fast-buck promoter who had made a killing with Steve Reeves as Hercules into a latter-day tycoon.

Louella became interested in Levine through Jimmy McHugh and Bill Doll. "Bill said, 'This is a guy you should know,' I said. 'Well, fine.' He said Levine was coming to California, so I put Bill on the phone with

---

* Even Charlton Heston, who arrived in Hollywood in the late 1940's, claimed he didn't know either Hedda or Louella well.

Louella," Jimmy recalled. "Now she didn't know who this guy Levine was when Bill started talking. You couldn't explain him. But Bill talked about *Hercules* and all these wonderful plans Levine had. I don't know if Louella even knew about any of it or believed it; but Louella liked Bill, and she ran something, a very nice little write-up on Levine."

"Well, Joe came to Hollywood to visit. Right away he brought me a great big silver vase or pitcher. Must have cost a thousand dollars. A gift before I started hustling him. The upshot was we started a music publishing company together, and he was going to have me do the music for his pictures. *The Law* or *Where the Hot Wind Blows*; *Jack, the Ripper; Aladdin; Boys Night Out*—all these pictures. So naturally Louella was great to that man. Dear Louella made it possible for him to meet everybody simply because I happened to be with Joe Levine. See, she thought it would be nice for me and everything else.

"He didn't give me any real work. I saw *Two Women.* I had a song "Mama Mia" for under the title. I knew I could win an Academy Award with it. Fine. Joe Levine wants it. Then Carlo Ponti says, anybody touches the picture, I get an injunction. That was the end of that. But I was still friendly with Joe when he came back next time, holding out more promises. I took him to the Academy Awards with Louella. We drive out in Louella's car with Collins, her chauffeur. Joe's star, Sophia Loren, won the award for *Two Women.* Louella and I went to his hotel, where we spent an hour waiting to get Sophia on the phone to tell her she'd won.

"So Louella was all the way through this—helping. Yet Levine never put anything in my hand. Never followed through on anything to speak of. But every time he came in, he'd call and I'd tell Louella, 'Joe and his dear Rosalie (whom, by the way, I still like very much) are in town,' and we'd take them out. But in a way, Joe Levine just uses you. If he can get anything out of you, fine, but if he knows you're of no help, he drops you very fast. To use is fine, but he accepted and forgot. An ingrate! So when people ask me about my work with him, I always say,

'Well, I don't know. He's doing *Never Be Rude to a Nude,* and titles like that aren't exactly inspiring.' "

As Jimmy's relationship with Levine waned, the producer's prominence in the column declined despite the fact that his projects had multiplied. By early 1961 Levine was often consigned to Louella's Siberia—the "Snapshots" at the end of the column. Then on July 17 of that year, Levine once again led off the column. During a brief visit to Hollywood "the supershowman" had signed a deal with Harriet to produce *I Married a Psychiatrist.*

The fruition of the Parsons-Levine project was no more satisfactory than that of the McHugh-Levine association had been. After a burst of enthusiasm in which Louella announced that Richard Morris, who had written *The Unsinkable Molly Brown,* and director Frank Tashlin had been signed, the project languished.

In the fall of 1961 G. P. Putnam's Sons published *Tell It to Louella,** a book of reminiscences for which the columnist had accepted an advance a couple of years earlier. Then, having spent the advance, she found it impossible to deliver a publishable manuscript. Finally, Dee Katcher was brought in to help put the book in shape, although this proved easier to contemplate than to accomplish since with each passing year, Louella had grown increasingly protective about Hollywood.

In a sense, the book, which consisted of profiles of superstars and personal reminiscences, served as a eulogy to the opulent days of Hollywood which Louella had helped create and had outlived. Clark Gable, Marion Davies, Gary Cooper and mogul Joseph Schenck died before the book appeared, and Marilyn Monroe, one of the last glamor stars developed under the major studio system, survived it by only a few months. Surrounded by intimations of her own mortality, Louella retreated more and more frequently into the comfort of prayer.

While her contemporaries languished, retired or died, Louella, sustained by prayer, continued to operate on high, making two trips to New York in 1961. The second in

* Title courtesy of Mrs. William Randolph Hearst, Sr.

October had all the trappings of a farewell tour, although Louella, being Louella, invested it with the enthusiasm of a young reporter visiting Manhattan for the first time. She was genuinely thrilled that a two-part excerpt of the book was being published in *McCall's* and worked like a neophyte in promoting the hard-cover version. She was feted by friends at prepublication parties in posh restaurants; appeared with Arlene Francis on *Luncheon at Sardi's;* was introduced on TV by Hedda's enemy Ed Sullivan; and naturally was interviewed by Hearst reporters, one of whom announced that Louella was no less a reporter in the great tradition than Arthur Krock, Floyd Gibbons, Bob Considine and Jim Bishop.

When the book was reviewed in November and December, the Hearst press found it admirable. To no one's surprise the liberal New York *Post* concluded that it was "at its best sentimental, and at its worst malicious-sounding." Somewhere in between were the estimates of critics John K. Hutchens, E. S. Hipp and Murray Schumach, who noted that the expected inaccuracies were present and that Louella's fondness for the inept cliché and the inapt generalization* had not diminished. Nevertheless, they credited the book—as they might have her columns—with reflecting the modes and manners, the traditions and aspirations of what one called that "tinsel El Dorado, Hollywood."

Upon her return to the Coast, Louella became increasingly nervous and anxiety-ridden. But having for so long resisted facing the toll that serious illnesses and advancing years entailed, she looked upon the malaise as temporary. Among her staff, friends and even casual acquaintances, there was no question that Louella was slowing down. "In her last years," said a prominent industry executive, "you'd see her coming into a party on the arm of Jimmy McHugh, moving at a turtle pace. She was like some old Russian princess exiled in Paris—still clinging to a few jewels and the royal manner. But really someone

* "Not until such great books as *War and Peace, The Red and the Black* and *Sons and Lovers* became motion pictures was there any demand for them."

to be viewed with sympathy or pity or contempt, depending on what kind of a person you were."

Jimmy McHugh, who had faced an identity crisis of his own as rock and country music largely supplanted the traditional Tinpan Alley output, was awed by Louella's tenacity. "She tried to go out every night," he said. "Even when she didn't feel like it. Somebody would be hustling her, and she'd call and say, we must do this and that. So this one night she said she had to go to see the new Millionaire's Club or something. I said okay. All evening she kept rubbing this place up by her eye, scratching. I told her not to do it, but she said it was itching and sore. I told her to put something on it and get a good rest. So anyhow when I called next morning, this little patch had spread to her eye. You never hear of shingles of the eyes, but they called this great, great doctor—I forget whether it was Dr. Myron Prinzmetal or Rex Kennemar and he had her taken right to the hospital."

Louella was admitted to Cedars of Lebanon on April 12, 1962, suffering from shingles of the optic nerve, an excruciatingly painful malady, plus pneumonia. Initially, the hospital announced that she would be released within a week. However, the illness aggravated an existing heart condition. For six weeks, she lay heavily sedated, so seriously ill that at one point the last rites of the Catholic Church were administered—and then miraculously she recovered. When she returned to Maple Drive, Hedda predicted that Louella would never write again.

Confounding the Cassandras, Louella returned to her typewriter in the fall of 1962 and seemed about to take up her old schedule when two disheartening events occurred. First, her beloved *Examiner,* a morning newspaper, folded, and Louella's column was transferred to the afternoon *Herald-Express.* This definitely gave Hedda an edge. Then in October, Ed Ettinger, Louella's younger brother, died at seventy-six.

Now more and more Louella retreated into her religion as one sad event followed another. A reporter who had always been conscientious about deadlines, she simply ignored them as she said her beads and offered prayers for family and friends. When she heard that Hedda was writing a book, she roused herself to call and suggest that Hedda treat her kindly as she had treated Hedda. What, she wanted to know, was Hedda writing? The truth, Hedda replied. "Oh, dear!" Louella whined. "That's what I was afraid of."

For Louella, 1963 was devoted to fighting the inevitable moment of retirement. While Docky lived, she had sometimes daydreamed of quitting work and allowing him to take care of her, but she had admitted to magazine writer Isabella Taves Mich that she knew she could never bring herself to do it. Privately, after a visit to the ailing, confused Joesph Schenck, she confided to friends that she desperately wanted to avoid that fate. She hoped, she said, that one morning someone would find her, clad in her nightgown, slumped over her typewriter, an unfinished scoop in the machine.

Louella's wish was not to be granted. In late September, 1964, she fell, breaking a hip. After a fifteen-day hospital stay, she returned to her home, attended by nurses around the clock. Periodically, she made halfhearted attempts to resume writing her column, but finally she shared the byline with Dorothy Manners during the week, while Harriet did the Sunday stories. Days passed in which Louella was wholly immersed in her religious concerns. On others, she talked of the past—of Dixon, Chicago and New York; of the Chief; and of stars who had long since passed into obscurity. By the end of the year, Louella's world was the circumscribed one of her Beverly Hills home, although occasionally she would be troubled by imaginary obligations.

Hedda told an anecdote that so neatly illustrated Louella's position it seems almost certainly apocryphal. Louella, the story went, announced one evening that she had to rush through dinner to attend a preview. All those accompanying her were to be ready to leave at once. Thereupon, she disappeared into her bedroom, reappearing shortly after wearing an ensemble that consisted in its entirety of a red hat, red shoes and a red purse. Not seeing her companions, she tapped her foot impatiently and announced that if no one was ready, she was going to the johnnie. Once more she disappeared. After a long absence, she finally reemerged, slammed down her purse, pulled off her hat and querulously announced: "Well! That was the worst damn picture I ever saw!"

Hedda was not the only person at attack Louella in private or in print. At a dinner in honor of Joseph Levine, a *Life* writer, Paul O'Neil, had been seated next to Louella. Later he allegedly told Harriet that he had always liked her mother very much. He suggested that he do a good, upbeat story on Louella. Harriet informed him that her mother was too ill to see anyone but promised to arrange an interview as soon as Louella recovered sufficiently. The promise was fulfilled, and the result was a piece entitled, "That Little Queen That Hollywood Deserved." It drew outraged protests from such disparate types as silent star Arlene Pretty and columnist Mike Connolly, who accused *Life* of exploiting an old, sick woman to support its sagging circulation.

The story appeared only a few weeks after Louella, despite the presence of a nurse, had fallen and broken her shoulder, necessitating further hospitalization. While there, the doctors also performed eye surgery, removing cataracts. Upon her release, there was no question that Louella would resume work. She spent her "good days" in a wheelchair; the others, in bed. Finally, consultation between Harriet and Louella's doctors resulted in the decision to transfer her to a nursing home. "People ask why she gave up the house," Jimmy McHugh said. "There really wasn't any necessity for it anymore. There were expenses for three nurses, a cook, Collins—it was running into a fortune."

The November 17 issue of the New York *Times* made it official that Dorothy Manners, who had been Louella's assistant for thirty years, would take over the column on December 1. Even as the story ran, Louella was already in a nursing home. The move from her Maple Drive mansion to the first of two nursing homes that she has since occupied was scarcely noted by Louella. At the homes, she spent her days with her face almost always as carefully made up as it had been when she was a young newspaper reporter (although she sometimes perversely resisted wearing her teeth). Initially, her staff and friends visited frequently. On days when she was alert, she chatted more animatedly than she had when she was a working reporter especially if the visitor was Jimmy McHugh, legman Neil Rau, chauffeur Louis Collins or some other male. But there were sad moments, too. Once in the midst of a visit, she turned to Jimmy, her large brown eyes brimming with tears, and asked whether he had heard the terrible news. Jimmy had not. "Jimmy McHugh passed away," she informed him. And when her beloved cousin Maggie Ettinger, thin, haggard and terminally ill with cancer, visited Louella for the last time, Louella, failing to recognize her, insisted that she was an impostor and berated her.

The spring after Louella entered the rest home, her china, silver, bronzes, clocks, crystal, nineteenth-century paintings, antiques and knickknacks went on the auction block There was no going back now.

Louella became less frequently alert. When former associates visited her, she knew she ought to recognize them but couldn't and she would weep. Finally, her doctors suggested that only intimates be allowed visiting privileges. Ironically, this woman who had survived tuberculosis, massive heart attacks and numerous other illnesses was now physically in good condition, but the aftermath of the visit left her agitated.

Louella became happiest alone with the shadows of the glittering personalities whom she had loved, tyrannized and protected. Lulled by the comforting sound of her television set for company, she passed the days uneventfully.

Now that she is no longer among them, what is the reaction of her associates?

Even after her retirement, actor Kirk Douglas apparently thinks of her only in the present tense. "Louella Parsons," he told a reporter, "is a paradox; she is a star and she is a fan. She functions with zest. She is synonymous with everything that is exciting about Hollywood."

Director George Cukor said: "What made Louella unique was her love of the movies, the people in them and Hollywood. She always had their interest at heart. She was a real 'fan,' a first-class newspaperwoman. There may have been questions about her style, but her columns were full of news."

Lew Wasserman, ex-agent and studio production head, said: "Louella held a mirror to Hollywood on most of its growing years. No one reflected the fables and foibles of our people and our industry more vividly. Her familiar by-line will be missing, but she has well earned her retirement, and she earned Hollywood's admiration and respect."

John Wayne spoke directly to Louella in his comments. "The announcement of your retirement has set a lot of us to brooding. You wrote the day-to-day history of this industry and its careers in the making. You knew some of us better than we knew ourselves. You hollered at us like a banshee when we had it coming.You defended us when no one else would. Your bowing out comes as a bit of a shock, but if anybody has earned the green pastures, you have. God bless and keep you."

"Louella couldn't *stand* it when she was no longer queen," Ruth Waterbury said, "when she had to have the afternoon paper and Hopper had a morning paper. Really, I don't mean to get mystical about it, but I think she just couldn't tolerate it—and so she didn't. I think unconsciously she just said I'm not going to take this anymore. Because Louis B. Mayer was dead, and Harry Cohn was dead and David Selznick wasn't David Selznick anymore . . . and all her friends had gone. I can remember her saying any number of times, '*What* will I use for a lead item?' I think temperamentally she couldn't put up with it. Physically she's all right. That's the sad thing. But she'd been a star all along, and she had no intention of becoming a supporting player. She just pulled down the curtain."

So tightly down was the curtain that less than three years after her retirement two magazines devoted to covering the Southern California scene ran apologies for referring to her as "the late Louella Parsons."

* * *

At the convalarium, Zelma Farmer, one of the employees, looks in on the old lady huddling in a chair that faces a television screen whose reflected light reveals the impatience that flickers in her eyes. Her darting tongue repeatedly wets her withered lips as she searches for an opportunity to speak. "Clark!" she calls out in her familiar whine. When there is no response, her irritation becomes apparent. The temper is intact. "Clark! Tell me— when are you and Carole going to tie the knot? Remember—I must be the first to know!"

Obviously the long-ago slight still rankles. But Gable's shade plays out the scene in the 1930's film, ignoring the old reporter, just as he and Carole Lombard ignored her when they eloped while she was attending a premiere in San Francisco. Gable ignores her as only Garbo, Katharine Hepburn and Marlon Brando dared do consistently in her heyday.

Now, even though her faculties are dimmed, her newspaperwoman's avidity for a scoop is strong as ever. She tries again and again. Finally, she curses Gable, and when that evokes no response, she falls silent. Tears of frustration roll down the now-withered cheeks of Louella O. Parsons—once fawned over, feared, loved, lied about, insulted, assaulted, catered to and courted, but seldom ignored. The old reporter is crying.

XVIII

I miss Hedda Hopper because she and I used to fight.
I didn't agree with her, but I liked her.
—MARY PICKFORD
to Aljean Harmetz

AT SEVENTY-SIX, Hedda, who had always emerged second-best in her endeavors, stood alone and triumphant, miraculously having outrun and outlasted her rivals. After all the years of being slighted, passed over and humiliated, Hedda was the acknowledged queen. Whether one entirely approved of her or not, there was a gallantry about her, undeniable courage, a sense of character. Blessed with the capacity to learn, she had taken her experiences—as a disillusioned young woman tossed aside by an older man; a young beauty who voluntarily rejected romantic entanglements; an actress who neither totally succeeded nor failed; a mother who had difficulty communicating with her son—and had utilized her failures as stepping-stones to success. Early on, she transformed herself into a kind of *grand dame*—giving rise to *Time*'s wisecrack that she had been blessed with eternal middle age.

Because Hedda flaunted her prejudices, wrote essentially about herself and her reactions, she fared better than Louella, when Hollywood productions became wracked with problems. In the 1940's and the 1950's Hedda had ridden her political hobbyhorses. In the 1960's the temper of the times had changed, but Hedda had no intention of doing so. She continued to discover conspiracies. At a New York luncheon in 1961, she revealed that the motto "In God We Trust" had been removed from the dollar bill, exhibiting one with, one without it. She was inclined to blame the Supreme Court for the deletion and brushed aside Alice Topping's suggestion that perhaps the words had been added rather than removed. Claiming she had written the story three times only to have it blue-penciled by "some Commie" at the Los Angeles *Times,* she challenged Cleveland Amory to get it into print. Amory checked with the Federal Reserve and discovered Miss Topping's speculation was correct. The motto had been added in 1957, as he reported in his *Saturday Review* column.

A less self-righteous person might have been embarrassed, but such mistakes never bothered Hedda. As far as she was concerned the "Demmies" could do no right. She criticized President John F. Kennedy for entertaining André Malraux, who, she said, was in the United States to raise funds for Spanish Reds. She saw no reason to open the doors of the White House to cellist Pablo Casals, who disapproved of the United States' recognition of Franco. She was almost—but not quite—left speechless that physicist Dr. Linus Pauling, who picketed the White House by day, dined there by night.

Even close friends sometimes became alarmed at possible consequences of her outspokenness. When Orry-Kelly was planning a party in honor of Mrs. Oscar Hammerstein II in 1962, he felt mildly apprehensive about exposing the guest of honor to his good friend Hedda. For Mrs. Hammerstein's liberalism was as rigid as Hedda's conservatism. Nevertheless, he dared not offend Hedda by excluding her. She arrived at the party and, after greeting other guests, stationed herself at Mrs. Hammerstein's side. All seemed to be progressing smoothly when Hedda's booming voice was heard proclaiming: "His election was a tragedy! I don't listen to him, and I don't look at him!" It was easy to surmise that she was speaking of President Kennedy. Jack Warner, whose studio was filming *PT 109,* immediately took over and approached Hedda, who was vociferously extolling the vertues of Richard M. Nixon. As the powerful head of a major studio and a heavy contributor to various Nixon campaigns, Jack Warner had impeccable credentials. "Do you mean to say that you don't know what your President says?" he asked Hedda.

"Oh, I know what he's up to," she shot back. "I read his speeches . . . painful as it is. But I don't listen to him, and I won't look at him!"

Jack Warner smiled. "You'd rather look at Dick Nixon than Jack Kennedy?"

"Yes, by God, I would!"

"Then I'm glad of one thing."

"What?" Hedda demanded.

"That you're not a casting director at Warner's."

Everyone laughed—Hedda as loud as the others. Hedda could laugh more easily now. All the years of hard work had paid off in making her a star personality. It was to be expected that when she returned to Altoona for "Hedda Hopper Day" that she would dominate the proceedings. But even on "Lucille Ball Day" at the New York World's Fair in September, 1964, Hedda nearly stole the headlines, kicking off her shoes and joining a group of Watusis in their native dances. Carried away with emotion, Hedda threw the Watusis kisses and tossed a treasured parasol to them as a toreador might award an ear. "She had an élan, a *joi de vivre* that just flipped me," Charles Pomerantz said. "She was younger than anyone. And in the newspapers, she rated almost as much space as Lucy, who was the most popular star on television."

When, as a member of the press, she visited Mason City, Iowa, for the world premiere of Warner's *The Music Man,* she evoked a greater response than any of the ninety marching bands or the stars of the film, a response that was exceeded only by the ovation given local son, Meredith Willson, who had written the show. Others might be put up at hotels, but Hedda and her fifteen-year-old granddaughter, Joan, were guests of Mason City's leading citizens, General and Mrs. Hanford McNider, at their country estate.

Hedda was inordinately proud of Joan, who was voted "The Brain" by her classmates when she graduated from high school at sixteen and who later performed brilliantly at college. With the separation of Bill and Jane Hopper after twenty-two years of marriage, Hedda sought to establish rapport with her son, too. It was not easy. Following his divorce, she made several abortive attempts, but progress was always followed by a setback. Yet Bill's success as Paul Drake on the *Perry Mason* television show gratified Hedda.

When, eventually, he chose a new bride, Bill called to tell Hedda, and she coldly informed him that she had heard all about it. "Nothing good, I suppose," Bill said banteringly. Hedda agreed. "Well, I suppose you might say she's a swinger," Bill said.

"How dare you say that to me?" Hedda demanded, slamming down the phone. Then she dialed Frances Marion, reported the converastion and asked, "Fan, what's a swinger?"

"I guess you could have called me that when I was young," Miss Marion told her. "I liked to dance and sing and I liked the boys. . . ."

"Oh," Hedda said. "That's not bad. I thought it was hopping into bed—"

"Oh, we did a little of that, too," Miss Marion cut in. Then she suggested Hedda call Bill and apologize. "The trouble with you," she said, taking the opportunity to speak a home truth, "is that you've been so busy criticizing everyone else you've missed out on all the fun." To Miss Marion's surprise, Hedda replied, "Fan, I think you're absolutely right."

Although Hedda's relationship with Bill was not immediately mended, Bill's new wife, Jan, suggested after meeting Hedda that her husband and his mother resolve their differences before she intruded. Thereafter a closer relationship was worked out, and when Hedda wrote the dedication for the book she was working on, it read: "To my son, Bill, who never took any sass from his mother and never gave her any."

Although the book was called *The Whole Truth and Nothing But,* the dedication was only partly true. Hedda may have wished it had been that way, but in at least two areas—politics and sex—Bill still consistently gave her sass. "We used to have many arguments after I began seeing her frequently again," Bill recalled. "She was so dead set on those subjects. I used to say to her, 'God damn it, honey, people's politics and sex lives are their own. If they don't bother anybody, what difference does it make? Everybody can't be a nun.' And I said, 'You've been around fags all your life, wonderful guys.' I don't know—I guess she was of the old school where something was either right or wrong. One time I was in a picture with this actor. After it was finished, she asked whether I'd liked working with so-and-so. I said I'd loved it. He was a quiet, good-natured guy. He was taller than I was, so I didn't have nine chins looking down at him. She came back with, 'Of course, you know he's a fag!' So I let her have it with both barrels. I said, 'Did you ever see him—' and I went through the whole thing. She said, 'How dare you talk to me like that! I'm your mother!' I said, 'Well, how dare you accuse him of something like that? Have you seen it?' She said, 'Well, of course not!' I told her then not to make those remarks. I didn't want to hear them. 'If he is, he is. That's his business. Not yours or mine.' She never did it anymore. And I'm sorry we didn't get closer sooner. I think I could have got her not to be so sweeping on politics."

Either Bill overestimated his influence on Hedda or she had already completed her book before the exchange about the actor. The former seems likely. She was in her seventies and having at last experienced the heady glow that accompanies power, she was undoubtedly unwilling to relinquish it. With the new candor in mass and fan magazines, Hedda fell in with the spirit of the times and was determined to turn out a book about Hollywood that would make the world take notice. With the help of newsman James Brough, she produced a highly readable, eyebrow-raising tome that clearly outdid *Tell It to Louella*.

Herbert Mayes of *McCall's* magazine, who had suggested the project, published installments in the October and November issues. The first shipment of the magazine sold out in twelve hours and was reordered five times. Hedda flippantly reported that every lawyer in town was reading it, a statement she lived to rue. Published in hard cover, *The Whole Truth* included racier material than that in the magazine and headed the best-seller list from February through June, 1963. Reviews ranged from ecstatic to mildly favorable. The paperback edition quickly sold 750,000 copies, and its acceptance encouraged a publisher to issue the earlier *From Under My Hat* in paperback too.

In England *News of the World* (circulation 15,000,000) serialized *The Whole Truth* with such success that chairman of the board William Carr eventually presented Hedda with a Silver Cloud Rolls-Royce as a bonus.

Hedda promoted the book relentlessly, in both England and the United States. She roamed the country, speaking to clubs, appearing on television, attending autograph parties and even managing to persuade Richard M. Nixon to attend a party for the book given by Russell V. Downing of Radio City Music Hall. "You've made so many appearances for me. It's time I made one for you," she quoted Nixon as saying.

It should have been a moment of gratification for a woman who had suffered so many defeats. Yet the reasons for its success contained the seeds of the difficulty that was to develop. "Hedda Hopper, the Queen of Hollywood reporters, tells *The Whole Truth and Nothing But,*" read the titillating promotional copy for *News of the World*. "There has never been a series like it. She knows the stars better than their mothers and lovers. They have told her their secrets and now frank, adult, astringent, she tells us."

In keeping with this promise to tell the stories behind the stories, Hedda worked over many favorite targets. Hedda later said she knew that Louella had read the book when they met on the steps at Saks. Hedda spoke, but Louella failed to respond. Hedda raised her voice and asked whether Louella had heard her. "I heard you," Louella responded and passed by.

Hedda attacked Louis B. Mayer for lacking generosity and gratitude but said nothing of a Louis Lurie luncheon at Jack's in San Francisco during which she and Mayer had quarreled over Hedda's assertion that Louella's column was ghostwritten. Mayer disputed the claim. He and Hedda exchanged a series of insults in which she called him a son of a bitch and he barred her from MGM.

She characterized Mario Lanza as a man who used his Cadillac to batter down the mailbox of a movie executive he believed had double-crossed him. She charged Grace Kelly with assuming royal airs that exceeded those of Prince Rainier. According to Hedda, Harry Cohn hired a hood to break up Kim Novak's romance with Sammy Davis, Jr., by telling Davis, "You've only got one eye; want to try for none?" She repeated the story of Elsa Maxwell's failure to pay for party lighting equipment but made no mention of the fact that when a film needed a black cat, Miss Maxwell suggested getting Hedda or another time enraged her by printing she was glad to help Bill by having him in her picture.

Hedda expended her greatest energy in paying off Elizabeth Taylor, of whom she had disapproved since Miss Taylor had taken Eddie Fisher away from Debbie Reynolds. Hedda not only quoted Miss Taylor as saying that was a lot of bull, but had said the actress had asked her (a woman who had been chaste for more than a quarter of a century) what she expected her to do after Mike Todd's death—sleep alone?

With great skill, Hedda drew a portrait of Miss Taylor as a spoiled, materialistic, callous woman. Had she stopped there, she might have avoided a costly mistake. But in detailing Miss Taylor's marital record, Hedda claimed that she had summoned the star and Michael Wilding to her home to try to persuade them that he was too old. She also claimed that she had accused him of having had a homosexual relationship with another international star.

Upon reading the manuscript, many who had Hedda's

welfare at heart urged her to delete the allegation. As an ex-newspaper reporter, Molly Merrick warned her that she was relying on hearsay. Bill Hopper read it and exploded, "Oh, Jesus, no! They can't let that go through." Frances Marion tried to explain that a reporter must have corroboration. "You must have four eyes," she explained. "Two pairs."

"Oh, Fan," Hedda laughed, as if the argument were unimportant and the charge minor, "you're so discreet."

Meanwhile, according to Miss Marion, Hedda was being encouraged to sensationalize the entire book by her friend Orry-Kelly, "who was great on giving advice. 'Don't be a fart in a bandbox, Hedda,' he told her. 'Go out and scare them. Nobody paid any attention to you until you started attacking people.'"

Members of her staff later maintained that Hedda was confident that there should be no repercussions and that if there were, she could defend herself. "She felt the item added spice," Suzie Traynor said. "There was no doubt that many people suggested that it might not be good to include it, but Miss Hopper insisted. Because, you see, Elizabeth Taylor was terrific copy at that time, and Miss Hopper thought she wrote the truth. It was one of the most dramatic incidents in her career—and a sorry one. She never let anyone know that there was any concern on her part at the time of the suit. But she was greatly concerned. She didn't want to lose the money. It was thought —and I'm speaking frankly—that Doubleday should have brought pressure to delete the story. I don't know why they didn't."

Actually a certain amount of libelous material referring to Louella, Louis B. Mayer, Mario Lanza and Michael Wilding had been deleted. In some cases, however, Hedda insisted upon retaining incendiary statements, thereby causing bad feeling to exist between the publisher and her. When in November, 1962, Henrietta Jelm, the publisher's Los Angeles representative, encountered Hedda at a literary luncheon, she introduced herself, only to have Hedda respond, "I don't want anything to do with double-crossing, double-dealing Doubleday." What provoked the outburst was that the quibbling over what should be included and what should be cut had delayed publication.

"As it happened, we turned the manuscript over to an insurance company, and their lawyer had held it up so long that the book didn't get the Christmas trade. I invited her to sit at my table when we met and she refused. I looked at her and said, 'Hedda, you're not looking pretty, and you're not acting pretty. You're hurting your book. As far as I'm concerned, I don't care whether I work on it or not.' I turned on my heel and left. When I got back to my table, Gene Fowler's widow, Agnes, her son Will and Adela Rogers St. John were there. I was very upset. They all laughed and agreed it was just Hedda. They said I'd love her when I got to know her. Well, the next day Hedda called and said she'd been rude and hoped I'd forget it. I said I'd forgotten already and from then on we were very good friends." *

On April 4, 1963, Michael Wilding filed a $3,000,000 libel suit against Hedda, her collaborator and Doubleday, charging that the book contained twelve misstatements of fact. Soon after, Miss Jelm was dispatched to England to attempt to find evidence. Spec McClure, who no longer worked for Hedda, was also hired to help gather corrobo-

* Later the women became close friends, but Hedda seemed to Miss Jelm always to be testing friendship. One day Hedda called to invite her to luncheon. Miss J., who had an autograph party for Bob Hope and a lunchtime interview set up for Cobina Wright, declined, but Hedda insisted. "I was in a vile mood, but I went. She served jellied madrilene and sour cream. I don't like sour cream, but she insisted I eat it, and we had a stupid, aimless lunch. Hedda purposely made it so because she had a flair for the dramatic," Miss Jelm said. "When we finished, she asked whether I hadn't had appointments with Bob and Cobina. I said I had, and she wanted to know why I'd come there. I told her she was as important as any of my people, and besides, I was fond of her. A moment later, she handed me a box and in it was a magnificent jade elephant pin like one of hers I'd admired. And then it was typical of her, she said, 'You wouldn't have gotten it if you hadn't come.' "

ration for the charges. "I knew it was hopeless. I told her so as soon as I read the book," he said. "If I'd been there or if I had seen the manuscript, it would never have gotten through. All she had was hearsay and the fact that they shared a hotel room during the blitz in London. She liked to say, 'You can't fool an old bag like me,' but Hopper was a naïve woman. The suit was a blow to her prestige, but a worse blow to her pocketbook."

In March, 1965, Wilding's lawyer, Ben F. Goldman, secured a six-figure out-of-court settlement in which the defendant admitted the charges "had been made in a reckless and wanton disregard of his [Wilding's] rights and feelings and with intent to injure his feelings." Hedda and Doubleday shared equally in payment of the $100,000 settlement. In subsequent printings, the passages were deleted.

Hedda was furious at Doubleday, according to Miss Jelm, and never forgave them. Although Bill, Molly Merrick and others felt she was deeply humiliated by the incident and never fully recovered from it, publicly Hedda held her head high and refused comment.

Meanwhile, she dashed about the country lecturing on Hollywood and patriotism, extolling the virtues of her new hero, Senator Barry Goldwater (she said he was handsome enough to be in films), labeling the Beatles as "the Dead End Kids of England" and attacking them for lacking wit and talent.* She constantly attempted to link increasing sexual candor in films with the Communists, confidently predicted a return to censorship and urged parent-teachers associations and women's clubs to exert pressure.

She clobbered *La Dolce Vita* on the grounds of immorality before seeing it. When public relations man Bill Doll persuaded her to attend, she renewed her attack, adding that it was not only immoral, but also Communistic. She was horrified by *Dr. Strangelove*. "No Com-

---

* When a Beatle fan demanded who she was to criticize the Beatles, Hedda retorted: "Who do you have to be?"

munist could dream up a more effective anti-American film to spread abroad than this one," she said. After seeing *The Loved One* at a preview, Hedda was approached by an anxiety-ridden press agent, who asked her what she thought they ought to do with it. "Burn it!" Hedda snorted and stalked off.

Her vigorous public image was something of a hoax, however. Her hearing had failed enough so that amplifiers had been installed on her telephones. Every night she took medication. And early in 1965 she suffered what she described to close friends as "fibulations." These, friends suspected, were something of a more serious nature, but Hedda did not allow them to pry. When Bill asked how she was, she told him, "They want me to rest all the time, but you know me. I'd rather be dead."

At about this time, the Los Angeles *Times* presented Hedda with one of its Woman of the Year awards and L. D. Hotchkiss, the editor, who had bought her column for the paper in the first place, observed in his presentation speech, "Can she write? That is irrelevant. Is she cautious? Is she always right? That too is not the question. The point is, she's Hedda—and for millions that's quite enough." And Hedda was determined to go right on being Hedda—at least in public. That she had become increasingly conscious of death can be seen in that, before setting out for the Berlin Film Festival in July, 1965, she not only made a will but wrote out detailed instructions concerning the disposition of her belongings. "She was amazing," Molly Merrick said. "Most people when they come to die don't remember all the little kindnesses, and I think it's an interesting light on her personality she did."

She also allowed herself the luxury of making arrangements for a real vacation,* turning the column over to a group of guests, including Gypsy Rose Lee, Walt Disney,

---

* Not, however, before blasting George Stevens, Jr., for sending only Lee Marvin to the Berlin event while rounding up Gregory Peck, Natalie Wood, Gene Kelly, Audrey Hepburn, Tony Curtis, Jack Lemmon and half a dozen others for the Moscow Festival.

Robert Q. Lewis, Carol Channing, Henry Hull, Jerry Lewis and Ida Lupino among others.

Upon Hedda's return home, she reported to Paramount for a cameo role in *The Oscar,* starring Stephen Boyd, who had received almost as many mentions in Hedda's column as Marion Davies had in Louella's in the old days. When Hedda arrived at Paramount, there were flowers in her dressing room from the head of the studio, the producer-director team and Boyd. It was only a brief bit as a columnist that Hedda was playing, but two makeup men —the Westmore brothers, no less—were on hand to take care of her. Briefly, Hedda, the actress, received the star treatment that she had envied real movie queens so long ago.†

When it was announced that Dorothy Manners was officially replacing Louella Parsons, Thomas Pryor, editor of *Daily Variety,* wrote: NOW THERE IS ONLY HEDDA.

But for how long? Intimates were aware that Hedda was far from top physical form. At one of her parties after Hedda had finished *The Oscar,* Gypsy Rose Lee was seated on a divan beside an old woman who had to be helped when she wanted to arise. "She looked like an old, old lady. Bent over, very wrinkled, a cane and snow white hair. A lovely lady with a wonderful sense of humor, a dear, darling person, but when she talked, her teeth would slip and she'd have to push them up again. She said, 'You know Hedda and I went to school together.' Well, it was proof that age is a fantasy. Hedda was still so beautiful, wearing a multicolored chiffon dress and looking so young. But once during the evening on the steps going into her living room, she tripped and fell. So to those of us who knew her well, it looked as if she had a dizzy spell. But she was up before you could assist her, and she brushed

† "There was a certain sadness in her last appearance," said Charles Champlin, entertainment editor of the Los Angeles *Times.* "I must say, this terrible movie *The Oscar,* Hedda's last, seemed heartbreaking. Her last word on the screen was 'good-bye.' And she looked so bored, so all-perceiving, I found it terribly moving. To me it suggested how the industry had changed for one thing and that at best you can sustain your enthusiasm for x number of years."

it off so gaily you couldn't possibly pay any attention to it. Not anyone but the old lady, who said, 'Elda's killing herself. She just won't admit her age, that's all. But she's killing herself.' "

The next morning Gypsy called to thank Hedda for the party and to ask if she had hurt herself in the fall. "She said she'd just skinned her knee, but she was going to take it easy for a while. She had been planning a big party we were all going to be on. When she had to call it off, she said, 'I'm going to lay real low for a couple of weeks, Gypsy. I'm going to take it very, very easy, because I'm tired out. I'm just exhausted.' She'd say she was tired, but never sick. She wouldn't even admit to a headache."

With the coming of the holidays, Hedda roused herself and flew to Burlingame to be with Mrs. Nion Tucker and in mid-January flew to Washington, D.C., for two weeks with Post Toasties heiress Mrs. Marjorie Merriweather Post. In Patsy Gaile's opinion, the trip contributed further to her deteriorating health. "It had begun with the Wilding lawsuit," she said, "because Miss Hopper had a terrible fight with herself as to whether she should have done it. She never talked about it openly, but she was disturbed by it. There was a certain declining of health, and she had to watch her diet. She was not supposed to have alcohol or caviar or any rich things. But she indulged in them. She came back having put on several pounds."

Upon her return to Hollywood from Washington, she plunged into a heavy schedule. On January 24, in addition to her work, she had Joy from Westmore's wash and set her hair, and George Masters combed it out. That night she attended a preview at Goldwyn Studios. On Tuesday, after turning out the column, she attended a cocktail party for Dolores Del Rio and two previews—one for *The Half-breed* and the other for *Harper*.

Wednesday and Thursday were equally busy, especially since Hedda's favorite escort, Jerome Zerbe, was in town. On that day Molly Merrick spoke to her on the phone and noticed that she was very hoarse. "You must be very tired, Hedda," Miss Merrick said. "Your voice is awful today." Hedda agreed and said she was going home to rest until Monday. On Friday, Patsy Gaile called Miss Merrick to say that Hedda wanted to speak to her. When Miss Merrick reminded Hedda that she had promised to stay home and rest, Hedda said she had to come down to the office since she had heard that Charlie Chaplin was being allowed back in the country. "Her voice was much worse, and I said, 'Oh, Hedda, this is foolhardy,'" Miss Merrick recalled. "I knew she was just going to crumble."

Instead of going directly home, Hedda attended a party for the editor of *Photoplay,* accompanied by Zerbe. Afterward, when Zerbe, who was leaving town, said that he would be seeing her, Hedda, who friends claimed had flashes of intuition, shook her head. "No, dear," she said, "this is good-bye."

On Saturday she stayed in bed. On Sunday she awoke feeling much worse. She immediately canceled her engagement with Abe Sapperstein to attend an exhibition game of the Harlem Globe Trotters. When her doctors arrived, he insisted that she enter Cedars of Lebanon Hospital. Hedda resisted, saying, "If I go, I'll never come back." She had a horror of hospitals, which had grown stronger after having seen Marion Davies during her last days.

Hedda was admitted—after calling Steve Boyd to explain her absence in Washington—and after that spoke to no one. Frances Marion, Molly Merrick, Patsy Gaile and Suzie Traynor went to the hospital at once. Attempts to locate Bill, who was in the desert supervising the construction of a new home, were unsuccessful until the fire department was pressed into service. When Bill arrived at Cedars of Lebanon, he found Lucille Ball, sitting outside Hedda's door in case her friend regained consciousness.

The nurses refused admittance to anyone. Finally, Bill insisted upon entering. There he found his mother in an oxygen tent, a tube inserted in an incision in her throat. She was unconscious.

On February 1, 1966, news that the double pneumonia had been conquered was announced, but the medication had produced adverse effects on Hedda's weakened heart and kidneys. A kidney specialist was called—but within two hours Hedda was dead.

Following her death, her Quaker upbringing revealed itself for one last time. Having attended the $10,000 funeral of a Hollywood star, Hedda said, "I don't want any of that. I'm going to have the plain blueplate. I'm going to limit them to four hundred dollars."

Hedda also specified that the location of the services be kept secret and that anyone wishing to send flowers make a contribution to the Blind Children's Cloister instead. On the day of the service at Pierce Brothers Mortuary in Beverly Hills, Howard Strickling sent guards from Metro to see that there were no intruders.

Inside the Chapel, Charlotte Greenwood, the star and Christian Science practitioner, read a simple service that was attended only by Hedda's family and staff. At its conclusion word was received that television cameramen were outside the mortuary, so the casket was removed by the rear door and transported to the crematorium. Hedda's ashes were then returned to her Pennsylvania birthplace, where her first cousin, Kenton R. Miller, oversaw the private interment.

When Louella had retired, *Time* had noted that even Hedda's enemies now conceded that she was alone on the throne. It was empty now. Her syndicated column was divided among a number of would-be successors. The $200,000, eight-room home on Tropical Drive was sold, and her personal possessions, including her famed hats and her gowns, were, as she wished, sold at public auction.

In a tribute, *Benediction Without Tears,* Molly Merrick revealed that in Hedda's last interview, which had been with Rod Steiger, Hedda had asked him to describe her, being as rough as he liked. Miss Merrick reported that he said: "I think of you as a woman who knows that in our society as it exists, as a woman alone you must fight to maintain yourself. I think you hate cowardice: I think you have verbal brilliance that hides a touch of loneliness."

Hedda agreed.

"Hedda loved parties but was never the last to leave," Miss Merrick wrote. " 'Don't be swept out,' was her creed.

'Go before the glow fades.' She lived up to it: she left the party of LIFE so swiftly, so quietly that only a handful of intimates knew that she had closed the door."

Epilogue

HOLLYWOOD "managed the news" long before U.S. Presidents or the military complex ever thought of it. This practice became so specialized a technique that within the publicity departments of major studios such powerhouses as Hedda and Louella each had a man assigned to plant items at the top of their columns and another to place squibs at the bottom.

Press departments, as adjuncts of the industry, created an aura around Hollywood personalities through gossip writers. They persuaded the public that a little hoyden from Brooklyn was the "It Girl," a well-endowed Kansas City kid was a platinum-haired "love goddess" and a lumberjack with big ears was an exciting new type of leading man. They transformed a not-so-young Broadway sex personality into a national rage and a vapid ingenue into America's favorite portrayer of neurotic women. Clara Bow, Jean Harlow, Clark Gable, Mae West and Bette Davis owed much to that public, but just as swiftly, the same public could turn upon and destroy such erstwhile favorites as Miss Bow, Fatty Arbuckle, Luise Rainer and (temporarily) Ingrid Bergman.

Yet make no mistake about it, aside from helping create

stars' images, Hedda and Louella were powerful, fearsome women within the industry. Their power lay in the built-in *fear* that permeated Hollywood. Behind the scenes were nervous executives with only shrewd guesses, luck and superstition to sustain the decisions upon which this multimillion-dollar business depended. Let disturbing elements intrude upon the prepackaged fantasies that these tycoons sold, and the sweet dreams could turn into nightmares. Hollywood built up the columnists as a means of communicating an air of benign envy, awe and wish fulfillment to people who lived uneventful lives.

In the earliest days, some producers did consult Louella for her opinion on dubious projects and untried talents, but as the industry expanded, this became impractical. However, since both Louella and Hedda were highly opinionated women, many of their responses could be predicted. They shared a preference for escapist entertainment over classical literature; wholesome over risqué material; comedy over tragedy; less talented, attractive players over gifted but unphotogenic performers—but in this they probably reflected, rather than formed, mass taste. Still, intelligent, knowledgeable people demand examples of how these women created and destroyed careers, caused scripts to be rewritten and altered the operation of a studio —if not the course of the industry. Rarely could they exert such power. Chaplin, Welles and Brando are proof of that. Louella and Hedda were no more capable of such things than Joseph Goebbles was of challenging the precepts upon which Adolf Hitler built Nazi Germany. Like Goebbels, they were the propagandists—and knew it.

What Hedda and Louella could and did was to publicize newcomers, assist in building featured players into stars and promote the careers of writers and directors. When offended, they ferociously attacked expensive publicity buildups of a given star or property. They also massaged the egos of executives who were eager for their colleagues —almost all of whom read the columns—to know what they were accomplishing.

These executives provided the columnists with access to the most important figures in the industry. In return, the columnists repaid news tips by printing gratuitous puffs, but when angered, they clamped down like pit bulls, refusing to let go until they took a part of the subject with them. They could damage a studio by battering away at one of its stars for filial ingratitude, moral turpitude, dubious political connections—or selfishness. Heavy investments in personalities were studios' lifeblood, and if Hedda or Louella attacked Ginger Rogers or Hedy Lamarr, it could influence the box office. On the other side, if an item reported that some unknown had written a great script, that helped sell it. However ridiculous, this was true.

In a time when many actors now consider marriage passé, when nude scenes are commonplace, when the star system is in disrepute, when sound stages are technologically outmoded and scandal can be hot box office, it is difficult to grasp the power bestowed upon these two adventuresses. To understand it is to evoke not only another Hollywood, but also a society that operated on another set of basic assumptions.

The benevolent dictatorship that was Hollywood is gone now, and the artistic autocrats surrounded by yes-yes-yes men, the hedonistic stars and the managerial tyrants survive only in memory—distorted by what happened and what ought to have happened.

Passing time and inevitable change have altered the course of the first mechanical art. The major studios are fragmented beyond reassembling. Even their artifacts have been sold at public auction. Louis B. Mayer, Samuel Goldwyn, Harry Cohn, the Warner brothers, David Selznick and the incredible Herbert J. Yates each ruled over his domain like a Far Eastern potentate—making and breaking careers, projecting their private fantasies upon millions, forging myths—and yet even they were eventually accountable to such mundane things as profit-and-loss statements and such unmagical creatures as stockholders and bankers. But at the zenith of their power, the tycoons demanded and received loyalty to their realms and their subjects. While freedom of speech might be guaranteed other citizens by the Constitution of the United States, no Hollywood reporter—not Hedda, not even Louella—could fully exercise it.

Sic transit gloria mundi.

Index

SUMMER, 1934: ADOLF HITLER MASSACRES
ERNST ROEHM AND THE SA "BROWN SHIRTS"

The Night
of Long Knives

☒ **By Max Gallo** ☒

an hour by hour account of the bloody purge that
changed the course of the Third Reich

"Unquestionably one of the most readable histories yet
produced on any aspect of the Nazi era. . . ." —**Newsday**

"A nightmarish work of narrative non-fiction."
—**Publishers Weekly**

"Engrossing reading (with the) cinematic style of an X-
rated newsreel." —**Business Week**

"Combines the fury of the Valkyries with the suspense of
a Gothic horror tale." —**Kirkus Reviews**